INSPIRE / PLAN / DISCOVER / EXPERIENCE

PARIS

PARIS

CONTENTS

DISCOVER 6

EXPERIENCE 64

NEED TO KNOW 306

Left: Classic Parisian rooftops
Previous page: The city of Paris in springtime
Front cover: Beautiful sunset over Arc de Triomphe, Paris

DISCOVER

A boat cruising along the Seine

WELCOME TO
PARIS

Sweeping, tree-lined boulevards and beautifully manicured parks. World-class museums and cutting-edge haute cuisine. The inspiration of countless artists, writers and philosophers, Paris is a city that speaks to the soul. Whatever your dream trip to Paris includes, this DK Eyewitness Travel Guide is the perfect travel companion.

1 Admiring art in the Musée du Louvre

2 Irresistible *macarons*, a patisserie favourite

3 The cobbled streets of Montmartre

4 Taking a break in Square Jean XXIII

The birthplace of the French Revolution, Paris is steeped in history. From the Gothic magnificence of Notre-Dame, through the Napoleonic opulence of the Opéra Garnier to the elegance of the Eiffel Tower, the city's landmarks are a testament to its enduring status as a political and cultural powerhouse. Art is everywhere: lose yourself in the galleries of the Louvre and marvel at the Impressionist masterpieces in the Musée d'Orsay, or visit Belleville to view the ever-changing street art on Rue Dénoyez. Paris's renowned food scene is equally rich, with an enticing array of boulangeries and bistros that reflect each neighbourhood's local flavour. Stalls overflow with fresh produce at the Marché d'Aligre, while La Cuisine offers the opportunity to learn to cook your own French classics.

The city's charms extend beyond its centre and it's well worth heading to Versailles to experience the royal splendour of the palace and gardens. Alternatively, escape the crowds and play *flaneur* for the day at the Bois de Vincennes or Bois de Boulogne, exploring their winding trails, stately châteaus and serene boating ponds.

Compact enough to travel around easily, Paris can still overwhelm with the volume of unmissable sites on offer. We've broken the city down into easily navigable chapters, with detailed itineraries, expert local knowledge and comprehensive maps. Add insider tips, and a need-to-know guide that lists the essentials to be aware of before and during your trip, and you've got an indispensable guidebook. Enjoy the book, and enjoy Paris.

REASONS TO LOVE
PARIS

It's soaked in history. It's steeped in culture. It's a gourmet's delight. Ask any Parisian and you'll hear a different reason why they love their city. Here, we pick some of our favourites.

1 EIFFEL TOWER

The most iconic symbol of Paris. Some people scale its full height while others view it from a distance, but no one forgets the first time they see the Iron Lady *(p200)*.

COFFEE AND CAFÉS *2*

Parisians caffeinate in style. Centuries-old cafés are the place to sit and stir the perfect espresso as you smell the caramel scent of roasters wafting through the city.

3 PLAYING FLANEUR

Parisians invented the concept of the *flaneur*, an aimless wanderer. Whether it's the Seine's footpaths *(p210)* or the boutique-filled Marais *(p84)*, there's always a reason to put one foot in front of the other.

MUSÉE DU LOUVRE 4

Home to the *Mona Lisa*, the Louvre *(p184)* houses over 30,000 works from across the ages. It's easy – and recommended – to get lost in its seemingly endless galleries.

NOTRE-DAME 5

The huge outpouring of grief that followed the 2019 fire at this massive cathedral *(p70)* is a testament to how dear it is to the city's heart. Damaged, but defiantly still standing, this national treasure is an enduring icon.

CLASSIC FRENCH CUISINE 6

French food is unrivalled, and eating in a restaurant is a total experience, where service is an art and every server can recommend a stellar wine.

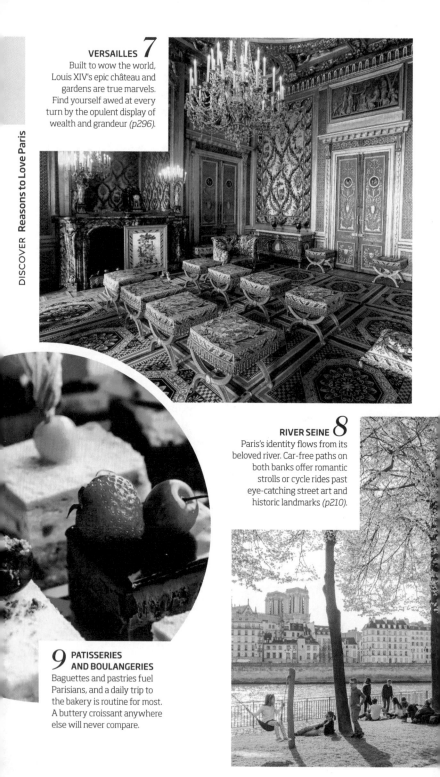

VERSAILLES 7

Built to wow the world, Louis XIV's epic château and gardens are true marvels. Find yourself awed at every turn by the opulent display of wealth and grandeur *(p296)*.

RIVER SEINE 8

Paris's identity flows from its beloved river. Car-free paths on both banks offer romantic strolls or cycle rides past eye-catching street art and historic landmarks *(p210)*.

9 **PATISSERIES AND BOULANGERIES**

Baguettes and pastries fuel Parisians, and a daily trip to the bakery is routine for most. A buttery croissant anywhere else will never compare.

10 MARKETS

Rain or shine, Paris's street sellers spring to life each day. Bustling food markets colour nearly every neighbourhood, while the flea markets brim with hidden treasure.

OPERA AND BALLET 11

France raised the bar on ballet and opera under the Sun King. Savour the spectacular fruits of that legacy in the ornate Opéra Garnier *(p172)* and the modern Opéra Bastille *(p106).*

HAUTE COUTURE 12

Paris is a fashion capital and its designer stores are veritable temples to couture. Marvel at the dazzling displays that elevate clothing into fine art.

EXPLORE
PARIS

This guide divides Paris into 15 colour-coded sightseeing areas, as shown on the map below. Find out more about each area on the following pages. For areas beyond the centre see p290.

Cimetière de
Montmartre

Place
de Clichy

**MONTMARTRE
AND PIGALLE**
p152

Parc
Monceau

**OPÉRA AND GRANDS
BOULEVARDS**
p168

Opéra National
de Paris Garnier

Place
de l'Opéra

Arc de
Triomphe

**CHAMPS-ÉLYSÉES
AND CHAILLOT**
p214

Place
de la
Concorde

Jardin des
Tuileries

**LOUVRE AND
LES HALLES**
p180

Palais de
Chaillot

La Seine

Musée du
Louvre

Jardins du
Trocadero

Musée du Quai Branly-
Jacques Chirac

Musée
d'Orsay

Eiffel
Tower

**EIFFEL TOWER
AND INVALIDES**
p196

Parc du
Champ-de-
Mars

Dôme des
Invalides

**ST-GERMAIN-
DES-PRÉS**
p234

Place
Jóffre

Place de
Breteuil

Jardin du
Luxembourg

WESTERN EUROPE

UNITED
KINGDOM

NETHERLANDS

BELGIUM

GERMANY

Lille •

PARIS

Rennes •

Strasbourg •

FRANCE

SWITZERLAND

Atlantic
Ocean

Bordeaux •

• Lyon

ITALY

Toulouse •

• Marseille

SPAIN

Mediterranean
Sea

**MONTPARNASSE AND
JARDIN DU LUXEMBOURG**
p278

Cimetière du
Montparnasse

Place
Denfert-
Rochereau

Cité des Sciences
et de l'Industrie

Parc de
la Villette

Sacré-
Coeur

LA VILLETTE
p138

Place de
Stalingrad

Parc des
Buttes-Chaumont

Canal St-Martin

**RÉPUBLIQUE AND
CANAL ST-MARTIN**
p114

Parc de
Belleville

Place
de la
République

**BELLEVILLE AND
MÉNILMONTANT**
p126

Pompidou
Centre

Musée
Picasso Paris

Cimetière du
Père Lachaise

Place
de l'Hotel
de Ville

THE MARAIS
p84

Place
Voltaire

**ÎLE DE LA CITÉ
AND ÎLE ST-LOUIS**
p66

**BASTILLE AND
OBERKAMPF**
p100

Place
de la
Bastille

Musée de
Cluny

**LATIN
QUARTER**
p248

La Seine

Panthéon

Jardin des
Plantes

Muséum National
d'Histoire Naturelle

Parc de
Bercy

**JARDIN DES PLANTES
AND PLACE D'ITALIE**
p262

Place
d'Italie

| 0 metres | 800 |
| 0 yards | 800 |

N

GETTING TO KNOW
PARIS

Paris is a patchwork of neighbourhoods, each with a history and essence of its own. The Seine runs through the heart of the city, creating its Right and Left banks, while the main sightseeing areas are enclosed by the Périphérique, a ring road that separates the city centre from the suburbs.

PAGE 66

ÎLE DE LA CITÉ AND ÎLE ST-LOUIS

Located at the heart of Paris, these two islands are cornucopias of must-see sights. Île de la Cité houses both Notre-Dame and Sainte-Chapelle, masterpieces of Gothic architecture, while Île St-Louis is full of cute boutiques and cafés. Former royal palaces double as administrative buildings, but it's not a place to mingle with the locals unless picnicking on the quays at night. Both islands are an essential, and usually inevitable, part of a Parisian excursion.

Best for
Sightseeing and strolling along the river

Home to
Notre-Dame, Sainte-Chapelle

Experience
The awe-inspiring Gothic architecture of Notre-Dame and Sainte-Chapelle

THE MARAIS

PAGE 84

Full of fashionable boutiques and restaurants, the Marais is the neighbourhood visitors return to over and over again. Its noble origins are apparent in the Renaissance mansions repurposed for the likes of Chanel and the Musée Carnavalet. Along Rue des Rosiers, the scent of freshly fried falafel wafts through the air as the city's best Jewish bakeries prepare poppy-seed pastries. Parisians spend afternoons mingling at the Place des Vosges, with its leafy green trees set against the rosy bricks of a former palace.

Best for
Shopping, dining, history, architecture, LGBT+ life

Home to
Musée Picasso Paris, Pompidou Centre

Experience
The trendy boutiques and the scenic Place des Vosges

BASTILLE AND OBERKAMPF

PAGE 100

Gritty and lively, these areas east of the Marais make up for a lack of major tourist attractions with stellar dining options. Trendy coffee shops, independent boutiques and innovative bars draw a younger, multicultural crowd from across the city. *Flaneurs* can enjoy the elevated Coulée Verte René-Dumont for a bucolic stroll above the streets, or wander the markets at Aligre and along Boulevard Richard Lenoir – both sell fresh flowers and mounds of seasonal produce. Those looking for a taste of local life will find it here.

Best for
Nightlife and restaurants

Home to
Place de la Bastille

Experience
The magnificent Colonne de Juillet and a stroll along the elevated Coulée Verte René-Dumont

$\rightarrow$

PAGE 114

RÉPUBLIQUE AND CANAL ST-MARTIN

These areas have recently transformed into exciting, somewhat quirky destinations. Characterized by the *bobos* (bohemian-bourgeois Parisians) who helped gentrify it, the canal is a hotspot for daytime coffee dates and evening picnics, fuelled by an extensive selection of cafés. Shoppers should head to the pockets of boutiques specializing in homewares, clothing and jewellery. This is the side of Paris that few visitors see but are exceedingly happy to find.

Best for
Coffee lovers and getting off the beaten track in style

Home to
Canal St-Martin

Experience
The Musée des Moulages medical museum and a pizza picnic beside the canal

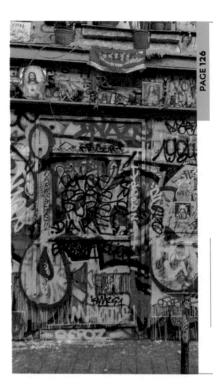

PAGE 126

BELLEVILLE AND MÉNILMONTANT

Far from the beaten path, Belleville and Ménilmontant are local enclaves that are little visited by tourists. Artists toil away in their galleries and in the streets, turning thoroughfares such as Rue Dénoyez into open-air artworks, while Asian restaurants and shops attract locals who want a break from duck *confit*. Hipsters and international residents have made their home in these characterful areas, which offer a rewarding glimpse into everyday Parisian life.

Best for
Ethnic food and experiencing local life

Home to
Cimetière du Père Lachaise

Experience
A hunt for the tombs of famous figures such as Edith Piaf and Oscar Wilde at the Cimetière du Père Lachaise

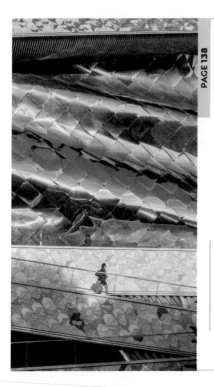

PAGE 138

LA VILLETTE

On the city's northeast edge, the canal cuts a broad path through this green park that's as family friendly as it is cultural. The stunning Jean Nouvel-designed Philharmonie towers like a spaceship while the science centre and playground across the water provide endless entertainment for kids. Joggers and cyclists appreciate the traffic-free pathways, and in spring and summer concerts and outdoor movies sound-track the evenings. Parisians of all ages head here to while away the time with a glass of rosé as the clinking of their *pétanque* balls echoes over the water.

Best for
Music lovers and getting some fresh air

Home to
Parc de la Villette, Cité des Sciences et de l'Industrie

Experience
Playing pétanque along the canal or taking in a show at the Philharmonie de Paris

PAGE 152

MONTMARTRE AND PIGALLE

Although the area around the Moulin Rouge is still dotted with sordid "love" shops and seedy bars, Montmartre and Pigalle have become fashionable destinations for diners and shoppers. Pigalle's red lights have given way to some of the city's best pastry shops, boutique hotels and designer stores. Visitors still love browsing the art at Place du Tertre and soaking up the view of Paris from atop hilly Montmartre, where the cobbled streets and quaint houses retain a 19th-century village feel that few other districts reproduce.

Best for
A night out and great views

Home to
Sacré-Coeur

Experience
The sound of buskers on the steps in front of the Sacré-Coeur while watching the sun set over the city

$\rightarrow$

PAGE 168

OPÉRA AND GRANDS BOULEVARDS

Studded with theatres and crowned by the Opéra Garnier, this district epitomizes Baron Haussmann's plans for Paris, with monuments at every intersection. Its broad avenues, lined with exquisite churches and wallet-emptying department stores, are filled with bustling crowds of Parisians. This is the place to stroll, shop and repeat, whether it's for rose-flavoured *macarons* from Ladurée's original shop or a luxury bag from Printemps.

Best for
Shoppers and theatre-goers

Home to
Opéra National de Paris Garnier

Experience
Shopping for perfume under the Art Nouveau cupola of Galeries Lafayette, before heading next-door to Printemps' rooftop café

PAGE 180

LOUVRE AND LES HALLES

Paris's former royal palace and central market are as lively as ever. The Musée du Louvre, with its infamous glass pyramid and the *Mona Lisa*, needs no introduction. The stately manicured gardens of the adjacent Tuileries house cafés and other art galleries. Les Halles was historically the hub of food distribution in the city, and the smells of ripened cheeses and fresh baguettes still tempt shoppers along Rue Montorgueil. It's all about cuisine here, from fine dining to street food, and wine bars and cocktail clubs shake up the nights.

Best for
Shopping, dining and history

Home to
Musée du Louvre

Experience
Coming face to face with the Mona Lisa before sampling pastries along Rue Montorgueil

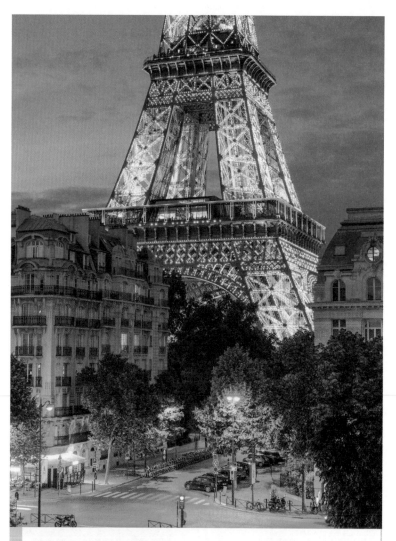

PAGE 196

EIFFEL TOWER AND INVALIDES

This corner of town is grandiose and ornate, with the gold-topped Dôme des Invalides soaring against the skyline. Full of history and artifacts, it plays second fiddle to the neighbourhood's real star: the Iron Lady herself, the Eiffel Tower, rising at the edge of the river. Away from the chaos of tours and elevator lines, this district also offers quaint streets such as Rue Cler, where colourful, buttery pastries await. Some of the city's top restaurants aren't far away. If Michelin stars are out of the budget then a picnic on the Champ-de-Mars underneath the tower will do, with the appropriate bottle of oaky red wine, of course.

Best for
Sightseeing and fine dining

Home to
Eiffel Tower, Dôme des Invalides, Musée du Quai Branly–Jacques Chirac

Experience
Stunning views from atop the Eiffel Tower before paying homage to Napoleon at his tomb at the Invalides

→

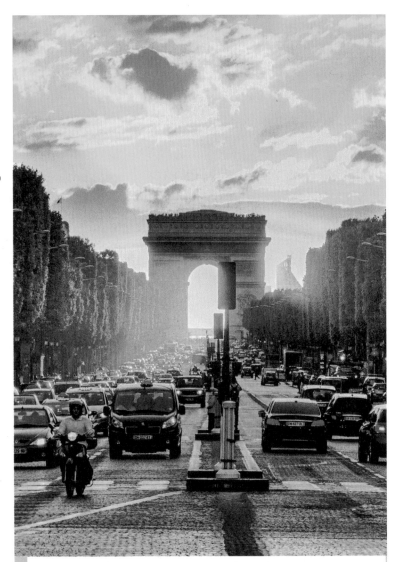

CHAMPS-ÉLYSÉES AND CHAILLOT

The world's most beautiful avenue still has a shine to it. Although its shops are mainly frequented by tourists, it's worth a visit for the iconic stores and the monumental Arc de Triomphe. Well-heeled Parisians do live nearby, but are more likely to be found at one of the museums at the Palais de Chaillot. Luxury shoppers will revel along the Avenue Montaigne, and the area's palace hotels are the perfect place for a ritzy afternoon tea or evening cocktail.

Best for
Window shopping and Michelin-starred dining

Home to
Arc de Triomphe, Palais de Chaillot

Experience
A dip into the Petit Palais exhibition hall before splashing out on a terrace coffee on the Avenue des Champs-Élysées

ST-GERMAIN-DES-PRÉS

PAGE 234

Cafés line the streets and squares of this iconic district – the chocolates and pastries are some of the city's best. Shoppers delight in the boutiques and art galleries found here – Le Bon Marché in particular captivates shoppers who walk through its perfume-laden halls. A smattering of museums and centuries-old churches attract tourists, but locals continue to lay claim to this bohemian enclave. There's no better place to rub elbows with true-blooded Parisians than in one of the neighbourhood's plentiful cafés and bars.

Best for
Strolling and people watching

Home to
Musée d'Orsay

Experience
Local life at one of the legendary cafés while nibbling macarons

LATIN QUARTER

PAGE 248

From Romans ruins to Hollywood backdrops, the Latin Quarter is beloved by Parisians and travellers alike. Café crowds are decidedly younger than most, filled with university students from the Collège de France and La Sorbonne. Every block seems to have a bookstore, from obscure academic shops to the bursting shelves of the famed Shakespeare and Company. Peppered along the tiny twisting streets are crêpe stands and dive bars, all offset by the grandeur of stunning sights such as the Panthéon, Musée de Cluny and Church of St-Étienne-du-Mont.

Best for
Budget travel and history lovers

Home to
The Panthéon

Experience
Shopping for a picnic at the Marché Maubert and discussing philosophy with students around the Sorbonne

→

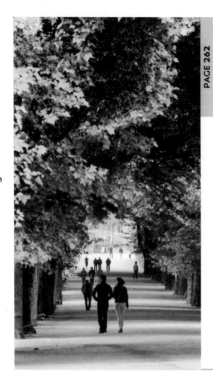

PAGE 262

JARDIN DES PLANTES AND PLACE D'ITALIE

Many people stop at the Latin Quarter, leaving this corner of the Left Bank less busy than the rest. The flowering Jardin des Plantes is home to natural history galleries and a zoo, and is a popular spot with Parisian families at weekends. A stroll along Rue Mouffetard delights with cheese and pastry shops, while architectural surprises such as the mosque or the national library make an exciting break from the traditional Parisian cityscape.

Best for
Family days out in any weather

Home to
Muséum National d'Histoire Naturelle

Experience
Sipping mint tea at the Grande Mosquée de Paris after visiting Europe's second-oldest zoo

PAGE 278

MONTPARNASSE AND JARDIN DU LUXEMBOURG

Old and new Paris come together in this lively area, where traditional cafés nestle alongside modern tower blocks. The gorgeous Jardin du Luxembourg attracts Parisians looking for a bit of fresh air, while in-the-know visitors head to the Tour Montparnasse and the Catacombs. Locals still congregate at the *belle époque* brasseries, where the appetizing smell of lentils and sausages is accompanied by the sound of clinking beers.

Best for
A day at the playground and belle époque dining

Home to
Cimetière du Montparnasse

Experience
The cavernous underground Catacombs before ascending the Tour Montparnasse for a unique perspective of the city

BEYOND THE CENTRE

Beyond the Périphérique (Paris's ring road), two natural parks act as the city's green lungs. The Bois de Vincennes and Bois de Boulogne offer lakes for boating, paths for strolling and châteaus for exploring, as well as attractions such as the contemporary Fondation Louis Vuitton art gallery and an innovative zoo. Disneyland® Paris grants families another daylong escape, while history buffs will enjoy an outing to the palace and gardens at Versailles, a 17th century Disneyland® in its own right.

Best for
Getting out of Paris

Home to
Bois de Boulogne, Bois de Vincennes, the Palace and Gardens of Versailles, Disneyland® Paris

Experience
The sumptuous estate of Versailles or taking some air in one of Paris's green lungs

←

1 The interior of Notre-Dame, before the 2019 fire

2 The Pont des Arts

3 Shakespeare and Company bookshop in the Latin Quarter

4 Jardin des Tuileries

Paris is a treasure trove of things to see and do, and its relatively compact size means that much exploring can be done on foot. These itineraries will inspire you to make the most of your visit.

5 HOURS

If you only have a few hours in Paris, a stroll along the River Seine is an ideal way to take in a plethora of sights. Begin in the Marais at the Hôtel de Ville (p95), the ornate city hall. Cross the river onto Île de la Cité, one of the oldest areas in Paris and home to major attractions such as Notre-Dame (p70). Pause outside the splendid cathedral to see the latest developments before continuing your walk past the similarly impressive Sainte-Chapelle (p74). At the island's western tip, a statue of King Henri IV stands on the Pont Neuf (p78), the city's oldest bridge. Cross the bridge and head west towards the Louvre (p184), rising unmistakably just a few blocks away. Walk through its courtyard and admire the elegant wings and iconic pyramid, after stopping for coffee and a snack at Le Fumoir, located on Rue de l'Amiral de Coligny, behind the massive museum. There's no time to go inside to admire the art, but the beautifully manicured Jardin des Tuileries (p191) offers an inviting stroll through flower beds and leafy walkways lined with statues. Enter the gardens through the Arc de Triomphe du Carrousel (p192), one of two monumental arches built by Napoleon.

At the gardens' far end, looking onto the Place de la Concorde (p224) and its Egyptian obelisk, sweeping views take in the Grand Palais (p225), the Arc de Triomphe (p218) and the Eiffel Tower (p200). Walk down to the square and cross the river towards the National Assembly (p210), home to the lower house of the French Parliament. Follow the reclaimed riverbanks of the Berges de Seine (p210) east towards the Musée d'Orsay (p238), identifiable by its twin clock towers. Continue on Quai Voltaire towards the Pont des Arts (p245), which affords great photo opportunities.

Proceed back along the Left Bank, browsing the stalls of the bouquinistes (used-book vendors), arriving at Place St-Michel (p256). Visit one of the many nearby bookshops, such as Shakespeare and Company (p258), before heading past Notre-Dame to intimate Île St-Louis. This little island sports no grand tourist attractions, but is the place to grab a cone of Berthillon ice cream (p77). End your stroll with a glass of wine and dinner at the Brasserie de l'Isle Saint-Louis on Quai de Bourbon, enjoying views of the Seine.

←

① Pretty Canal St-Martin

② The Colonne de Juillet in Place de la Bastille

③ Les Philosophes café

④ An exhibit in the Muséum National d'Histoire Naturelle

24 HOURS

Morning

Start with coffee and a pastry along the Canal St-Martin (p118). Hipster coffee joints are in abundance here, and a take-away cappuccino pairs perfectly with a chocolate croissant from Du Pain et des Idées, the district's best bakery, on Rue Yves Toudic. Sit with your breakfast beside the canal, its green bridges arching gracefully over the water. Stroll the area and its shops on your way to the Upper Marais, just across nearby Place de la République, then live out noble fantasies while exploring the 17th-century mansion that houses the Musée Picasso (p88). Browse the art and relax with a drink on the rooftop terrace before continuing.

Afternoon

Enter the heart of the Marais by foot, stopping for lunch in a café such as Les Philosophes on Rue Vieille du Temple, or queueing for the entirely worthwhile falafel at L'As du Fallafel (p92) on Rue des Rosiers. Indulge in some retail therapy before ducking down onto the Seine, along the Berges Rive Droite. This riverside pathway allows traffic-free strolling and features boats doubling as cafés. Cross a bridge onto Île St-Louis and make your way over to the Left Bank. Just to the east is the pristine Jardin des Plantes (p268), an enclave for botany enthusiasts and a haven for anyone who appreciates natural beauty. It's also home to the Muséum National d'Histoire Naturelle (p266), which is worth a quick look. At the far end of the garden, pause for some mint tea at the Grande Mosquée de Paris (p268), just beyond the garden's gates.

Evening

Head back to the river and cross, walking along the stretch of canal that leads towards Place de la Bastille (p104). Its Colonne de Juillet is visible from a distance. Plan on eating somewhere in the neighbourhood, such as Bistrot Paul Bert on Rue Paul Bert or Septime (p107) on Rue de Charonne, for a true Parisian dinner. Then hang around for drinks and cocktails in the vicinity of Rue de la Roquette (p107), where the nightlife is sure to catch you up in its excitement.

1 The opulent Hall of Mirrors in the palace of Versailles

2 Cruising the Seine at sunset

3 A classic French breakfast

4 Art for sale in Place du Tertre in Montmartre

3 DAYS

Day 1

Morning Start the day in St-Germain-des-Prés with coffee and a croissant at any café, then take a leafy stroll through the nearby Jardin du Luxembourg *(p286)*. Dip into St-Sulpice church *(p243)* to inspect the Delacroix paintings before going shopping along Boulevard St-Germain.

Afternoon Follow Rue de Seine towards the river, stopping for lunch at La Palette, a traditional café serving delicious *croque monsieur*. Stroll the Île St-Louis, home to Notre-Dame *(p70)*, before taking the Metro west to spend the rest of the afternoon exploring the Eiffel Tower *(p200)*. Dare to walk the stairs if the queue for the elevator is too long.

Evening Have dinner nearby at Café Christian Constant *(p208)*, which serves classic French dishes. Follow this with a boat ride down the Seine as the sun sets.

Day 2

Morning Begin in hilly Montmartre, with a quick visit to the Sacré-Coeur basilica *(p156)*. Browse the artists selling their wares in the open-air gallery of Place du Tertre *(p158)*, then visit the Musée de Montmartre *(p160)* for a quick lesson on the 19th-century artists that made the district famous.

Afternoon Have lunch at Le Sancerre on Rue des Abbesses before heading down the hill towards Rue des Martyrs *(p165)*,

laden with pastry shops and boutiques. Consider a late afternoon jaunt through the Louvre *(p184)* to see the highlights, including *Mona Lisa* and the *Venus de Milo*. Soak up the views of the exterior with a coffee stop at the Café Marly, under the arcades of the Richelieu wing.

Evening Head to Les Halles for dinner at Champeaux *(p189)*. Sip wine and people-watch for the rest of the evening along bustling Rue Montorgueil, or see what shows are playing at the nearby venues in the Opéra district, such as the historic Olympia music hall.

Day 3

Morning Travel less than an hour out of the city to Versailles *(p296)*. Wander the world-famous gardens and 17th-century château, renowned for its opulent Hall of Mirrors.

Afternoon Splurge on lunch at Ore *(p299)*, an ornate little restaurant situated inside the château. Be sure to visit the outer estates, including the queen's fairy-tale hamlet with a working farm.

Evening Head back to Paris and share a bottle at an intimate venue like Willi's Wine Bar on Rue des Petits Champs, near the Louvre. If you've still got room after your lunch, have dinner in style at one of the city's iconic belle époque brasseries such as Bofinger *(p107)* or La Rotonde *(p147)*.

PARIS FOR
ART LOVERS

Numerous figures have shaken up the art scene from the French capital, from Monet and the Impressionists to Dalí and the Surrealists. Countless masterpieces adorn Paris's greatest museums, while private galleries and even the streets offer a more personal look at contemporary art in the city.

World-Class Museums

Whatever your interest in art, one of Paris's museums has a collection of it. Highlights include the soaring gallery of the Musée d'Orsay *(p238)*, a former train station famed for its Impressionist works, and the fascinating modern galleries of the Fondation Louis Vuitton *(p292)*. Try to escape Mona Lisa's gaze while exploring the superlative collection at the Louvre *(p184)*, before snaking up the panoramic escalator of the Pompidou Centre *(p90)* to marvel at Mondrian's deceptively simple squares. Smaller museums dedicated to Monet *(p304)* and Picasso *(p88)* will leave you swooning for these artistic icons.

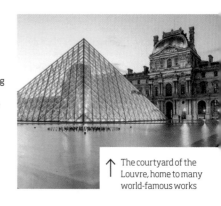

↑ The courtyard of the Louvre, home to many world-famous works

Create Your Own Collection

Paris is a nirvana for art collectors with any budget. High-end art galleries along the Left Bank sell some of the city's most sought-after works, while at Place du Tertre in Montmartre (p158) you can mingle with local artists selling their canvases for a bargain. Visit the studios of little-known artists in Belleville (p137) – they might end up selling you something you didn't even know was for sale.

← Place du Tertre in Montmartre, a hotspot for local artists exhibiting and selling their work

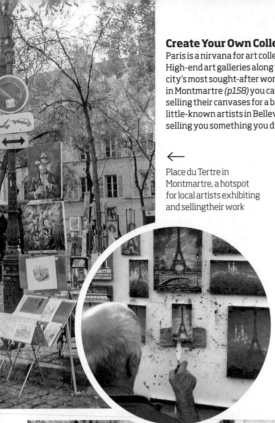

TOP 5 ART MUSEUMS

Musée du Louvre
The world's most visited museum and home of the Mona Lisa (p184).

Musée d'Orsay
Dedicated to Western art between 1848 and 1914, its main draw is Impressionism (p238).

Musée Picasso Paris
The greatest collection of the legendary artist's iconic works (p88).

Pompidou Centre
An eye-catching modern building that houses an equally memorable art collection (p90).

Palais de Toyko
A daring, and often overlooked, contemporary collection (p231).

Striking Street Art

From the wily Space Invaders that dot the city to work of the iconic Miss.Tic, Paris is a haven for street art. Some of it appears clandestinely overnight while other murals, especially around the Canal St-Martin or even along Rue Dénoyez in Belleville (p133), are city initiatives to encourage street artists. Explore these ever-changing works by taking a wander around eastern Paris, or booking a tour with Street Art Tour Paris.

↑ An alley in the Marais decorated with some of the city's colourful street art

Rue Cremieux

Located by the Gare de Lyon *(p108)*, Rue Cremieux and its colourful buildings are the stuff of Instagram lore. While the rest of the neighbourhood provides precious little beauty, these pastel façades shine on a sunny day.

→

Rue Cremieux, one of the prettiest streets in Paris

PARIS FOR
PHOTOGRAPHERS

Paris can't help being photogenic – it's where photography was born in the 1800s with the daguerreotype, so the city has a history of smiling at the camera. Here's an insider's guide to finding Paris's most picturesque spots.

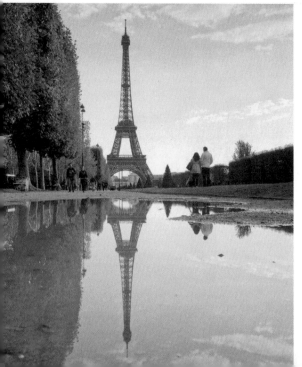

Eiffel Tower in a Puddle

It's as clichéd as it comes, but who cares? Put a rainy day in Paris to creative use. The Champ-de-Mars *(p211)* is riddled with puddles after a shower, so score your own artful photo by taking a low-angled shot of the Eiffel Tower reflected in a pool of water. To pack your picture with extra punch, use the trees along the park's avenues to create leading lines that draw the viewer's eye to the tower in the middle – a framing technique that works just as well if you're shooting in dry weather.

 ←

A classic shot of the Eiffel Tower and its watery reflection

Rooftop View

Shots of the the roofs of Paris are best taken from atop Printemps *(p177)*. Ride the escalator to the department store's roof for a postcard-perfect view. Looking northward in the early evening, the Sacré-Coeur glistens as Paris illuminates itself.

→ The view from the top of Printemps at twilight

FAMOUS PHOTOGRAPHERS OF PARIS

Parisian painter Louis Daguerre was one of the fathers of modern photography and the inventor of the daguerreotype. It was here in the city, on Boulevard du Temple, that he experimented with his innovative technology to take what became known as the first candid photo of a person: a man getting a shoe-shine. Later French photographers such as Henri Cartier-Bresson and Robert Doisneau helped turn photography into an art with their inventive shots of the city.

↑ The illusory "sinking house" on a bright summer day

INSIDER TIP
Sunset Shot

Capture the golden hour in Paris on a bridge by Île de la Cité, looking west at the sunset.

The "Sinking House"

The "sinking house" in Montmartre is a popular shot with travellers and locals alike. Walk up the stairs to the Sacré-Coeur *(p156)* and look to the right on the final flight, where you will see the corner of a perfectly upright orange-and-cream apartment building peeking out behind the lawn. To create the optical illusion, tilt your camera to follow the angle of the grass.

Go Wild at the Zoo

Paris has two zoos, and both will captivate small children and teens alike. Meet the world-famous primates at the Ménagerie in the Jardin des Plantes (p268), Europe's second oldest zoo, with enclosures dating back to the time of Napoleon. At the modern zoo in the Bois de Vincennes (p294), visitors are immersed in animal habitats such as the grassy African savannah, where lanky giraffes and lazy lions await.

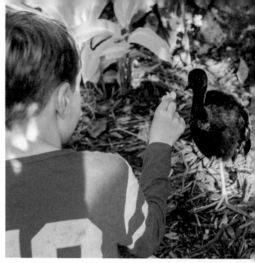

→

Exotic birdlife at the Parc Zoologique de Paris in the Bois de Vincennes

PARIS FOR
FAMILIES

Paris is a playground for kids, with engaging parks and family-friendly events throughout the year. Children – and adults – will delight in riding the carousel in the Jardin des Plantes, watching a puppet show at the Jardin du Luxembourg or enjoying the beaches of the Paris Plages.

Take a Boat Trip

Boat cruises along the Seine or the canal at La Villette are a family favourite. Parents have the chance to relax while kids watch the city pass them by. Options along the Seine include Bateaux Mouches, Vedettes du Pont Neuf and Bateaux Parisiens, while the main company for the canal is Canauxrama. The 19th-century locks of the canal are especially curious, as is the cavernous tunnel that the tour takes you through.

A boat tour cruising along the Seine, past the Eiffel Tower ↑

Be a Chef for the Day

The kitchen is the heart of any family, so learn to cook together with a class at La Cuisine Paris (p96). This well-appointed cooking school in the Marais offers English-language lessons in making a variety of traditional French dishes. Discover how to make buttery croissants or roll out your own baguettes before tasting the fruits, or rather pastries, of your labour. It's a sure-fire way to keep the whole family busy and smiling for a few hours, even if you end up covered in flour.

← Learning the basics of French baking at a cooking school

TOP 5 RAINY DAY MUSEUMS

Muséum National d'Histoire Naturelle
Home to thousands of impressive animal specimens (p266).

Musée de la Chasse et de la Nature
A collection of hunting trophies (p96).

Aquarium de Paris - Cinéaqua
An underwater wonderland situated across from the Eiffel Tower (p223).

Cité des Sciences et de l'Industrie
A huge science museum, packed with interactive exhibits (p144).

Palais de la Découverte
Science for kids just off the Avenue des Champs-Élysées (p228).

💬 INSIDER TIP
Eating Out

Parisians don't typically take their children to higher-end restaurants, so choose somewhere more family oriented, such as the chain Hippopotamus or the budget-friendly Chez Gladines (p255), where the food is still good but the atmosphere more relaxed.

Search for Hidden Treasure

Paris's museums are huge, but a treasure hunt provides an exciting new way of exploring them. A little rivalry, a bit of learning and a whole lot of fun await anyone who embarks on a hunt with THATMuse at the Louvre (p184) or Musée d'Orsay (p238).

→ Posing for a photograph as part of a treasure hunt at the Louvre

Daily Bread

Although French bread needs no introduction, there is, nevertheless, an art to choosing it. In Paris, all baguettes are not created equal. Ask for a *baguette à la tradition* to get the Parisian favourite, a regulated loaf that has nothing beyond the essentials inside. Crusty and handmade, these baguettes are tastier and delectably chewier than some regular crumbly baguettes. Try a *baguette bien cuite* if you like your bread well-baked and extra crispy.

$\rightarrow$

Fresh, crunchy baguettes, available for sale at any neighbourhood boulangerie

PARIS FOR
FOODIES

Paris is legendary for its cuisine, so make sure you pack your appetite. Whether it's haute cuisine, rich, buttery pastries or rustic regional dishes, the city's delectable array of fresh, quality produce will delight your taste buds – though perhaps not your waistline.

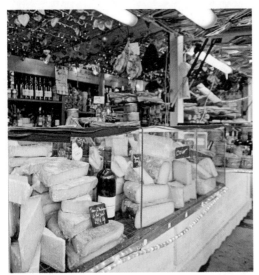

Flavourful fromage

Cheese is a way of life in France and punctuates any worthwhile meal. Cheesemongers dot Paris's streets and markets with hundreds of different pungent, subtle and salty varieties, their shops lined with huge, aged wheels and fresh, delicate discs. Try a bit of everything, following the vendor's suggestions. A mix of creamy, stinky but irresistible goat, cow and sheep's milk cheese is a perfect example of France's finest *fromages*.

$\leftarrow$

An array of delicious cheeses on display at a market stall

TOP 4 ETHNIC CUISINES IN PARIS

With its multicultural population, the city also offers diners an amazing selection of world flavours – particularly those of France's former colonies.

North African
Couscous and tagine are popular dishes.

Vietnamese
Waves of immigration mean stellar *bo bun* and *bao minh*.

Middle Eastern
Falafel in the Marais is unparalleled.

Japanese
Ramen around Rue Ste-Anne is worth the wait.

→

Mouthwatering pastries for sale in one of the city's many patisseries, where delicate *macarons (above)* are a regular feature

MARKET STREETS

Shop like a Parisian on market streets, where stores focus on specific goods and outdoor stalls often pop up at weekends. Trendy Rue Montorgueil is a good stop for bread and cheese, while pastries are the draw on Rue Cler *(p209)*. Sample caramels and candies on Rue des Martyrs *(p165)* or shop for fresh produce along Rue Mouffetard *(p269)*.

Heavenly Patisserie

From the mighty *macaron* and spongy madeleines to creamy éclairs and tangy lemon tarts, Paris's patisseries are where taste buds go to be reawakened. Every corner bakery produces its own sweet, buttery or otherwise decadent versions of the classics. If there's a queue at your chosen boutique, chances are you've made the right choice.

Opera and Ballet

The palatial Opéra Garnier (p172), home to the ballet, is a fairy-tale experience. Showing both opera and dance productions, it's a classic dose of Paris's musical heritage. The more modern Opéra Bastille (p106), a stunning glass venue, lacks the romance but delivers on acoustics. There's not a bad seat in the house from which to take in a production.

←

A ballet performance at the Opéra Garnier, the historic home of the ballet

PARIS FOR
LIVE MUSIC

From elegant symphonies to buskers in the Metro, Paris is a constant concert. World-class singers belt out centuries-old operas on stages that also welcome contemporary musical comedies or the latest pop artist. In the streets, the hum of accordions and funky jazz renditions infuse the air.

Paris Philharmonic

The glittering Philharmonie de Paris (p147) immerses spectators in the musical experience. You're never more than 32 m (105 ft) from the conductor, and cutting-edge acoustics mean you won't miss even the softest flute. Home to Paris's symphony, it's a daring space that will envelop you in sound.

↑ Chinese pianist Lang Lang performing at the Philharmonie de Paris

Contemporary Music

Contemporary music flourishes in Paris, and local venues such as La Maroquinerie *(p134)* host up-and-coming artists. Familiar faces grace the stages of L'Olympia, where Edith Piaf famously sang, while smaller venues like La Cigalle offer a more intimate concert experience. Major pop and rock acts pass through the arena by Bercy *(p113),* or even the Stade de France, for massive, bass-blowing concerts.

Major Lazer performing at L'Olympia

> 💬 **INSIDER TIP**
> **Music Festival**
>
> Celebrate the summer solstice with street buskers and concerts during June's all-night Fête de la Musique *(p58).*

Musical Theatre

Paris has no Broadway or West End, but its growing musical theatre scene has French audiences applauding at the stage call. Experience classics such as *My Fair Lady* and *Singin' in the Rain* in English amid the splendour of the revamped 19th-century Théâtre du Châtelet. For French versions of modern musicals, from *Grease* to *Mamma Mia!*, head to the Théâtre Mogador *(p175)* in the Opéra district.

TOP 5 JAZZ VENUES

Sunset-Sunside
An intimate venue in Châtelet.

La Petite Halle
A newcomer on the scene in La Villette.

Duc des Lombards
In the Latin Quarter and practically a pilgrimage for musical artists.

New Morning
An obligatory stop for real jazz enthusiasts.

Chez Papa
An elegant jazz venue with restaurant.

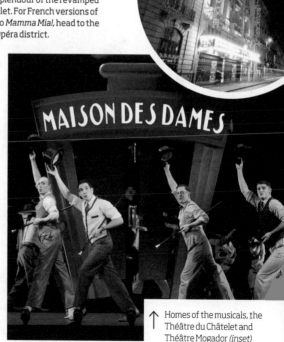

↑ Homes of the musicals, the Théâtre du Châtelet and Théâtre Mogador *(inset)*

Idyllic Gardens

Flowers seem to bloom year-round in Paris's gardens. The hidden Jardin du Palais-Royal *(p188)* features fragrant roses, while the Jardin des Plantes *(p268)* grows exotic specimens from around the globe. The Luxembourg *(p286)* and Tuileries *(p191)* gardens are exquisite examples of royal property turned public.

An avenue of trees within the arcade-lined enclosure of the Jardin du Palais-Royal

PARIS FOR
GREEN SPACES

Perfectly manicured flower beds, sheared and shaped shrubbery, and spouting fountains decorate every corner of Paris. Former royal hunting grounds and private gardens are today lush green spaces where locals congregate to stroll or play a friendly game of *pétanque*.

TOP 4 LOCAL FAVOURITES

These lesser-known green spaces are popular spots where locals relax.

Parc des Buttes-Chaumont
Hilly, pristine and popular on weekends *(p146)*.

Parc Monceau
Well-heeled Parisians picnic here *(p228)*.

Parc de la Villette
The place for football matches and jogging *(p142)*.

Place des Vosges
A tiny green space in a royal setting *(p92)*.

Innovative Reclaimed Space

Some of Paris's most successful modern green spaces have flourished out of former industrial expanses. Visit the Coulée Verte René-Dumont (p106), an elevated train track that traded trains for tulips – the entire walkway is akin to a hanging garden sitting above the city. The Berges de Seine (p210), a pedestrianized roadway along the river, features barges doubling as floating gardens.

→

The Coulée Verte René-Dumont, on a former railway track

INSIDER TIP
Flower Market

The Marché aux Fleurs Reine Elizabeth II (p77) is a gardener's playground. Flowers spill onto the street, while bulbs, seeds and tools fill the market stalls.

Relaxing Parks

In the 19th century, city planners built two green lungs – the Bois de Boulogne (p292) and Bois de Vincennes (p294) – on either side of Paris. Natural woodland, peaceful ponds and seemingly endless trails form this pair of bucolic havens. Each houses botanical gardens and various architectural features, as well as surprises such as an open-air theatre. Beyond the gardens of Versailles (p296), the vast Parc de Versailles allows visitors to wander through pristine parkland.

↑ The verdant parkland of the Bois de Vincennes and Bois de Boulogne (inset)

43

On Stage and Screen

As the location of Molière's final performance (at the Palais Royal) and home of the world's oldest continuing theatre - the Comédie-Française, founded in 1680 - Paris has a rich pedigree when it comes to the stage. On the silver screen, the city has notably provided the backdrop to New Wave classics such as *Breathless* and *Jules et Jim*, and more recently to *Amélie*'s heartfelt quest for love in Montmartre - the Café des 2 Moulins, where she worked, can be visited on Rue Lepic.

←

Audrey Tautou as the title character in 2001's charming *Amélie*

  INSIDER TIP
Famous Tombs

Visit icons such as Oscar Wilde and Edith Piaf at their final resting place in the Cimetière du Père Lachaise *(p130)*.

PARIS FOR
INSPIRATION

Paris has inspired countless thinkers and artists over the years. The centre of the Enlightenment, a fashion hub and a popular location for films since the Lumière brothers invented the cinema, the city is rich in cultural capital. Trace the steps of its icons to stimulate your own imagination.

Iconic Residents

From Chanel and Marie-Antoinette to Voltaire and Pasteur, Paris has hosted a long list of world-famous icons who have contributed to philosophy, art, science and culture. See Marie-Antoinette's bedchamber at Versailles (p296), sip coffee in Les Deux Magots as Hemingway did (p244) and pay homage to Chanel at her first boutique on Rue Cambon.

↑ The legendary Chanel clothing boutique at 31 Rue Cambon

← Inside the opulent bedchamber of Marie-Antoinette at the Palace of Versailles

Literary Paris

The iconic Shakespeare and Company bookshop (p258) is always bustling, a testament to the staying power of the written word. Paris has been the backdrop for countless epic novels, including Notre Dame de Paris and Les Misérables. Search for the phantom at the Opéra Garnier (p172), stroll Rue Montorgueil like Florent in The Belly of Paris and keep an eye out for Les Misérables' Gavroche around the Bastille (p104) – or maybe in Victor Hugo's house (p93), where he penned his most famous work.

← The Opéra Garnier, the setting for The Phantom of the Opera

TOP 5 FOREIGN WRITERS WHO LIVED IN PARIS

Ernest Hemingway
The US author wrote A Moveable Feast about his time living in Paris from 1921 to 1926.

F Scott Fitzgerald
US writer Fitzgerald lived in Montparnasse in the 1920s.

George Orwell
The English novelist tells of his experiences living in poverty in Down and Out in Paris and London (1933).

James Joyce
Irish writer Joyce lived in Paris from 1920 to 1940. Ulysses was published here in 1922.

Anaïs Nin
Novelist Nin met her lover, fellow American Henry Miller, in Paris.

Visitors walking through ↑
the beautifully landscaped
Jardin des Tuileries

PARIS ON A
SHOESTRING

Paris attracts droves of budget travellers with good reason. Free museums and green spaces keep visitors active during the day, while low-cost street food and happy hours make evenings a pleasure. And what beats a picnic along the Seine with a bargain bottle of wine, a baguette and some cheese?

Churches

Most churches in Paris are public property, open to visits for no fee. Avoid the tourist crowds at Notre-Dame and the Sacré-Coeur, and instead head for the beautiful St-Sulpice *(p243)*, Paris's second largest church, which houses paintings by Delacroix. St-Étienne-du-Mont *(p257)*, next to the domed Panthéon, is often deserted, despite containing the tomb of St Geneviève – the patron saint of Paris. With stunning stained glass and countless artworks, these monuments are as awe-inspiring as they are budget-friendly.

→

The magnificent St-Étienne-
du-Mont church

Parks and Gardens

From the top of Parc des Buttes-Chaumont (*p146*) to the furthest reaches of the Bois de Boulogne (*p292*) and the Bois de Vincennes (*p294*), greenery in Paris is, generally, free. Discover the ornate Médici Fountain in the Jardin du Luxembourg (*p286*) and view the obelisk at Place de la Concorde from the Jardin des Tuileries (*p191*). Have a pond-side picnic in Parc Monceau (*p228*) or join a game of *pétanque* in the Jardin du Palais-Royal (*p188*). It's astonishing that these pristine parks and gardens require no fee, but such is the magic of Paris.

← Locals playing a game of *pétanque* in the Jardin du Palais-Royal courtyard

TIPPING

The great mystery of tipping has a simple answer: tip sometimes. For meals, round the bill to the closest euro if you must. For taxis, add a euro or two. In hotels, express gratitude to housekeeping. Your tour guide was stellar? Let it be known. But never feel like you have to add 15 percent for every experience. Employees in France get paid real salaries, so your tip expresses pure gratitude.

Did You Know?

Many ticketed museums are free on the first Sunday of the month – check websites for details.

One of the lavishly decorated rooms in the Musée Carnavalet ↑

Municipal Museums

A number of city-run institutions such as the Maison de Victor Hugo (*p93*) and the Musée Carnavalet (*p97*), dedicated to Parisian history, are free. While special exhibitions are ticketed, the main collections are open to the public. Even contemporary art at the Musée d'Art Moderne de la Ville de Paris (*p230*) is accessible for visitors to view. The quaint Musée Cognacq-Jay (*p92*) fills a historical mansion, while the soaring Petit Palais (*p225*) is housed in an exhibition hall built for the 1900 Exposition Universelle.

High-End Shopping

The home of Chanel, Dior and Gaultier, Paris excels at high-end boutiques. Avenue Montaigne *(p228)* is a sight in and of itself, with all of the designer names that most will recognize and few can afford. These aren't places to wander in casually in your trainers and shorts, they are the real deal – just ask the security guards who double as bouncers. Equally prestigious shops exist around Rue St-Honoré and in the St-Germain neighbourhood *(p241)*, while the Marais has recently become a centre for men's haute couture.

→

Rue St-Honoré and Avenue Montaigne *(inset)*, two of the city's most pretigious shopping streets

PARIS FOR
SHOPPERS

Paris is synonymous with fashion, and for many people Parisian style is the ultimate in chic. In addition to clothing, the city is also a treasure trove of boutiques selling one-of-a-kind items that you can't get elsewhere. Whether it's a flea market find or a scarf from Hermès, the fun is in the hunt.

Department Stores

Paris brought department store shopping to life with Le Bon Marché *(p243)*. Today there are several emporiums to choose from, but the formula is the same. Browse the designer outlets on the ground floors, amid masses of visitors queueing for the latest bag, before ascending the escalators through floor after floor of multi-brand bliss. When it all gets too much, take a breather on the rooftop in the scenic café at Printemps *(p177)* or the deck at Galeries Lafayette *(p175)*.

←

The stunning Art Nouveau interior of Galeries Lafayette

COCO CHANEL

Born into poverty and raised in an orphanage, the iconic Coco Chanel (1883-1971) opened her first shop in Paris in 1913. It sold hats and sportswear made from simple fabrics such as jersey, which proved popular with women seeking relief from restrictive corsets. The designer revolutionized fashion in the 1920s with the introduction of the little black dress and the launch of Chanel No.5, the first perfume to bear the name of a designer.

Did You Know?

The "Made in France" label signifies products that are authentic local items.

Shoppers browsing the ↑ wares at the Marché aux Puces de St-Ouen

Flea Markets

Parisians frequently sell their belongings, and flea markets attract shoppers each weekend. The maze-like Marché aux Puces de St-Ouen at Porte de Clignancourt *(p305)* is the place to spend money on antique lamps, chairs and other homewares to create your own personal Versailles. Browse, feign interest and bargain when necessary – perhaps not on the €5 trinket box, but the €5,000 Louis XV chair may be negotiable.

World War II Scars

Hitler gave orders for Paris to be levelled at the end of the Nazi Occupation, but they were disobeyed by the general in charge of the city, who instead surrendered. Relatively few physical scars remain from the Occupation of 1940–44, but marks on the front of the police office on Île de la Cité *(p77)* recall skirmishes between Resistance fighters and German forces.

←

The police office on Île de la Cité, the scene of fighting during World War II

PARIS FOR
HISTORY BUFFS

There are more than two millennia of history to visit in Paris. From Viking invasions and plagues to Revolution and Nazi Occupation, the past comes alive in the museums, streets and cafés - basically everywhere.

TOP 4 HISTORY MUSEUMS

Musée de l'Armée
Military history from medieval knights to Charles de Gaulle *(p206)*.

Musée Carnavalet
An in depth exploration of the history of Paris, located in two former mansions *(p97)*.

Pavillon de l'Arsenal
Houses an exhibition charting the evolution of architecture in Paris *(p93)*.

Musée de Cluny
Specializes in medieval history, and also houses Gallo-Roman ruins *(p254)*.

→
The Arc de Triomphe du Carrousel at the entrance to the Jardin des Tuileries

Napoleonic Memorials

The mark of the 19th-century emperors Napoleon I and his nephew, Napoleon III, is visible throughout the city. If you see an "N" on a bridge or monument, as on the façade of the Louvre *(p184)*, it's easy to date that particular work to one of those men. Napoleon I also commissioned several monuments in his own honour, including the Arc de Triomphe *(p218)*, the smaller Arc de Triomphe du Carrousel *(p192)* and the bronze column in Place Vendôme *(p193)*.

Roman Remains

Few are aware that Paris was once a bustling Roman town. Boulevard St-Michel is a former Roman road, and ruins of the baths there are still on display next to the Musée de Cluny (p254). The enormous Arènes de Lutèce (p268), which today hosts football matches and playdates, once was a staging ground for Roman theatre and combats.

→

The ruins of the Arènes de Lutèce, once a vast Roman arena

 INSIDER TIP
Historic Tales

Test your French by reading the 700 or so Histoire de Paris signs all over the city, which recount historic events at the location where they happened. The oar-shaped plaques were designed by Philippe Starck.

The Flame of Liberty

More recent history is commemorated by impromptu memorials such as the Flame of Liberty. A copy of the torch held by the statue of the Lady Liberty in New York, it originally symbolized French-US relations. Today it informally honours Princess Diana, who tragically met her fate in 1997 in a car accident in the road tunnels below.

The golden Flame of Liberty, a tribute to Princess Diana ↓

↑ Napoleon's commemorative column in Place Vendôme

PARIS
RAISE A GLASS

Parisians have always enjoyed their tipples. Wine, imported from all over France, remains a staple, while a new wave of cocktail bars have reinvented how the city enjoys spirits. Beer, once brewed in belle époque brasseries, now gets the craft treatment in hip, upstart breweries.

Craft Beer

French beer has historically never been something to write home about. Today, however, bolshy breweries like Goutte d'Or and Paname Brewing Company *(p151)* are changing all that. The brasseries of the 19th century have ceded their hops and barley to younger brewers bringing craft beer to Paris. Sample their wares at establishments like La Fine Mousse *(p108)*, which specializes in French and international craft beers.

$\rightarrow$

The impressive beer
selection at La Fine Mousse

Innovative Wine

Parisian wine tastes have moved far beyond the clichés of red with meat and white with fish. While there's no reason to stray from French wine in the city, prepare to experiment with pairings that you might not have considered. When in doubt, always trust your server, who can advise you which bottle will suit your needs. And if you're still unsure, sample the house wine – often a sure-fire monthly offering.

←

Red wine flowing at a dinner among friends, and for sale at one of the city's many wine shops *(below)*

WINE TASTING

Booking an official tasting is often the best way to engage more fully with French wine. At Ô Chateau *(p193)*, English-speaking specialists offer tastings, a Champagne cruise and even a dinner where you can discover multiple vintages. Classes at Le Foodist include a cheese pairing, doubling as lunch with charcuterie, olives and various wine samplings. Events at Wine Tasting in Paris introduce participants to the various winemaking regions in France through different samplings.

Creative Cocktails

Bars like Candelaria and Prescription Cocktail Club have fully opened Parisian eyes to cocktails, a revolution that began over a century ago with the legendary Harry's Bar *(p175)*. A new wave of bartenders play with a variety of ingredients and flavours, creating a host of inventive concoctions. Sit back and enjoy the show, and have your patience rewarded with an Instagram-worthy cocktail that also tickles the tastebuds.

↑ The attractive façade of the cocktail bar Candelaria

Above the Skyline

Paris rose to new heights in the modern era. At first declared an eyesore, the 19th-century Eiffel Tower *(p200)* became a symbol of the city with its brown iron lattices. Enjoy a bird's-eye perspective of Paris from its viewing gallery. Alternatively, ascend the 20th-century Tour Montparnasse *(p284)* for panoramic views from a different angle. While not as elegant as the Iron Lady, its green makeover for the 2024 Olympic Games promises a change, joining shimmering contemporary structures like the Fondation Louis Vuitton *(p292)* and the Philharmonie de Paris *(p147)*.

$\rightarrow$

The view from the Tour Montparnasse, looking towards the Eiffel Tower

PARIS FOR
ARCHITECTURE

Planned and perfected, Paris showcases centuries of architectural styles. Jagged Gothic façades, soaring Neo-Classical domes and dazzling modern buildings dot the city. Admire Paris from a fresh perspective by tracing the city's architecture from its subterranean depths to the tip of the Eiffel Tower.

KEY ARCHITECTURAL STYLES

Gothic: this imposing style flourished in France, most famously at Notre-Dame *(p70)*.

Baroque: the lavish decoration of Versailles *(p296)* is typical of this style.

Neo-Classical: inspired by ancient Greece and Rome, this style is epitomized by the Panthéon *(p252)*.

Art Nouveau: incorporating curves and natural motifs, Art Nouveau details are still visible in the Metro station entrances.

Overhead

Most of Paris's architecture dates from the 19th century, when the city planner Baron Haussmann redesigned most of the city. His fashionable architectural innovations spread across France, and even to other countries. Amble along Haussmann's sweeping tree-lined boulevards and gaze up at the uniform façades that are a signature of his style. He was also known for the monumental intersections he created around lofty buildings, such as the cupcake-like Opéra Garnier *(p172)*.

Avenue de la Grande Armée, designed by Baron Haussmann $\uparrow$

Street Level

Medieval half-timbered houses and Renaissance palaces still dot the Marais, where history survived the ravages of conflict and city planning. See examples on Rue François Miron, or head over to the palatial Place des Vosges (p92), lined with pretty pink brick façades, for a taste of French Renaissance architecture under Henri IV.

The courtyards of these mansions once welcomed the regal carriages of Parisian nobility.

← Hôtel de Soubise, one of the numerous historic mansions in the Marais

BARON HAUSSMANN

Lawyer by training and civil servant by profession, Georges-Eugène Haussmann worked under Emperor Napoleon III to redesign Paris. Working with the best architects and engineers of the day, he tore down old buildings and cut new boulevards across the city. His controversial plans angered many, but the result was, arguably, quite striking. During his time, modern sewers, green leafy parks and strict building regulations gave us the Paris that we adore today.

Below Ground

Underground, Paris is a world unto itself. Discover the 18th-century Catacombes (p285), a dark and twisted tangle of limestone quarries that house the bones of millions of Parisians, transferred from overflowing cemeteries. The 19th-century sewers (p209) are also open for visits, showcasing the potent and often rat-infested network to daring tourists.

↑ The macabre Catacombes de Paris, decorated with millions of bones

Walk the Canal Towards La Villette

Head to the Canal St-Martin *(p118)* to experience a local vibe. Few tour groups make it to the green bridges arching over the water, flanked by cute boutiques and coffee shops. Walk north along the canal to La Villette, a district worth the trek. The modern park *(p142)*, with its concert hall and science museum, draws Parisian families.

←

Canal St-Martin, a popular spot with locals for strolling and picnicking

PARIS OFF THE
BEATEN TRACK

It's easy to escape the crowds without going too far. Hidden courtyards and museums in the centre lure those who want something different, while the outer districts hold charming cafés, monumental churches and oddball galleries. Discover where the Parisians live and see the local side of the city.

Explore Multicultural Belleville

A bustling Vietnamese and Chinese district, Belleville is an enclave for Parisian artists and a new generation of hipsters. Take a rewarding excursion through the hilly Parc de Belleville *(p132)* for sweeping panoramas of the city, then be enticed by the smell of *pho* (Vietnamese soup) wafting along Rue de Belleville *(p132)*. Street art and quaint cafés decorate the district, which is especially lively during the market on Tuesday and Friday.

↑ Shoppers browsing a neighbourhood flea market in Belleville

Shop with Parisians at the Marché d'Aligre

Live like a Parisian for a day at the Marché d'Aligre *(p106)*, one of Paris's most vibrant food markets. Barter for strawberries and have some mid-morning wine and oysters while filling your canvas bags with treats. The covered market, the Beauveau St-Antoine, is the best place to head for succulent sausages or tangy goat's cheese, while outside are fresh flowers, mountains of lettuce and stalls full of seasonal produce that will provide endless meal inspiration. The outdoor market also features stalls selling bric-a-brac and second-hand books.

Food stalls at the Marché d'Aligre, packed with an array of quality fresh produce

 INSIDER TIP
Quiet Spots in the Louvre

You can even escape the crowds within the heart of the Louvre, the world's most-visited museum. Head where tourist groups rarely go, upstairs to the Northern European painters or to the wings housing Islamic art and Near Eastern antiquities.

Make an Excursion to Paris's Green Lungs

Rowing lazily across one of the lakes in the Bois de Vincennes *(p294)* or the Bois de Boulogne *(p292)*, you'll wonder why all the tourists are still queuing for a boat ride along the Seine. These two large parks - lush green spaces situated on the outskirts of Paris - are often overlooked by visitors to the city. Stunning châteaus, exotic botanical gardens, a zoo, a mini amusement park and even the Fondation Louis Vuitton contemporary art gallery *(p292)* await those who make the trip across the Périphérique into these natural havens.

→ The Bois de Boulogne, home to the Fondation Louis Vuitton *(above)*

A YEAR IN
PARIS

JANUARY

△ **Fête des Rois** *(6 Jan)*. Feast on *galettes des rois* (a puff pastry cake) to celebrate the Epiphany.
Prix d'Amérique *(end Jan)*. World-famous trotting race, first held in 1920.

FEBRUARY

△ **Chinese New Year** *(early Feb)*. Parades and street festivals in Chinatown.
Salon International d'Agriculture *(end Feb–early Mar)*. One of the world's largest farming fairs.

MAY

Shakespeare Garden Festival *(throughout until Oct)*. Plays performed in Bois du Boulogne.
Nuit Européenne des Musées *(mid-May)*. Museums open for one spring evening.
Taste of Paris *(mid-May)*. Four-day food festival at the Grand Palais.
△ **French Tennis Open** *(end May–early Jun)*. Major tennis tournament.
Le Printemps des Rues *(end May)*. Art and performance festival in east Paris.

JUNE

Fête de la Musique *(21 Jun)*. All-day celebration of music, with many free events across the city.
Les Grandes Eaux-Nocturnes *(mid-Jun–mid-Sep)*. Music and light show in Versailles gardens.
△ **Gay Pride** *(end Jun)*. Lively parade and festivities.
International Paris Air Show *(end Jun)*. One of the oldest and largest air shows in the world.
Fête du Cinema *(end Jun–early Jul)*. Four-day film festival with discounted tickets.
Paris Jazz Festival *(end-Jun–end Jul)*. A celebration of jazz music held in the Park Floral de Paris.

SEPTEMBER

Jazz à La Villette *(mid-Sep)*. Programme of jazz-related music, films and exhibitions.
Journées du Patrimoine *(mid-Sep)*. Historical buildings open their doors to the public.
△ **La Parisienne** *(mid-Sep)*. A running race just for women.
Techno Parade *(end Sep)*. Electronic music festival.

OCTOBER

Nuit Blanche *(1st Sat)*. All-night art installations.
△ **Prix de l'Arc de Triomphe** *(1st Sun)*. Renowned flat race at the Hippodrome de Longchamp.
Mondial de l'Automobile *(1st fortnight, alternate years)*. Commercial motor show.
Foire International d'Art Contemporain (FIAC) *(end Oct)*. Modern and contemporary art fair.
BNP Paribas Masters *(end Oct–early Nov)*. Prestigious indoor tennis tournament.

MARCH

Printemps du Cinema *(late Mar)*. Discounted tickets available for films shown citywide.
Festival des Arts Martiaux *(late Mar)*. Martial arts fair.
△ **Foire du Trône** *(Mar–May)*. Funfair held in Bois de Vincennes with hundreds of rides and attractions.

APRIL

Easter *(10–13 Apr)*. Religious services plus chocolates galore.
△ **Paris Marathon** *(12 Apr)*. A lengthy run through the streets of Paris.
Foire de Paris *(Apr–May)*. Lifestyle, leisure, fashion and food at an enormous trade fair.

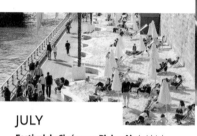

JULY

Festival du Cinéma en Pleine Air *(mid-Jul–mid-Aug)*. Outdoor cinema in La Villette.
△ **Paris Plages** *(Jul–Aug)*. The seaside comes to the Seine.
Paris Quartier d'Été *(mid-Jul–early Aug)*. Citywide dance, music, theatre and ballet.
Bastille Day *(14 Jul)*. Fireworks and festivities.
Tour de France *(end Jul)*. The world's greatest cycle race arrives in Paris.

AUGUST

Festival Classique au Vert *(mid-Aug–early Sep)*. Classical music in the Parc Floral.
△ **Rock en Seine** *(end Aug)*. Major international rock music festival.

NOVEMBER

△ **Beaujolais Nouveau** *(3rd Thu)*. Celebrations to mark the arrival of a new vintage wine on Parisian shelves.
Salon des Vins des Vignerons Indépendants *(end Nov–early Dec)*. Independent festival for wine lovers and winegrowers.

DECEMBER

Christmas illuminations *(until Jan)*. Paris lights up to celebrate Christmas.
Nautic *(early to mid-Dec)*. International boat show presenting the latest from the seas.
△ **New Year's Eve** *(31 Dec)*. Light shows at the Arc de Triomphe bring in the new year.

1

A BRIEF
HISTORY

For over 2,000 years, Paris has survived endless invasions, wars and plagues that have tested the spirits of its citizens. The seat of power for world leaders such as Louis XIV and Napoleon, and the backdrop for events including revolution and Nazi invasion, Paris has endured – and with style.

From Roman Outpost to Capital City

The first permanent settlers, the Parisii, landed here around 2,500 years ago – though artifacts show that others were here before them. In 52 BC, Rome conquered the Parisii, creating an outpost called Lutetia. By the fall of the Roman Empire in the 3rd century AD, Paris was on the rise. Clovis I, King of the Franks, made the city his kingdom's capital in 508 and, despite outbreaks of plague and English occupation hammering at the city's morale over the following centuries, art and culture flourished. Notre-Dame rose from Île de la Cité and the University of Paris became a centre for European education.

1 A medieval map of Paris

2 The Sorbonne, seat of the University of Paris, in 1550

3 The Hundred Years' War between France and England

4 Revolutionaries storming the Bastille

Timeline of events

508

Clovis I, King of the Franks, establishes Paris as the capital of his kingdom, which becomes France

987

Hugh Capet, forbearer of all future kings of France, rules the Kingdom of Franks

1240

Church bells are regulated by clocks for the first time, facilitating the regulation of work hours in Paris

1429

Joan of Arc fails to retake Paris from English control and is burned at the stake one year later

A Cultural Centre

By the 1500s, the Italian Renaissance had arrived in Paris by way of the Medici family of Florence, and the city began to shine. Despite severe religious wars, exacerbated by the Protestant faith of King Henri IV, culture thrived with new foods, fashions and even ballet. The Louvre became a royal palace and the nobility constructed mansions in the Marais. The French monarchs made Paris a world capital, epitomized by Louis XIV's opulent château and gardens at Versailles.

Revolution

In the 1700s the Enlightenment blossomed in Paris while the monarchy shrivelled. Famine and excessive spending at Versailles, as well as near-constant war, led to a call to arms. The French Revolution put a turbulent end to divine right as citizens stormed the Bastille prison on 14 July 1789. In 1793, Louis XVI and Marie-Antoinette both met their ends at Place de la Concorde, subjected to the guillotine. Parisians shook their city – and country – to the core, and a new government strove to regain order in a country divided by various ideologies.

FIRSTS IN PARIS

1348 Bubonic Plague first arrives
1660 Coffee first arrives from the East
1728 First street signs are erected
1827 First giraffe arrives in Paris, a gift from the ruler of Egypt
1907 First woman gets a taxi licence in Paris
1986 First Paris Marathon takes place
2014 Anne Hidalgo, first female mayor, is elected

1528
François I returns the monarchy to Paris after a century-long hiatus

1546
Work starts on the new Louvre palace and the first stone quay is built along the Seine

1572
St Bartholomew's Day Massacre ends with some 2,000 Protestants dead in Paris, following the wedding of future King Henri IV and Marguerite de Valois

1671
Louis XIV moves the entire royal court to Versailles

1789
French Revolution dethrones Louis XVI and Marie-Antoinette from Versailles

1

2

The Napoleonic Era

The rise to power of military leader Napoleon Bonaparte saw France's influence spread throughout its newly created Empire. The Bourbon kings briefly returned to power after Napoleon's downfall, before giving way to Louis-Napoleon Bonaparte, known as Napoleon III, who pursued France's Second Empire in his great-uncle's tradition. During the latter half of the 1800s, he charged administrator Baron Haussmann with modernizing Paris, creating the sweeping boulevards that define the city. By 1860, towns such as Montmartre and Belleville had been incorporated into Paris, establishing the present-day city limits.

The Belle Époque

The end of the brief and bloody Paris Commune of 1871, in which the citizens of Paris rose up against the French government, marked the emergence of the new Third Republic, which flourished during the belle époque (beautiful age) of the late 19th and early 20th centuries. The Eiffel Tower soared over Paris in 1889 and in 1900 the Metro opened. Paris truly was a glittering city at the cutting edge of art and technology.

↑ Louis-Napoleon Bonaparte, Emperor Napoleon III

Timeline continued

1804
Napoleon crowns himself Emperor of France

1853
Baron Haussmann's renovations of Paris begin

1871
The Bloody Week sees up to 10,000 French citizens killed at the hands of the army during the Paris Commune uprising

1941
The first Jewish Parisians are arrested by occupying forces

1944
Paris is liberated from Nazi occupation

Occupation and Recovery

In 1940, during World War II, the republic fell to Nazi Germany. Parisians survived the Occupation – albeit emerging beaten and subdued – and the city slowly recuperated. In 1968, student protests threatened to upturn the government, but the unrest quickly subsided. A series of ambitious architectural projects began at this time, and by the turn of the millennium, Paris was a world-class city with modernization firmly in its sights The Vélib bike service changed the way Parisians travel, and cars were banned from the riverbanks, creating new green spaces.

Paris Today

Paris is a model city, attracting new businesses, embracing innovation and serving as an example for its European – and global – counterparts, while still retaining its traditional elements. The city was shaken again in 2015 by the Charlie Hebdo and Bataclan terrorist attacks, but it refuses to be cowed. Recently elected leaders, including future-facing mayors and a new president, have confirmed a commitment to Paris's status as a global city.

1 The Champ-de-Mars and Eiffel Tower during the Exposition Universelle of 1900 ↑

2 Students marching during the protests of 1968

3 The Vélib bike scheme, launched in 2007

4 A streetside memorial following the Charlie Hebdo attacks

1961–62
Often-deadly protests are held by Algerians in Paris over the French-Algerian War

1992
EuroDisney (now Disneyland® Paris) officially opens

1977
Jacques Chirac is installed as the first elected mayor of Paris since 1871

1968
Student riots and worker strikes take place in the Latin Quarter

2017
Emmanuel Macron, France's youngest president, moves into the Palais de l'Élysée

EXPERIENCE

A Notre-Dame gargoyle surveying the city

ÎLE DE LA CITÉ AND ÎLE ST-LOUIS

The history of Paris started on the Île de la Cité, an island formed by two meanders of the Seine. Inhabited by the Parisii Gauls from the 3rd century BC and taken over in 52 BC by Caesar's Romans, the Île de la Cité was the birthplace of river commerce, and in medieval times it became a centre of political and religious power. Some imposing evidence of this power can still be seen in the Conciergerie, a medieval palace-turned-prison, and in Notre-Dame, the island's world-famous Gothic cathedral. The huddles of tiny houses and narrow streets that once characterized the island were swept away by the spacious thoroughfares built in the 19th century, but there are still charming snippets of another time around the romantic Square du Vert-Galant and the venerable Place Dauphine.

At the island's eastern end, the Pont St-Louis connects it to the smaller Île St-Louis. This former swampy pastureland was transformed into an elegant 17th-century residential area, with picturesque tree-lined quays. More recently, it has been home to rich artists, actresses and heiresses.

ÎLE DE LA CITÉ AND ÎLE ST-LOUIS

Must Sees
1 Notre-Dame
2 Sainte-Chapelle

Experience More
3 Mémorial des Martyrs de la Déportation
4 Conciergerie
5 Crypte Archéologique
6 Hôtel Dieu
7 Marché aux Fleurs Reine Elizabeth II
8 Palais de Justice
9 Place Dauphine
10 Pont Neuf
11 Square du Vert-Galant
12 St-Louis-en-l'Île

Eat
1 Berthillon

Stay
2 Paris Perfect Flat Place Dauphine
3 Saint-Louis en l'Isle
4 Hôtel du Jeu de Paume

ÎLE DE LA CITÉ AND ÎLE ST-LOUIS

Centre Georges Pompidou

Archives Nationales

RUE RAMBUTEAU

RUE DU RENARD

RUE DES ARCHIVES

RUE DES BLANCS MANTEAUX

RUE DES FRANCS BOURGEOIS

RUE DU TEMPLE

RUE STE-CROIX

DE LA BRETONNERIE

RUE LA VERRERIE

Ⓜ Hôtel de Ville

ℹ Hôtel de Ville

RUE VIEILLE DU TEMPLE

Musée Cognacq-Jay

Musée Carnavalet

RUE DES ROSIERS

MARAIS

RUE DES FRANCS BOURGEOIS

Hôtel de Lamoignon

RUE DE LOBAU

RUE DE RIVOLI

RUE DU ROI DE SICILE

RUE PAVÉE

PLACE ST-GERVAIS

RUE FRANCOIS MIRON

St-Paul Ⓜ

Maison Européenne de la Photographie

Hôtel de Sully

QUAI DE L'HOTEL DE VILLE

🚇 Quai de l'Hôtel de Ville

RUE DE L'HOTEL DE VILLE

Mémorial de la Shoah

St-Paul-St-Louis

RUE CHARLEMAGNE

RUE ST-ANTOINE

RUE SAINT PAUL

Pont-Marie Ⓜ

Pont Louis Philippe

THE MARAIS
p84

QUAI DES CELESTINS

RUE DU PETIT MUSC

AUX FLEURS

RUE DU BELLAY

QUAI DE BOURBON

Pont Marie

Pont St-Louis

Square de l'Île de France

RUE LE REGRATTIER

RUE

RUE BUDE

RUE ST

③

④

RUE DES DEUX PONTS

Île St-Louis

① LOUIS

QUAI POULLETIER

QUAI D'ANJOU

BOULEVARD HENRI IV

SQUARE H GALLI

③ Mémorial des Martyrs de la Déportation

QUAI D'ORLEANS

Musée Adam Mickiewicz

St-Louis-en-l'Île

⑫

RUE POULLETIER

EN

L'ÎLE

Ⓜ Sully Morland

Pavillon de l'Arsenal

QUAI DE LA TOURNELLE

Pont de la Tournelle

LATIN QUARTER
p248

QUAI DE BETHUNE

Square Barye

Préfecture de Paris

BOULEVARD MORLAND

RUE DE PONTOISE

BLVD ST-GERMAIN

Pont de Sully

QUAI HENRI IV

RUE CARDINAL LEMOINE

RUE DES FOSSES SAINT BERNARD

QUAI SAINT-BERNARD

Institut du Monde Arabe

La Seine

SQUARE TINO ROSSI

RUE DU

RUE JUSSIEU

Université Pierre et Marie Curie

0 metres		250
0 yards		250

N ↑

PLACE JUSSIEU

Ⓜ Jussieu

❶ 🖊 🖊

NOTRE-DAME

📍 K8 🏠 Pl du Parvis Notre-Dame 75004 Ⓜ Cité 🚌 21, 38, 47, 58, 70, 72, 81, 82
Ⓝ Notre-Dame 🕐 Closed until further notice Ⓦ notredamedeparis.fr

No other building is more associated with the history of Paris than Notre-Dame (Our Lady). The "heart" of the country, both geographically and spiritually, the cathedral rises majestically at the eastern end of the Île de la Cité. A Gothic masterpiece, it was severely damaged by fire in 2019 – including the loss of its spire – and is currently closed to visitors while reconstruction is carried out.

Notre-Dame was built on the site of a Roman temple. After Pope Alexander III laid the first stone in 1163, an army of architects and craftsmen toiled for 170 years to realize Bishop Maurice de Sully's magnificent design. At the time it was finished, in about 1334, it was 130 m (430 ft) long and featured flying buttresses, a large transept, a deep choir and 69-m- (228-ft-) high towers.

Within the cathedral's hallowed walls, kings and emperors were crowned and royal Crusaders were blessed. But Notre-Dame was also the scene of turmoil. Revolutionaries ransacked it, banished religion, changed it into a temple to the Cult of Reason, and then used it as a wine store. Napoleon restored religion in 1804 and architect Viollet-le-Duc later restored the building to its former glory. Tragedy struck again in 2019, however, when a devastating fire engulfed the roof of the cathedral. Following a flood of high-profile donations, French President Emmanuel Macron vowed to rebuild Notre-Dame in time for the Paris 2024 Olympics.

↑ Jean Ravy's spectacular flying buttresses, with a span of 15 m (50 ft), at the east end of the cathedral

↑ The cathedral's legendary gargoyles (chimères), hiding behind a large upper gallery between the towers

> After Pope Alexander III laid the foundation stone in 1163, an army of architects and craftsmen toiled for 170 years to realize Bishop Maurice de Sully's magnificent design.

Timeline

1163
▲ Foundation stone laid by Pope Alexander III

1708
▲ Choir remodelled by Louis XIV, fulfilling his father's promise to honour the Virgin

1793
▲ Revolutionaries loot the cathedral and rename it the Temple of Reason

2019
▲ The cathedral's roof and spire are destroyed by a catastrophic fire

The West Front, featuring superb ↑
statuary, a central rose window
and an openwork gallery

Inside Notre-Dame

The high-vaulted central nave is bisected by a huge transept, at either end of which are medieval rose windows, 13 m (43 ft) in diameter. Although damaged by the collapse of the roof and spire in the 2019 fire, much of Notre-Dame's interior survived intact. This includes some of the works by major sculptors that adorned the cathedral – such as Nicolas Coustou's *Pietà* – which have been temporarily rehoused while the cathedral is rebuilt.

The spire was completely destroyed during the fire in 2019.

Galerie des Chimères

South tower

Portal of the Virgin

West rose window

Transept

The King's Gallery

387

steps up the north
tower lead to the
famous gargoyles.

Flying buttresses

South rose window

Treasury

1 A 14th-century screen
enclosed the chancel, offering
canons at prayer peace from
noisy congregations.

2 Behind the high altar is
Nicolas Coustou's *Pietà*,
standing on a gilded base.

3 Only the north
window retains its 13th-
century stained glass.

A MEDIEVAL ROMANCE

The 12th-century romance
between the monk Pierre Abélard
and the young Héloïse began in the
cloisters of Notre-Dame. Abélard
was hired as a tutor to the 17-year-
old niece of a canon, and a love
affair soon developed between the
teacher and his pupil. In his wrath,
Héloïse's uncle had the scholar
castrated and Héloïse took refuge
in a convent.

2 ⚡ Ⓜ 🛍

SAINTE-CHAPELLE

📍 J7 🏠 Blvd du Palais 75001 Ⓜ Cité 🚌 21, 27, 38, 85, 96 to Île de la Cité
🚇 St-Michel 🚢 Notre-Dame 🕐 Apr-Sep: 9am-7pm daily; Oct-Mar: 9am-
5pm daily 🚫 1 Jan, 1 May, 25 Dec 🌐 sainte-chapelle.fr

Ethereal and magical, Sainte-Chapelle has been hailed
as one of the greatest architectural masterpieces
of the Western world. In the Middle Ages, the devout
likened this church to "a gateway to heaven". Today,
no visitor can fail to be transported by the blaze
of light created by the 15 magnificent
stained-glass windows.

A Gothic Masterpiece

The chapel was built in 1248 by Louis IX
to house Christ's purported Crown of
Thorns (now housed in the Notre-
Dame treasury). A Gothic masterpiece,
its stunning stained-glass windows –
the oldest extant in Paris – are
separated by narrow columns that
soar 15 m (50 ft) to the star-studded,
vaulted roof. The windows portray over
1,000 biblical scenes, from Genesis
right through to the Crucifixion, in a
kaleidoscope of red, gold, green, blue
and mauve. Servants and commoners
worshipped in the Lower Chapel, while
the Upper Chapel was reserved for the
use of the king and the royal family.

Spire

Crown of
Thorns
decoration

Rose
window

Main portal

Lower Chapel

↑ The rose window,
telling the story of
the Apocalypse

Did You Know?

The spire is 75m (245 ft) high. It was erected in 1853 after four previous spires burned down.

Angel

Upper Chapel

① The Lower Chapel is not as light and lofty as the Upper Chapel, but is still magnificent.

② The windows of the Upper Chapel contain 600 sq m (6,458 sq ft) of stained glass.

③ Carved stone statues of the Apostles adorn the 12 pillars of the Upper Chapel.

ST LOUIS' RELICS

Louis IX was extremely devout, and was canonized in 1297, not long after his death. In 1239, he acquired the Crown of Thorns from the Emperor of Constantinople and, in 1241, a fragment of Christ's Cross. He built this chapel as a shrine to house them. Louis paid nearly three times more for the relics than for the construction of Sainte-Chapelle. The Crown of Thorns is now kept in Notre-Dame.

EXPERIENCE MORE

3

Mémorial des Martyrs de la Déportation

📍K8 🏛 Sq de l'Île de France 75004 ☎ 01 46 33 87 56 Ⓜ St-Paul, Maubert Mutualité, Pont Marie 🚆 St-Michel ⏰10am–5pm Tue–Sun (to 7pm Apr–Sep) 🚫1 Jan, 1 May, 15 Aug, 1 Nov & 25 Dec

The memorial to the 200,000 French men, women and children deported to Nazi concentration camps in World War II is covered with the names of the camps to which they were deported. Earth from these camps has been used to form tombs and the interior walls are decorated with poetry and thousands of glass crystals. At the far end is the tomb dedicated to the Unknown Deportee.

4

Conciergerie

📍J7 🏛2 Blvd du Palais 75001 Ⓜ Cité ⏰9:30am–6pm daily 🚫1 Jan, 1 May, 25 Dec 🌐paris-conciergerie.fr

The Conciergerie, part of the larger Palais de Justice (p78), was under the administration of the palace "concierge", the keeper of the king's mansion. When the monarch moved to the Marais (in 1417), the palace remained the seat of royal administration and law; the Conciergerie became a prison, with the "concierge" as its chief gaoler. Henry IV's assassin, Ravaillac, was imprisoned and tortured here.

During the French Revolution, the Conciergerie housed more than 4,000 prisoners, including Marie-Antoinette, who was held in a tiny cell,

and Charlotte Corday, who stabbed Revolutionary leader Marat as he lay in his bath. Ironically, the Revolutionary judges Robespierre and Danton also became "tenants" before being sent in turn to the guillotine.

The Conciergerie has a superb, four-aisled Gothic Salle des Gens d'Armes (Hall of the Men-at-Arms), the dining hall for the castle's 2,000 members of staff. The building, renovated in the

The old Conciergerie prison, with its medieval turreted towers, overlooking the River Seine ↑

↑ The Marché aux Fleurs, with its wonderful variety of seasonal and exotic flowers and plants

> During the French Revolution, the Conciergerie housed more than 4,000 prisoners, including Marie-Antoinette, who was held in a tiny cell.

19th century, retains the 14th-century clock on the Tour de l'Horloge (Clock Tower). It is the city's oldest public clock and is still operating.

⑤

Crypte Archéologique

📍 K8 🏠 7 Pl du Parvis Notre-Dame 75004 Ⓜ Cité, St-Michel 🕐 10am–6pm Tue–Sun 🚫 1 Jan, 1 May, 8 May, 25 Dec & religious hols 🌐 crypte.paris.fr

Situated on the main square (the *parvis*) in front of Notre-Dame and stretching 120 m (393 ft) underground, the Crypte Archéologique exhibits the remains of foundations and walls that predate the cathedral by several hundred years. The foundations of Paris's oldest rampart, dating from the 3rd century BC, are displayed, as are the medieval foundations of the Hôtel Dieu. Interactive touchscreens help to bring the exhibits to life. Within the crypt are also traces of a hypocaust, a sophisticated underground heating system used for heating ancient Roman thermal baths.

⑥

Hôtel Dieu

📍 K7 🏠 1 Pl du Parvis Notre-Dame 75004 📞 01 42 34 82 34 Ⓜ Cité

On the north side of the Place du Parvis Notre-Dame is the Hôtel Dieu, the city's oldest hospital, dating back to the 12th century. The original building stretched across the island to both banks of the river, but was demolished to make way for one of Baron Haussmann's urban-planning schemes. It was rehoused on the site of an old orphanage in 1878. The building now faces an uncertain future, as its services are being wound down and transferred elsewhere. It was nearby, at the Préfecture de la Police *(p82)*, in 1944, that the Paris police courageously resisted the German army; the battle is commemorated by a monument on Cour du 19-Août, within the Préfecture.

(p82)

EAT

Berthillon
Parisians flock to this ice-cream parlour for its unusual flavours.

📍 L8 🏠 29–31 Rue St-Louis-en-l'Île 75004 🚫 Mon, Tue 🌐 berthillon.fr.

€€€

⑦

Marché aux Fleurs Reine Elizabeth II

📍 K7 🏠 Pl Louis-Lépine 75004 Ⓜ Cité 🕐 8am–7pm Mon–Sat

The year-round flower market adds colour and scent to an area otherwise dominated by administrative buildings. It is the most famous and, unfortunately, one of the last remaining flower markets in the city of Paris, its attractive iron pavilions harbouring both seasonal flowers and a wide range of specialist varieties such as orchids. Each Sunday, it makes way for the Marché aux Oiseaux, an animal and bird market, which is probably best avoided by sensitive animal lovers.

Palais de Justice

9 J7 **△** 4-10 Blvd du Palais 75001 (main entrance by the Cour de Mai, 10 Blvd du Palais) **M** Cité **◷** 9am–6pm Mon–Fri **w** ca-paris.justice.fr

The monumental block of buildings stretching the entire width of the Île de la Cité was formerly the home of the central law courts, most of which have now moved into brand-new premises in the Clichy-Batignolles quarter in the 17th arrondissement. The site, occupied since Roman times, was the seat of royal power until Charles V moved the court to the Hôtel St-Paul in the Marais during the 14th century. In April 1793, the Revolutionary Tribunal began dispensing justice from the Première Chambre, but this court eventually degenerated during Robespierre's Reign of Terror. Plans are afoot to open up more of the site to the public.

---

9 Place Dauphine

9 J7 **△** 75001 (enter by Rue Henri-Robert) **M** Pont Neuf, Cité

Southeast of Pont Neuf is this ancient square, laid out in 1607 by Henri IV and named after the Dauphin, the future Louis XIII. It is actually triangular in shape and lined with cafés, wine bars and restaurants. In the middle is a park with trees and benches. No 14 is one of the few buildings to have avoided any subsequent restoration. This haven of 17th-century charm is popular with *pétanque* (boules) players.

→

The tranquil Square du Vert-Galant, at the extreme point of the Île de la Cité

Pont Neuf

9 J7 **△** Quai de la Mégisserie and Quai des Grands Augustins 75001 **M** Pont Neuf, Cité

Despite its name (New Bridge), this is the oldest of the existing bridges in Paris and has been immortalized by major literary and artistic figures since it was built. The first stone was laid by Henri III in 1578, but it was Henri IV who inaugurated it and gave it its name in 1607. His statue stands in the central section.

The bridge, which was the widest of its kind in Paris, has 12 arches and spans 275 m (912 ft). The first stone bridge in the city to be built without houses and with pavements for pedestrians, it heralded a new era in the relationship between the Île de la Cité and the river.

From its very beginning, the Pont Neuf has had heavy traffic, and it has undergone many renovations and repairs over the centuries.

⑪ Square du Vert-Galant

9 J7 **△** Île de la Cité 75001 **M** Pont Neuf, Cité

One of the most magical spots in Paris, this peaceful, tree-lined garden bears the nickname of Henri IV, *"vert-galant"*. This colourful monarch did much to beautify Paris in the early 17th century, and his popularity has lasted right up to this day. From here, there are splendid views of the Louvre and the Right Bank of the river, where Henri was assassinated in 1610. This is also the point from which the Vedettes du Pont Neuf pleasure boats depart.

Did You Know?

Henri IV's nickname, *vert-galant*, means "old flirt". The king was infamous for his womanizing.

The ornate interior of the Baroque church of St-Louis-en-l'Île

 St-Louis-en-l'Île

📍 L8 🏠 19 Rue St-Louis-en-l'Île 75004 📞 01 46 34 11 60 Ⓜ Pont Marie 🕐 10am-1pm & 3-7:30pm Tue-Fri, 10am-1pm & 3-8pm Sat, 10am-1pm & 3-7pm Sun

The construction of this church began in 1664 from plans by the royal architect Louis Le Vau, who lived on the island. It was completed and consecrated in 1726. Among its outstanding exterior features are the 1741 iron clock at the entrance and the pierced iron spire.

The interior, in the Baroque style, is richly decorated with gilding and marble. There is a statue of St Louis holding a Crusader's sword. A plaque in the north aisle bears the inscription "in grateful memory of St Louis in whose honour the City of St Louis, Missouri, USA is named". The church is also twinned with Carthage cathedral in Tunisia, where St Louis is buried.

STAY

Paris Perfect Flat Place Dauphine

Individual apartments with hotel service make this an ideal place for families or visitors who want to feel like a local.

📍 J7 🏠 25 Place Dauphine 75001 🌐 parisperfect.com

€€€

Saint-Louis en l'Isle

Elegantly decorated and offering comfort without going over the top.

📍 L8 🏠 75 Rue St-Louis-en-l'Île 75004 🌐 saintlouisenlisle.com

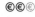

€€€

Hôtel du Jeu de Paume

The exposed wooden beams in this 17th-century building, along with the great location, make it a huge draw.

📍 L8 🏠 54 Rue St-Louis-en-l'Île 75004 🌐 jeudepaume hotel.com

€€€

Pont Neuf, straddling the Seine and the tip of the Île de la Cité

A SHORT WALK
ÎLE DE LA CITÉ

Distance 1.5 km (1 mile) **Nearest Metro** Cité
Time 15 minutes

The origins of Paris are here on the Île de la Cité, the boat-shaped island on the Seine first inhabited over 2,000 years ago by Celtic tribes. There is no older place in Paris, and remains of the first buildings can still be seen today in the archaeological crypt under the square in front of Notre-Dame. A stroll in this part of the city takes you from one Parisian icon – the great medieval cathedral – to another: the Gothic masterpiece that is Sainte-Chapelle.

A grisly antechamber to the guillotine, the Conciergerie prison was much used in the Revolution (p76).

The colourful, lively Marché aux Fleurs Reine Elizabeth II is one of Paris's few remaining flower markets. Birds are sold at the Sunday market (p77).

The Cour du Mai is the impressive main courtyard of the Palais de Justice.

START

A jewel of Gothic architecture, Sainte-Chapelle is one of the most magical sights in Paris, noted for the magnificence of its stained glass (p74).

The Quai des Orfèvres owes its name to the goldsmiths (orfèvres) who frequented the area from medieval times onwards.

With its ancient towers lining the quays, the Palais de Justice has a history that extends back over 16 centuries (p78).

The Préfecture de Police was the scene of intense battles during World War II.

Deep under the square, in the Crypte Archéologique, lie the remains of houses from 2,000 years ago (p77).

← A riverside view of the Conciergerie, a former prison

Patrons sitting outside one of the delightful cafés on the quaint Rue Chanoinesse

Locator Map
For more detail see p68

Did You Know?

In ancient times the island was used as a river crossing between northern and southern Gaul.

Once an orphanage, the Hôtel Dieu is now a city hospital (p77).

Point Zéro is the point from which all distances are measured in France.

Rue Chanoinesse has many charming old restaurants, cafés and shops.

The quaint streets of the Ancien Cloître Quartier were once home to medieval clergymen and students.

Notre-Dame cathedral is a superb example of French medieval architecture (p70).

The Square Jean XXIII is a peaceful square close to the river.

0 metres 100
0 yards 100
N

The Statue of Charlemagne commemorates the King of the Franks, who was crowned emperor in 800. He united all the Christian peoples of the West.

THE MARAIS

This district was little more than a muddy swamp until Henri IV built the Place Royale (now Place des Vosges) in 1605. But its position of prestige as a royal residence was soon swept away by the Revolution, which saw the Marais all but abandoned, before later descending into an architectural wasteland. Towards the end of the 19th century, a large number of Jewish settlers from Eastern Europe moved to the neighbourhood, establishing the Jewish Quarter around Rue des Rosiers. Beginning in the 1960s, sensitive restoration brought the Marais' historic buildings to life again; some of Paris's most popular museums are now housed in its elegant mansions, while the main streets and narrow passageways bustle with trendy restaurants, bars and chic boutiques. A hot spot for eclectic art galleries, the Marais is also the heart of the Parisian LGBT+ community.

THE MARAIS

Must Sees
1 Musée Picasso Paris
2 Pompidou Centre

Experience More
3 Musée Cognacq-Jay
4 Place des Vosges
5 Maison de Victor Hugo
6 Rue des Rosiers
7 Pavillon de l'Arsenal
8 St-Paul-St-Louis
9 Maison Européenne
de la Photographie
10 Mémorial de la Shoah
11 Hôtel de Ville
12 La Cuisine Paris
13 Enceinte de Philippe August
14 Hôtel de Guénégaud
(Musée de la Chasse et de la Nature)
15 Musée d'Art et d'Histoire
du Judaïsme
16 Musée Carnavalet

Eat
1 L'Ambassade d'Auvergne
2 L'As du Fallafel

Stay
3 Hôtel Jules et Jim
4 Hôtel de la Bretonnerie
5 Le Pavillon de la Reine

Shop
6 Mazet de Montargis
7 Edwart Chocolatier
8 Village St-Paul

BASTILLE AND
OBERKAMPF
p100

① ⊘⊗⊡⊡⊡
MUSÉE
PICASSO PARIS

📍M6 🏠Hôtel Salé, 5 Rue de Thorigny 75003 Ⓜ️St-Sébastien Froissart, St-Paul, Chemin Vert, Rambuteau
🚌29, 69, 75, 96 to St-Paul, Bastille, Pl des Vosges
🕐10:30am-6pm Tue-Fri; 9:30am-6pm Sat & Sun
🕐1 Jan, 1 May, 25 Dec 🌐museepicassoparis.fr

The Musée Picasso Paris holds the world's largest Picasso collection. Comprising over 5,000 works and tens of thousands of archived pieces, it offers an unparalleled insight into the artist's creative process.

↑ *Head of a Woman* (1931)

A visitor contemplating Picasso's *Femmes à leur Toilette* (1938) ↑

Spanish-born Pablo Picasso lived most of his life in France. Upon his death in 1973, the French state inherited many of his works in lieu of death duties. It used them to establish the Musée Picasso Paris, which opened in 1985. The museum is housed in a large 17th-century mansion, the Hôtel Salé, which was built in 1656 for Aubert de Fontenay, a salt-tax collector (*salé* means "salty"). The original character of the mansion has been preserved, and large sculptures adorn the garden and courtyard. Reopened in 2014 following a five-year renovation, the museum holds works spanning a full range of media – paintings, sculptures, ceramics, drawings and etchings – covering all of Picasso's creative periods. Be sure not to miss Picasso's own collection of paintings on the third floor.

↑ The Hôtel Salé, considered to be one of the most exquisite historic houses in the Marais

PICASSO IN FRANCE

Born in Malaga, Spain, Picasso first visited Paris in 1900. He moved to the city in 1904, before later settling in the south of France. After 1934, Picasso never returned to his homeland due to his rejection of Franco's regime. However, throughout his life in France he used Spanish themes in his art, such as the bull (often in the form of a minotaur) and the guitar, which he associated with his Andalusian childhood.

↑ *The Kiss* (1969), one of many works concerned with the theme of the couple painted by Picasso during his later years

2 🛷 🎨 🍴 🖥 🛍

POMPIDOU
CENTRE

📍K6 🏠Pl Georges Pompidou Ⓜ Rambuteau, Châtelet, Hôtel de Ville
🚌21, 29, 38, 47, 58, 69, 70, 72, 74, 75, 76, 81, 85, 96 🕐MNAM & temp
exhibitions: 11am-9pm Wed-Mon (to 11pm Thu); library: noon-10pm
Wed-Mon (from 11am Sat, Sun & pub hols); Atelier Brancusi:
2-6pm Wed-Mon 🌐centrepompidou.fr

Home to the Musée National d'Art Moderne, with over 60,000 works of art
by more than 5,000 artists, the Pompidou holds Europe's largest collection of modern and contemporary art. Looking like a building turned
inside out, its exterior is as eye-catching as the works on display within.

Blue: air
conditioning

Did You Know?
—
The Pompidou Centre's
collection was originally
housed in the Palais
de Tokyo *(p231)*.

← *With the Black Arc* (1912) by Vassily Kandinsky

← *Le Rhinocéros* (1999) by Xavier Veilhan

Museum Guide

The "historical" collections bring together the great artistic movements of the first half of the 20th century, from Fauvism to Abstract Expressionism. A rich collection of Cubist sculptures is displayed, as well as examples of the great masters of the 20th century. Matisse, Picasso, Braque, Duchamp, Kandinsky, Léger, Miró, Giacometti and Dubuffet command large areas at the heart of the collection, which also shows the groups and the movements on which the history of modern art is based, or by which it has been affected, including Dada, Abstract Art and Informal.

The contemporary art section occupies the fourth floor. The collection starts with works by leading French artists of the second half of the 20th century: Louise Bourgeois, Pierre Soulages, Jean-Pierre Raynaud, François

↑ The escalator overlooking the piazza

Morellet and Bertrand Lavier. The display is organized around a central aisle from which the rooms lead off. Certain areas have been designated to bring together different disciplines around a theme, such as minimalist painting or conceptual art, rather than a school or movement, while other rooms are artist-specific. Design and architecture are also covered, and there is a "global" room bringing together major pieces by African, Chinese, Japanese and American artists. A graphic arts exhibition room and a video area complete the collection.

— *Red: elevators and escalators*

— *Green: water*

Yellow: electricity

← The distinctive exterior of the Pompidou, with service pipes that are colour-coded according to their various functions

BRANCUSI'S STUDIO

The Atelier Brancusi, on the piazza, is a reconstruction of the workshop of the Romanian-born artist Constantin Brancusi (1876–1957), who lived and worked in Paris from 1904. He bequeathed his entire collection of works to the French state on condition that his workshop be rebuilt as it was on the day he died.

EXPERIENCE MORE

Musée Cognacq-Jay

📍M7 🏛Hôtel Donon,
8 Rue Elzevir 75003
Ⓜ St-Paul, Chemin Vert
🕙10am–6pm Tue–Sun
🚫Public hols 🌐musee
cognacqjay.paris.fr

This small, fine collection of
18th-century French works of
art and furniture was formed
by Ernest Cognacq and his
wife, Louise Jay, founder of the
Art Deco La Samaritaine, on
the Quai du Louvre, which was
once Paris's largest department store. The collection was
bequeathed to the city and is
now housed here in the Hôtel
Donon, an elegant building
dating from 1575 with an
18th-century façade and
wood-panelled rooms.

EAT

L'Ambassade
d'Auvergne

Regional cooking with
lots of cabbage and pork
dishes. Shared tables
are good for solo diners.

📍K6 🏛2 Rue du
Grenier-St-Lazare 75003
🌐ambassade-
auvergne.fr

€€€

L'As du Fallafel

The best Middle
Eastern food in Paris,
if the queues at
this bustling local
favourite are any
indication.

📍L7 🏛32 Rue des
Rosiers 75004
📞01 48 87 63 60

€€€

Place des Vosges

📍M7 🏛75003, 75004
Ⓜ Bastille, St-Paul

This square is considered
among the most beautiful in
the world by Parisians and
visitors alike. Its impressive
symmetry – 36 houses, nine
on each side, of brick and
stone, with deep slate roofs
and dormer windows over
arcades – is still intact after
400 years. It has been the
scene of many historic events
over the centuries. A three-
day tournament was held
here to celebrate the marriage
of Louis XIII to Anne of Austria
in 1615. Cardinal Richelieu,
pillar of the monarchy, stayed
here in 1615; the famous
literary hostess Madame de

Sévigné was born here in
1626; and the writer Victor
Hugo lived here for 16 years.
The arcades surrounding the
square are full of art galleries
and upmarket fashion
boutiques and often ring out
with the sound of buskers
playing classical music or jazz,
while at the centre of the *place*
is a lovely formal garden with
fountains and sandpits,
popular with young families.

> 💬 INSIDER TIP
> **Marais Mansions**
>
> Many of the former
> mansion houses in
> the Marais are open
> to the public; just walk
> through any doors that
> you see open.

A room decorated in ↑
Chinese style, in the
Maison de Victor Hugo

5
Maison de Victor Hugo

📍M7 🏠6 Pl des Vosges 75004 Ⓜ️Bastille, Chemin Vert, St-Paul 🌐maisons victorhugo.paris.fr

The French poet, dramatist and novelist lived on the second floor of the former Hôtel Rohan-Guéménée from 1832 to 1848. It was here that Victor Hugo wrote most of *Les Misérables* and completed many other famous works. Closed for renovation until spring 2020, the museum inside displays reconstructions of the rooms in which the writer lived, his vivid pen-and-ink drawings and caricatures, and books and mementos from the crucially important periods in his life, from his childhood to his exile between 1852 and 1870. It also holds temporary ticketed exhibitions on Hugo.

6
Rue des Rosiers

📍L7 🏠75004 Ⓜ️St-Paul, Chemin Vert

The Jewish quarter in and around this street is one of the most colourful areas of Paris. The street's name refers to the rose bushes within the old city wall. A Jewish community first settled here in the 13th century, with a second wave of immigration occurring in the 19th century from Russia, Poland and Central Europe. Sephardic Jews arrived from North Africa in the 1950s and 1960s. Some 165 students were deported from the Jewish boys' school nearby at 10 Rue des Hospitalières-St-Gervais in World War II. *"N'Oubliez" pas* (Lest we forget) is engraved on the wall. Today, this area contains synagogues, bakeries and kosher restaurants.

7
Pavillon de l'Arsenal

📍M8 🏠21 Blvd Morland 75004 Ⓜ️Sully Morland, Bastille 🕐11am–7pm Tue–Sun 🚫1 Jan 🌐pavillon-arsenal.com

The Pavillon de l'Arsenal houses a small but fascinating exhibition illustrating the architectural evolution of Paris. Using films, models and panoramic images, this permanent exhibition explores how Paris was built over the centuries, as well as looking at future plans for the city. The centrepiece of the exhibition is a large ground-level interactive screen showing Google Earth images of Paris and onto which are superimposed all the city's building projects planned for the next few years. Up to three temporary exhibitions are also programmed each year.

Paris's imposing town hall (Hôtel de Ville), with its elaborate façade ↑

8

St-Paul-St-Louis

📍 M7 🚪 99 Rue St-Antoine 75004 📞 01 42 72 30 32 Ⓜ St-Paul 🕐 8am-8pm daily

A Jesuit church, St-Paul–St-Louis was an important symbol of the influence that the Jesuits held from 1627, when Louis XIII laid the first stone, to 1762, when they were expelled from France. The Gesù church in Rome served as the model for the nave, while the 60-m-(180-ft-) high dome was the forerunner of those of the Invalides (p204) and the Sorbonne (p255). Most of the church's treasures were removed during periods of turmoil, but Delacroix's masterpiece Christ in the Garden of Olives can still be seen. The church sometimes hosts concerts. It is on one of the main streets of the Marais, but can also be approached by the ancient Passage St-Paul.

9

Maison Européenne de la Photographie

📍 L7 🚪 5-7 Rue de Fourcy 75004 Ⓜ St-Paul, Pont Marie 🕐 11am-7:45pm Wed-Fri, 10am-7:45pm Sat-Sun 🚫 Public hols 🌐 mep-fr.org

Located in the elegant 18th-century Hôtel Hénault de Cantobre, the Maison Européenne de la Photographie (MEP) hosts some of the best exhibitions of contemporary photography in Europe. It organizes cutting-edge shows alongside retrospectives on major photographers, and since opening its doors in 1996, it has hosted displays by such celebrated photographers as Elliott Erwitt, Don McCullin, Annie Leibovitz, Robert Doisneau and Henri Cartier-Bresson. The MEP's huge permanent collection on the history of photography is a must-see for anyone interested in exploring this medium.

THE MANSIONS OF THE MARAIS

In the 1500s, noble men and women began building sumptuous residences in the newly drained marshlands called the Marais. Many of these mansions, such as the Musée Carnavalet (p97) and Musée Cognacq-Jay (p92), have now been restored as museums.

DOOR DETAIL

10

Mémorial de la Shoah

📍L7 🏠17 Rue Geoffroy-l'Asnier 75004 Ⓜ Pont Marie, St-Paul ⏰10am–6pm Sun–Fri (to 10pm Thu); multimedia & reading rooms: 10am–5:30pm Sun–Fri (to 7:30pm Thu) 🗓Public & Jewish hols 🌐memorialdelashoah.org

The eternal flame burning in the crypt here is the memorial to the unknown Jewish martyr of the Holocaust. Its striking feature is a large cylinder that bears the names of the concentration camps where Jewish victims of the Holocaust died. In 2005, a stone wall engraved with the names of 76,000 Jews – 11,000 of them children – who were deported from France to the Nazi death camps, was put up here. Various drawings, letters and artifacts from the camps are also on display, as well as photos of deportees. Every other Sunday at 3pm, guided tours take place in English.

11

Hôtel de Ville

📍K7 🏠Pl de l'Hôtel de Ville 75004 (visitor entrance 29 Rue de Rivoli, exhibitions entrance 5 Rue de Lobau) Ⓜ Hôtel de Ville ⏰Hours vary for temporary exhibitions 🗓Public hols, official functions 🌐paris.fr

Home of the city council, the town hall is a 19th-century reconstruction of the original building erected between 1533 and 1628, which was burned down during the Paris Commune of 1871 *(p62)*. It is highly ornate, with elaborate stonework, turrets and statues overlooking a pedestrianized square whose fountains are lit up at night.

The square was once the main site for hangings, burnings and other gruesome executions. It was here that Ravaillac, Henri IV's assassin, was quartered alive in 1610, his body ripped to pieces by four strong horses.

Inside, a notable feature is the long Salle des Fêtes (ballroom), with adjoining salons devoted to science, literature and the arts. The impressive staircase, the decorated ceilings with their chandeliers, and the statues and caryatids all add to the air of ceremony and pomp. While these parts are mostly closed to the public (except during some of the Journées du Patrimoine in September), certain annexes are used for free, acclaimed temporary exhibitions on various themes related to Paris.

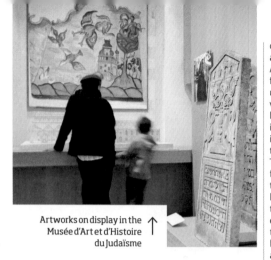

Artworks on display in the Musée d'Art et d'Histoire du Judaïsme ↑

city from attacks while he was away fighting in the Crusades. A hallmark of the wall was a fortress where the Louvre now stands; its remnants are visible today in the museum's lower levels. The section here in the Marais, however, hides in plain sight. It is still possible to see the large tower, the Tour Montgomery, that formed part of the gates through which everyone had to pass in order to enter the city. The wall was an effective means of regulating trade, allowing the king to levy taxes on imports such as wine and furs, as well as many other goods.

La Cuisine Paris

L7 **80 Quai de l'Hôtel de Ville 75004** **St-Paul** **lacuisineparis.com**

With Paris having so many restaurants and bakeries, few visitors stop to think about learning to make their own French-inspired dishes. La Cuisine offers a variety of cooking classes run by real French cooks, who teach you how to make classic savoury dishes as well as sweet pastries in a slick kitchen boasting views over the Seine. English-speaking instructors demonstrate the techniques behind buttery croissants and crusty baguettes, and demystify many of France's most iconic dishes, such as fluffy soufflés and perfectly prepared crêpes. Some of the classes offered even combine a market visit with a cooking

class where you prepare a whole lunch. After rolling up their sleeves for a few hours, La Cuisine students walk away with either a full belly or a package of flaky, buttery, or otherwise decadent pastries. The school also offers culinary walking tours of the Marais and nearby neighbourhoods for visitors wanting to discover local shops and flavours. Classes and tours are open to all ages and levels of experience.

Enceinte de Philippe Auguste

L7 **13 Rue Charlemagne 75004** **St-Paul, Sully Morland**

Dating back to 1190, these fortifications are the remains of Paris's oldest wall. King Philippe Auguste built the wall around Paris to protect the

Hôtel de Guénégaud (Musée de la Chasse et de la Nature)

L6 **62 Rue des Archives 75003** **Hôtel de Ville** **chassenature.org**

The celebrated architect François Mansart built this superb mansion in the mid-17th century for Henri de Guénégaud des Brosses, who was Secretary of State and Keeper of the Seals. One wing now contains the Musée de la Chasse et de la Nature

RIVERBANK WALK

After the success of the Left Bank renovation, Berges de Seine, Paris City Hall decided to tackle the Right Bank. In 2017, the two banks were joined as the Parc Rives de Seine, offering Parisians a place to stroll and jog along the waterfront. Citizens embraced the change, already acquainted with the car-free zone during the annual Paris Plages beach festival. Now, the festive atmosphere lasts all year long, with bars and cafés lining the promenade.

(Hunting Museum), inaugurated by André Malraux in 1967. Currently closed for renovations, the museum holds the collections of industrialist François Sommer and his wife Jacqueline; exhibits include a fine collection of hunting weapons and stuffed animals. There are also drawings and paintings by Jean-Baptiste Oudry, Peter Paul Rubens (including *Diane and her Nymphs Preparing to Hunt*) and Rembrandt.

Musée d'Art et d'Histoire du Judaïsme

L6 **Hôtel de St-Aignan, 71 Rue du Temple 75003** **Rambuteau** **11am-6pm Tue-Fri, 10am-6pm Sat & Sun** **1 Jan, 1 May, Rosh Hashanah & Yom Kippur** **mahj.org**

Housed in an elegant Marais mansion, the museum unites collections formerly scattered around the city, and commemorates the culture of French Jewry from medieval times to the present. There has been a sizeable Jewish community in France since Roman times, and some of the world's greatest Jewish scholars were French. Much exquisite craftsmanship is displayed, with elaborate silverware and Torah covers. There are also historical documents, photographs, paintings and cartoons.

Musée Carnavalet

M7 **16 Rue des Francs-Bourgeois 75003** **St-Paul, Chemin Vert** **carnavalet.paris.fr**

Currently closed for major building work, this fascinating museum, which charts the history of Paris, is scheduled to reopen in 2020 with completely refurbished displays of its vast collection. It occupies two adjoining mansions. The Hôtel Carnavalet, which was built as a town house in 1548, was transformed in the mid-17th century by architect François Mansart, while the neighbouring 17th-century Hôtel Le Peletier de St-Fargeau features superb early-20th-century interiors. In both, entire rooms are lavishly decorated with gilded wood panelling, furniture and objets d'art, including paintings and sculptures of prominent personalities, and engravings showing Paris being built. One of the most engaging parts of the museum is a section covering the French Revolution.

> After rolling up their sleeves for a few hours, La Cuisine students walk away with either a full belly or a package of flaky, buttery, or otherwise decadent pastries.

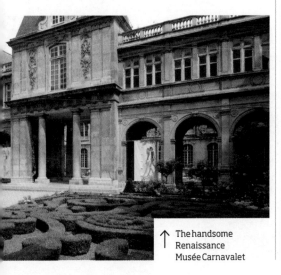

↑ The handsome Renaissance Musée Carnavalet

A SHORT WALK
THE MARAIS

Distance 1.5 km (1 mile) **Nearest Metro**
St-Paul **Time** 20 minutes

Once an area of marshland as its name suggests (*marais* means swamp), the Marais grew steadily in importance from the 14th century, by virtue of its proximity to the Louvre, the preferred residence of Charles V. Its heyday was in the 17th century, when it became the fashionable area for the monied classes. They built many grand and sumptuous mansions (*hôtels*) that still dot the Marais today – some of these *hôtels* have been restored and turned into museums. Once again fashionable with the monied classes, designer boutiques, trendy restaurants, art galleries and cafés now line the streets.

The renovated Hôtel Salé is the setting for the Musée Picasso Paris. It boasts the largest collection of Picassos in the world, many of which came from Picasso's own collection after his death (p88).

START

The ancient street of Rue des Francs-Bourgeois is lined with intriguing buildings and trendy shops.

The smell of hot pastrami and borscht wafts from restaurants and shops on Rue des Rosiers, the heart of the Jewish area (p93).

Discover the exquisite collection of 18th-century paintings and furniture at the Musée Cognacq-Jay (p92).

Behind the ornate doorway of the fine Hôtel de Lamoignon is Paris's historical library.

←

Cycling down the shopping street of Rue des Francs-Bourgeois

Locator Map
For more detail see p86

↑ The façade of the Musée Carnavalet, housed in two adjoining mansions

Did You Know?

It took Victor Hugo nearly two decades to write *Les Misérables*.

The Hôtel Le Peletier de St-Fargeau adjoins the Hôtel Carnavalet to form the Musée Carnavalet (p97).

The statue of Louis XIV in Roman dress by Coysevox is in the courtyard of the Hôtel Carnavalet, home to the Musée Carnavalet.

```
0 metres       100      N
0 yards        100      ↑
```

Once the site of jousting and tournaments, the historic Place des Vosges, in the very heart of the Marais, is a square of perfect symmetry (p92).

Author of Les Misérables, *Victor Hugo lived at No 6 Place des Vosges. The Maison de Victor Hugo is now a museum of his life and work (p93).*

FINISH

The Hôtel de Sully was built for a notorious gambler.

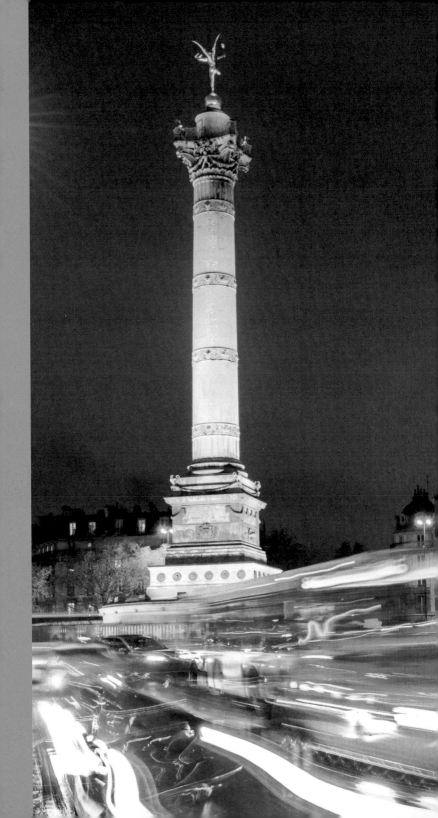

BASTILLE AND OBERKAMPF

East of the Marais, Bastille and Oberkampf were once Parisian *faubourgs*, or suburbs, well outside the main city wall in the Middle Ages. Furniture-makers inhabited the area around Bastille, capitalizing on wood delivered at the nearby docks, while Oberkampf was a working-class neighbourhood filled with artisans, including leather-makers. Where the Opéra National de Paris Bastille stands today, Parisians once gaped at the mighty Bastille – an imposing medieval prison fortress and symbol of royal repression, which famously met its demise in 1789 during the French Revolution. Throughout the 19th century, this largely working-class neighbourhood grew into one of Paris's most densely populated districts. In 1840, the Colonne de Juillet rose in Place de la Bastille, joined some 150 years later by the modern Opéra. Many of the artisans disappeared during this time, but an energetic nightlife grew up in their wake, fuelled by the culturally diverse and generally younger populations living here.

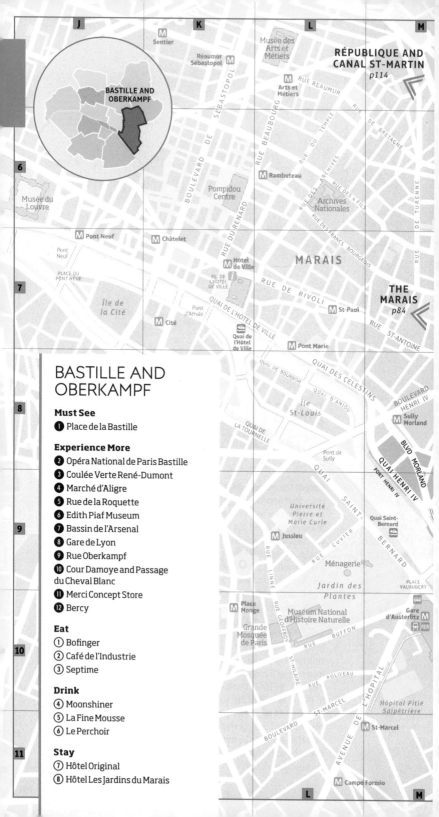

Sentier

Réaumur
Sébastopol

Musée des
Arts et
Métiers

RÉPUBLIQUE AND
CANAL ST-MARTIN
p114

Arts et
Métiers

RUE REAUMUR

BASTILLE AND
OBERKAMPF

RUE DE BRETAGNE

Musée du
Louvre

Rambuteau

Pompidou
Centre

Archives
Nationales

Pont Neuf

Châtelet

Hôtel
de Ville

MARAIS

Pont
Neuf

PLACE DU
PONT NEUF

PL. DE
L'HÔTEL
DE VILLE

RUE DE RIVOLI

St-Paul

THE
MARAIS
p84

Île de
la Cité

Pont
d'Arcole

QUAI DE L'HÔTEL DE VILLE

RUE ST-ANTOINE

Cité

Quai de
l'Hôtel
de Ville

Pont Marie

QUAI DE BOURBON

QUAI DES CÉLESTINS

QUAI D'ANJOU

BOULEVARD
HENRI IV

Île
St-Louis

Sully
Morland

QUAI DE
LA TOURNELLE

BLVD MORLAND

Pont de
Sully

QUAI HENRI IV

PORT HENRI IV

BASTILLE AND
OBERKAMPF

Must See

① Place de la Bastille

Experience More

② Opéra National de Paris Bastille
③ Coulée Verte René-Dumont
④ Marché d'Aligre
⑤ Rue de la Roquette
⑥ Edith Piaf Museum
⑦ Bassin de l'Arsenal
⑧ Gare de Lyon
⑨ Rue Oberkampf
⑩ Cour Damoye and Passage
du Cheval Blanc
⑪ Merci Concept Store
⑫ Bercy

Eat

① Bofinger
② Café de l'Industrie
③ Septime

Drink

④ Moonshiner
⑤ La Fine Mousse
⑥ Le Perchoir

Stay

⑦ Hôtel Original
⑧ Hôtel Les Jardins du Marais

Université
Pierre et
Marie Curie

Jussieu

QUAI SAINT-BERNARD

Quai Saint-
Bernard

RUE CUVIER

BERNARD

Ménagerie

RUE LINNÉ

Jardin des
Plantes

PLACE
VALHUBERT

Place
Monge

RUE GEOFFROY

Muséum National
d'Histoire Naturelle

Gare
d'Austerlitz

Grande
Mosquée
de Paris

RUE BUFFON

ST-HILAIRE

RUE POLIVEAU

AVENUE DE L'HÔPITAL

Hôpital Pitié
Salpêtrière

ST-MARCEL

BOULEVARD

St-Marcel

AVENUE DE

Campo Formio

N
P
Q

Edith Piaf
Museum
6

Ⓜ Ménilmontant

5

BELLEVILLE AND
MÉNILMONTANT
p126

RUE JP TIMBAUD
BLVD R LENOIR
RUE DE
RUE
Parmentier
Ⓜ
RUE OBERKAMPF
RUE OBERKAMPF
RUE TERNAUX
AVENUE DE LA RÉPUBLIQUE
Rue
St-Maur
Ⓜ
RUE DES BLUETS
6
5
BLVD DE MÉNILMONTANT
AVENUE GAMBETTA

Oberkampf
RUE ST-AMBROISE
RUE ST-MAUR
LACHARRIÈRE
RUE SERVAN
RUE DU CHEMIN VERT
Père Lachaise Ⓜ
Cimetière du
Père-Lachaise

Filles du
Ⓜ Calvaire
9 Rue
Oberkampf
RUE ST-SÉBASTIEN
SQUARE
RICHARD
LENOIR
St-Ambroise Ⓜ
RUE PASTEUR
RUE ST-AMBROISE
AVENUE PARMENTIER
RUE OMER
TALON
RUE DE LA
FOLIE REGNAULT
RUE MERLIN
RUE SERVAN
6

BLVD DES FILLES DU CALVAIRE
St-Sébastien
Ⓜ Froissart
8
RUE PELÉE
Richard
Ⓜ Lenoir
RUE DURANTI
RUE CAMILLE
DESMOULINS
RUE DE LA ROQUETTE
Ⓜ Philippe
Auguste

11
Merci
Concept Store
ALLÉE VERTE
BOULEVARD VOLTAIRE
BLVD DE
CHARONNE

BLVD BEAUMARCHAIS
RUE DES TOURNELLES
RUE AMELOT
RUE RICHARD
LENOIR
SQUARE
BREGUET
SABIN
RUE DU CHEMIN VERT
RUE BREGUET
RUE SÉDAINE
RUE FROMENT
Voltaire Ⓜ
RUE POPINCOURT
PLACE
LÉON
BLUM
RUE DE LA ROQUETTE
RUE GODEFROY CAVAIGNAC
RUE RICHARD LENOIR
RUE MERCOEUR
RUE DE
BELFORT
RUE LÉON
FROT
7

Chemin
Ⓜ Vert
Bréguet
Ⓜ Sabin
4
2
Rue de la
5 Roquette
AVENUE LEDRU ROLLIN
RUE BASFROI
RUE DE CHARONNE
RUE LA VACQUERIE
Charonne Ⓜ
RUE DE CHARONNE
AVE PHILIPPE AUGUSTE

7
10 Cour Damoye
RUE DE LAPPE
RUE KELLER
RUE DE
CHARONNE
3
RUE
DE
FAIDHERBE
RUE CHANZY
Rue des
Boulets Ⓜ
BOULEVARD VOLTAIRE
8

1 Place de
la Bastille
Bastille Ⓜ
1
i
10 Passage
du Cheval Blanc
2
Opéra National
de Paris Bastille
RUE DU FAUBOURG ST-ANTOINE
Ledru-
Rollin
Ⓜ
PGE DE LA
MAIN D'OR
RUE TROUSSEAU
RUE ST-BERNARD
RUE DU
DAHOMEY

Port de
l'Arsenal
3
Coulée Verte
René-Dumont
RUE DE CHARENTON
RUE DE
LYON
RUE DE
COTTE
RUE DE
PRAGUE
RUE D'ALIGRE
CITEAUX
Faidherbe-
Ⓜ Chaligny
RUE DU FAUBOURG ST-ANTOINE

4 Marché
d'Aligre
RUE E. CASTELAR
RUE DE REUILLY
BOULEVARD DIDEROT

7 Bassin de
l'Arsenal
AVENUE LEDRU ROLLIN
RUE TRAVERSIÈRE
RUE BECCARIA
RUE DE
CHARENTON
CHALIGNY
Reilly-
Diderot
Ⓜ
9

Quai de
la Rapée
Ⓜ
BLVD BOURDON
BLVD DE LA BASTILLE
RUE LACUÉE
RUE JULES CESAR
AVENUE DAUMESNIL
RUE PARROT
RUE ABEL
RUE
DE
LYON
RUE
MALOT
RUE
CROZATIER
AVENUE DE CHARENTON
AVENUE DAUMESNIL
Ⓜ Montgallet

PLACE
MAZAS
BLVD. DIDEROT
RUE VAN GOGH
RUE DE BERCY
Gare de
Lyon
Ⓜ 4
RER
i
8 Gare
de Lyon
PLACE H
FRENAY
PLACE
RUTEBEUF
REUILLY

Pont
d'Austerlitz
QUAI DE
LA RAPÉE
La Seine
PORT DE LA RAPÉE
Pont C de
Gaulle
RUE VILLIOT
RUE DE BERCY
10

QUAI D'AUSTERLITZ
JARDIN DES PLANTES
AND PLACE D'ITALIE
p262
BERCY
Bercy Ⓜ
BLVD DE BERCY
RUE DE BERCY
Paris-Bercy -
Bourgogne-
Pays d'Auvergne
BLVD DE REUILLY
Dugommier Ⓜ

Pont de
Bercy
AccorHotels
Arena
Bercy
12
Parc de
Bercy

Ⓜ Quai de
la Gare

0 metres   400
0 yards   400
N
↑

11

N
P
Q

1

PLACE DE LA BASTILLE

📍N8 🏠Place de la Bastille 75004 Ⓜ Bastille 🚌20, 29, 65, 69, 76, 86, 87, 91

This busy square was the scene of one of the most important events in French history – the storming of the Bastille on 14 July 1789. Little trace of the infamous prison remains, and today the square is a hub for nightlife and cultural events such as concerts.

↑ The Marché Bastille on nearby Boulevard Richard Lenoir

At the centre of the large square that marks the site of the prison is the Colonne de Juillet. Topped by the elegant, gilded statue of the winged "genius of liberty", this column of hollow bronze reaches 50.5 m (166 ft) into the sky. It is a memorial to those who died in the street battles of July 1830 that led to the overthrow of the monarch. The crypt contains the remains of 504 victims of the violent fighting and others who died in the 1848 revolution.

Place de la Bastille was once the border between central Paris and the eastern working-class areas *(faubourgs)*. Gentrification, however, is well under way. Just east of the Opéra Bastille is the starting point of the Coulée Verte René-Dumont *(p106)*, an elevated walking trail built on a disused railway line, while work to pedestrianize half of the square and connect it to the Bassin de l'Arsenal marina *(p108)* is currently in progress. The project is scheduled to be completed in 2020.

←

The Opéra National de Paris Bastille *(p106)*, designed by Carlos Ott

---

THE FRENCH REVOLUTION

In 1789, most Parisians were living in squalor and poverty. Rising inflation and opposition to Louis XVI culminated in the storming of the Bastille, the king's prison; the Republic was founded three years later. However, the Terror soon followed, when those suspected of betraying the Revolution were executed without trial: more than 60,000 people lost their lives.

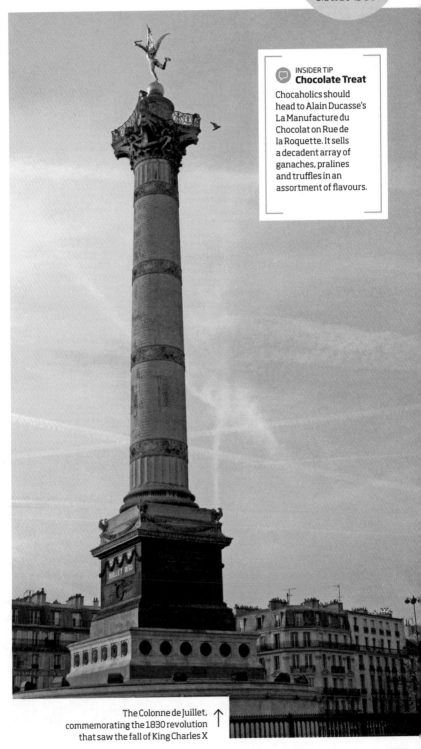

> **INSIDER TIP**
> **Chocolate Treat**
>
> Chocaholics should head to Alain Ducasse's La Manufacture du Chocolat on Rue de la Roquette. It sells a decadent array of ganaches, pralines and truffles in an assortment of flavours.

The Colonne de Juillet, commemorating the 1830 revolution that saw the fall of King Charles X ↑

EXPERIENCE MORE

Opéra National de Paris Bastille

◉N8 🏠120 Rue de Lyon 75012 Ⓜ Bastille ⓦoperadeparis.fr

The controversial "people's opera" was officially opened on 14 July 1989 to coincide with the bicentennial celebrations of the storming of the Bastille. Carlos Ott's imposing building is a notable break with 19th-century opera-house design, epitomized by Charles Garnier's opulent Opéra in the heart of the city (p172). The Bastille opera house is a massive, modern, curved, glass building. The main auditorium seats an audience of 2,700; its design is functional and modern, the black upholstered seats contrasting with the granite of the walls and the impressive glass ceiling. With its five moveable stages, this opera house is certainly a masterpiece of technological wizardry and it's well worth seeing a performance here; the website has full details of what's on and also has information about guided tours (in French).

Coulée Verte René-Dumont

◉P9 🏠1 Coulée Verte René-Dumont 75012 Ⓜ Bastille ◷8am-7:30pm (to 6pm in winter)

This former elevated railway hosts Paris's most exclusive verdant walkway. Rising up to 10 m (33 ft) above the streets, the promenade, planted with many varieties of flowers and trees, stretches for about 5 km (3 miles) between the Opéra Bastille and the Périphérique city boundary to the east.

The original railway closed in 1969 but the city preserved the structure and opened the Coulée Verte René-Dumont (also known as the Promenade Plantée) in 1993, serving as a model for urban renewal that has been replicated around the world. The topography varies from planted gardens and larger parks to narrow walkways snaking between apartment buildings. A stroll or jog along the Coulée Verte René-Dumont is a delightful traffic-free experience, with epic views of the city. Underneath the red-brick railway arches by the opera house, the Viaduc des Arts houses artisan and craft shops and fashion boutiques. All along the promenade, staircases lead down to street level, where cafés and bakeries are rarely far away for a quick pick-me-up while exploring Paris's eastern extremities in bucolic bliss.

Did You Know?

Remnants of the moat of the Bastille prison can be seen in the Bastille Metro.

Marché d'Aligre

◉P8 🏠Place d'Aligre 75012 Ⓜ Ledru-Rollin ◷7:30am-1pm Tue-Sun (indoor market 9am-1:30pm & 4-7:30pm Tue-Sat, 9am-1:30pm Sun)

On Sunday mornings, this lively and good-value market offers one of the most colourful sights in Paris. French, Arab and African traders hawk fruit, vegetables, flowers, clothing, bric-a-brac and second-hand books on the

> A stroll or jog along the Coulée Verte René-Dumont is a delightful traffic-free experience, with epic views of the city.

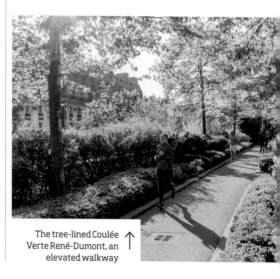

The tree-lined Coulée Verte René-Dumont, an elevated walkway ↑

Busy Rue de la Roquette with its lively cafés and restaurants ↑

streets, while the adjoining covered market, the Beauveau St-Antoine, offers fruit, vegetables, a great selection of cheese, charcuterie and olive oils, plus many intriguing international delicacies.

The Marché d'Aligre is where old and new Paris meet. Here, the established community of this old artisan quarter coexists with a more recently established group of hip urban professionals, lured here by the transformation of the nearby Bastille area. Some parts of the indoor market have been renovated following a fire in 2015.

5

Rue de la Roquette

📍N7 Ⓜ Bastille, Voltaire

This bustling street, lined with bars, cafés and restaurants, stretches from the Opéra Bastille towards Père Lachaise Cemetery (p130). At No 17 stands the house of Symbolist poet Paul Verlaine, a 19th-century regular in the neighbourhood. At No 70, a 19th-century fountain once brought water from the canal into the densely populated district. The five stone slabs in the road where the street meets Rue de la Croix Faubin are an eerie reminder of a much darker history. They are the foundations of the guillotine where inmates of the Prison de la Roquette met their fate, usually in front of a crowd of onlookers. Around 200 executions were carried out between 1851 and 1899, while some 4,000 women, members of the French Resistance, were incarcerated in the prison in 1944. The former entrance can still be seen across the street, on Square de la Roquette. Rue de la Roquette and the surrounding area, particularly cobbled Rue de Lappe, with its numerous bars, gets pretty animated at night.

EAT

Bofinger
This classic 19th-century brasserie serves up Alsatian fare in a glitzy setting.

📍M7 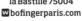 5 Rue de la Bastille 75004
🌐 bofingerparis.com

€€€

_____

Café de l'Industrie
Simple food and a funky setting make this a neighbourhood favourite.

📍N7 16 Rue St-Sabin 75011
🌐 cafedelindustrie paris.fr

€€€

_____

Septime
Innovative cuisine and a relaxed atmosphere combine for perfect Michelin-star dining.

📍P8 🏠 80 Rue de Charonne 75011
🚫 Sat & Sun 🌐 septime-charonne.fr

€€€

→
Memorabilia, paintings and artifacts in the small Edith Piaf Museum

Edith Piaf Museum

📍P5 🏠5 Rue Crespin du Gast 75011 📞01 43 55 52 72 Ⓜ Ménilmontant 🕐By appt 1-6pm Mon-Wed, 10-noon Thu

Legend has it that singer Edith Piaf was born in the street in nearby Belleville (p132). Historians debate that story, but she did actually live in this tiny apartment, now a museum dedicated to the singer's legacy. It is privately owned by a fan who has curated a collection of memorabilia and personal artifacts that belonged to the chanteuse. Just 1.42 m (4 ft 8 inches) tall and known as the "Little Sparrow", her voice was anything but small, echoing across concert halls worldwide. Buried in nearby Père Lachaise Cemetery (p130), Piaf is today best known for songs such as "La Vie en Rose". An engaging collection of souvenirs, prints and Piaf's signature black dresses are on display. The museum, unlike most in Paris, requires visitors to call and book in advance. A charming, intimate experience, it should appeal to both die-hard fans and visitors with just a casual interest.

Bassin de l'Arsenal

📍M9 🏠5 Quai de la Rapée Ⓜ Bastille

Between Place de la Bastille and the Seine, this pleasure-boat arena hides below street level. A lock joins it to the River Seine. The location of a weapons storehouse since the 16th century, the arsenal eventually fell into disuse as revolutionaries removed the Bastille fortress, stone by stone. Nowadays, the tiny marina hosts private watercraft and is also the starting point for tour cruises along the Canal St-Martin (p118). There is a café, Le Grand Bleu, at the north end, though on warm evenings most Parisians picnic along the traffic-free waterfront. Two bridges crossing the water offer picture-postcard views of the Colonne de Juillet in Place de la Bastille.

Gare de Lyon

📍N9 🏠Place Louis-Armand 75012 Ⓜ Gare de Lyon. Le Train Bleu: 🌐le-train-bleu.com

Built for the 1900 Exposition Universelle, this station is the third busiest in France,

With high-end restaurants, gourmet coffee shops, craft beer and spicy Mexican fare, Rue Oberkampf caters to all sorts of flavours and fancies.

> **INSIDER TIP**
> ## Chambelland
>
> Chambelland, at 14 Rue Ternaux, is one of the few gluten-free bakeries in Paris, serving a delicious array of bread, biscuits and pastries.

with about 90 million annual passengers. It welcomes trains from throughout France, as well as Italy, Switzerland and other international destinations. In the summer months you'll notice many sun-kissed travellers returning from the Côte d'Azur, as this station serves Nice and other southern French destinations. On the exterior of the station looms the iconic clock tower, reminiscent of the UK Parliament's Big Ben tower. Inside the Gare de Lyon is the illustrious restaurant Le Train Bleu, a glitzy dining experience that has been in operation for over a century. The ornate dining rooms are decorated with gilded carvings, mouldings and chandeliers, as well as 41 paintings representing French cities or regions by prominent French artists including François Flameng and Henri Gervex. Even if you're not catching a train to some sun-soaked destination, it's worth a visit to the station to sip a glass of wine amid the restaurant's sumptuous décor.

9

Rue Oberkampf

M6 Ⓜ **Oberkampf, Parmentier**

Rue Oberkampf stretches from the Upper Marais all the way to Ménilmontant, with most of the action happening around Metros Parmentier and Oberkampf. Dating back to the 1500s, the street gained its name in the 19th century from the German-born industrialist Christophe-Philippe Oberkampf, who contributed to the manufacturing of painted French cloth *(toile)*. Today, the area is anything but old-fashioned. With high-end restaurants, gourmet coffee shops, craft beer and spicy Mexican fare, Rue Oberkampf caters to all sorts of flavours and fancies in its many bars and eateries. The street becomes especially lively at night, with younger Parisians congregating at watering holes like Café Charbon or Le Quartier Général and crowds gathering under clouds of smoke at the live-music venues that dot the street. There are few, if any, tourist attractions here. It's all about local colour. Plan on spending an evening or afternoon hopping from venue to venue in search of the perfect fit.

The opulent interior of Le Train Bleu restaurant, inside the Gare de Lyon ↑

The Bassin de l'Arsenal, a pleasure boat arena

Cour Damoye and Passage du Cheval Blanc

◙ N7 Ⓜ Bastille, Voltaire, Bréguet Sabin

Amid the bustle of Place de la Bastille, there are tiny enclaves of calm hidden in two historic passages, the Cour Damoye and the Passage du Cheval Blanc. Most people walk right by their entrances without daring to enter, but they are public walkways. This area has been a centre of carpentry and French furniture design since the time of the Middle Ages. Its location near a port on the Seine that dealt with wood and timber made it popular with craftsmen, and many high-end artisans producing fine furnishings can still be found in the district. The late-18th-century Cour Damoye is today largely residential, with a few small businesses still functioning,

but remnants of its former artisan workshops are visible in the façades. The Passage du Cheval Blanc, just off Rue de la Roquette, is named after the sign of a horse that once adorned the entrance. Offering a peaceful respite from the busy Faubourg St-Antoine, its small labyrinth of cobbled courtyards, named after the months of the year (Cour de Janvier etc), hide architecture companies and apartments, with wooden beams still visible in some buildings. The Cité Parchappe spills you back out onto the main road.

FURNITURE-MAKING DISTRICT

Close to the former docks at Quai de la Rapée, this district east of the Place de la Bastille served to stock lumber, leading to its renown as a centre for furniture- and cabinet-making and their related trades. The craftsmen even caught the eye of Louis XIV, and his Minister of Finances, Colbert, established the royal mirror factory here. Today, there are still antique sellers, cabinet-makers and craftsmen dotted around Rue du Faubourg St-Antoine, especially on Le Passage du Chantier.

Merci Concept Store

◙ M6 ⌂ 111 Boulevard Beaumarchais 75003
Ⓜ St-Sébastien Froissart
◷ 10am-7:30pm Mon-Sat
◷ Sun ◨ merci-merci.com

Paris has grand department stores and luxury boutiques aplenty, but around Bastille, Merci is the place for retail therapy. A concept store housed in an old wallpaper factory, it opened in 2009 and curates the best in fashion and design. Homewares, clothing and kitchen products are housed under a glass atrium, spread across multiple floors. It has none of the glitz or brand names of big-brother department stores like Printemps or Le Bon Marché.

↓ The bold new architecture of Bercy, a former wine-trading district

Instead, it reflects the neighbourhood's character, featuring up-and-coming designers and local brands. If you're not interested in swiping your cards on trendy accessories, you could join the locals at Merci's popular restaurant and two cafés. The Used Book Café, set among towering shelves of literature, is especially appealing for afternoon tea or coffee. Fresh salads, egg dishes and *tartines* are all on the menu. The shop also houses temporary exhibitions and pop-up events that manage to keep it feeling fresh and exciting for locals and visitors alike.

Bercy

P11 75012 Bercy, Cour St-Émilion

This former wine-trading quarter east of the city centre, with its once-grim warehouses, pavilions and slum housing, has been transformed into a modern district. An automatic Metro line (Line 14) links it to the heart of the city. The centrepiece is the AccorHotels Arena, whose vast pyramidal structure has become a contemporary landmark. Many sports events are held here, as well as operas and rock concerts.

Other architecturally adventurous buildings dominate Bercy, notably Chemetov's gigantic building for the Ministry of Finance, and Frank Gehry's American Center. This houses the Cinémathèque Française, a wonderful cinema museum that hosts frequent retrospectives of famous directors.

At the foot of these structures, the imaginatively designed 70-ha (173-acre) Parc de Bercy provides a welcome green space for this part of the city.

Former wine stores and cellars along Cours St-Émilion have been restored as bars, restaurants and shops, and one of the warehouses now contains the Musée des Arts Forains (Fairground Museum), open for private tours only.

↑ The contemporary landscape design of the attractive Parc de Bercy

RÉPUBLIQUE AND CANAL ST-MARTIN

Lying beyond central Paris, this area was once farmland. The Knights Templar established their European headquarters here during the medieval period, at which time it was also home to a community of lepers. In the 17th century, King Henri IV built a hospital for plague victims, while the 18th century saw a new wall envelop these districts within the city limits. Following industrialization of the area in the 19th century, thanks to Napoleon's canal, the neighbourhood became largely working class. It suffered from dereliction in the 20th century, although strong African communities grew up here, especially around Chateau d'Eau. In the 1990s, a class of bohemian-bourgeois Parisians – known as *bobos* – began to gentrify the district. Place de la République, totally redesigned in 2013, now welcomes street fairs and public demonstrations. Even Gare du Nord, hub for the London-bound Eurostar, has cleaned up in recent years.

RÉPUBLIQUE AND CANAL ST-MARTIN

Must See
1. Canal St-Martin

Experience More
2. Square du Temple
3. Musée des Arts et Métiers
4. Musée des Moulages
5. Hôpital St-Louis
6. Rue Ste-Marthe
7. Gare de l'Est
8. Gare du Nord

9. Portes St-Denis et St-Martin

Eat & Drink
1. Le Plomb du Cantal
2. Pink Flamingo
3. Le Comptoir Général
4. La Barav
5. Le Mary Celeste

Shop
6. Marché des Enfants Rouge

1

CANAL ST-MARTIN

📍M4 Ⓜ Jacques Bonsergent, Goncourt, République 🚌 26, 46, 75

Dating back to the time of Napoleon, this 4.5-km (2¾-mile) waterway flows through one of Paris's trendiest districts. Colourful shops and cafés line its banks, where locals spend weekends picnicking or cycling along the waterfront.

Stretching between the Seine in the south and the Bassin de la Villette in the north, the Canal St-Martin opened in 1825 as a means of bringing fresh water to Paris's polluted city centre. However, in the late 19th century part of the canal was covered to make way for new roadways, and within a few decades the canal and the boats that worked upon it had become obsolete. City officials almost drained and filled the entire waterway in the 1970s, but by the turn of the millennium it had became a popular location for wealthy young Parisians to buy and renovate properties. This once-derelict district is now one of the Right Bank's most desirable areas, a culturally mixed neighbourhood where Paris's hipsters mingle among families and international arrivals.

INSIDER TIP
Canalside Pizza Delivery

Order a pizza from Pink Flamingo *(p125)*, grab a bright pink balloon, then find a comfortable spot along the canal and wait for the restaurant to deliver it to you.

DRINK

Here are the best coffee shops around the canal.

Ten Belles
📍M4 🏠10 Rue de la Grange aux Belles 75010 🌐tenbelles.com

—

Holybelly
📍L4 🏠5 Rue Lucien Sampaix 75010 🌐holybellycafe.com

—

Craft
📍M4 🏠24 Rue des Vinaigriers 75010 🌐cafe-craft.com

—

Radiodays
📍M4 🏠15 Rue Alibert 75010 🌐radiodays.cafe

—

DonAntónia
📍M4 🏠8 Rue de la Grange aux Belles 75010 🌐donantonia.paris

① Cafés and restaurants populate the neighbourhood around the canal.

② A selection of treats is sold at the Bakery du Pain et des Idées on Rue Yves Toudic.

③ The Canal St-Martin is punctuated by romantic bridges, including two swing ones.

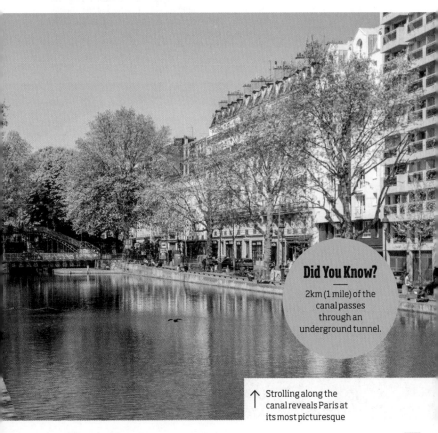

Did You Know?

2km (1 mile) of the canal passes through an underground tunnel.

↑ Strolling along the canal reveals Paris at its most picturesque

EXPERIENCE MORE

2

Square du Temple

📍 L5 🏠 75003
Ⓜ Temple

A quiet and pleasant square today, this was once a fortified centre of the medieval Knights Templar. A state within a state, the area contained a palace, a church and shops behind high walls and a drawbridge, making it a haven for those who were seeking to escape from royal jurisdiction. Louis XVI and Marie-Antoinette were held in the Temple fortress after their arrest in 1792. The king set out from here for his execution by guillotine.

Did You Know?

The Square du Temple contains 70 species of trees, including an 18-m- (59-ft-) tall Turkish hazel.

3

Musée des Arts et Métiers

📍 L5 🏠 60 Rue Réaumur 75003 Ⓜ Arts et Métiers
🕐 10am–6pm Tue–Sun (to 9:30pm Thu) 🚫 1 May & 25 Dec 🌐 arts-et-metiers.net

Housed within the old Abbey of St-Martin-des-Champs, the Arts and Crafts Museum was founded in 1794. After major renovations in the 1990s it reopened in 2000 as an excellent museum of science and industry displaying 5,000 items (it has 75,000 additional artifacts in storage that are available to academics and researchers). The museum's theme is man's ingenuity and the worlds of invention and manufacturing, covering such topics as textiles, photography and machines. Among the most entertaining displays are those of musical clocks, mechanical musical instruments and automata (mechanical figures). One of these figures, the "Joueuse de Tympanon", is said to represent Marie-Antoinette.

4

Musée des Moulages

📍 M4 🏠 1 Ave Claude Vellefaux 75010
📞 01 42 49 99 15
Ⓜ Goncourt, Colonel Fabien
🕐 9am–4:30pm Mon–Fri

Housed inside the Hôpital St-Louis, this museum boasts 4,807 wax moulds of horrific skin diseases of the 1800s. Dr Lallier of the Hôpital St-Louis hired Jules Baretta, a wax-fruit maker, to create models of real diseases to teach students about things

↑ The pretty Square du Temple garden with its bandstand and pond

↑ A plane on display at the Museé des Arts et Métiers, housed in a former church

SHOP

Marché des Enfants Rouges

This historical market on shop-laden Rue de Bretagne is full of food stalls and international cuisine, and is usually packed at lunchtime.

📍 M6 🏠 39 Rue de Bretagne 75003 🕐 Mon

such as syphilis and elephantiasis. Baretta would spend time with patients in the hospital, carefully using plaster of Paris to create his moulds. He would then paint them in great detail, even adding hair to keep them realistic. While many of the faces and body parts are unsettling in their realism, they are true works of art. Cyclopoid babies, various stages of then-fatal syphilis, and all sorts of abnormal skin growths are as fascinating as they are gruesome. The collection is an enlightening look into how far medicine has come in the past 150 years, to a time before the discovery of antibiotics that could cure

many of these diseases. Today, few students visit the antiquated learning tools, so the museum is often empty. Call ahead to arrange an appointment, and purchase tickets within the modern hospital's register adjacent to the original structure.

Hôpital St-Louis

📍 M4 🏠 1 Ave Claude Vellefaux 75010 Ⓜ Goncourt, Colonel Fabien

Built by order of King Henri IV in 1607 and completed after his death, this hospital originally served the growing number of plague victims at the time. Patients crowded into the rooms surrounding the square courtyard, reminiscent of Place des Vosges in the Marais (p92), and constructed by the same architect. Most would never see the sky again except for a rare stroll through that grassy courtyard. Conditions in the hospital worsened over time, but eventually

the plague passed. The building later served as a dermatology hospital and a prison for nuns during the French Revolution. Today, modern facilities next to the 17th-century buildings still function as a hospital. A small adjacent chapel – built for local farmers and not for plague victims – was used for King Henri IV's funeral in 1610. The main courtyard is open to the public and is an almost hauntingly calm respite in the heart of Paris. One of its wings is home to the Musée des Moulages, a museum dedicated to skin diseases.

→ A statue at the Musée des Arts et Metiers

The Gare de l'Est, lit up at night

6

Rue Ste-Marthe

N4 **75010**
Goncourt, Belleville

Just north of the Hôpital St-Louis, this tiny little street feels more like a walk through some southern provincial French town than central Paris. Colourful doors and façades contrast with the often grey Parisian skies. Each one opens up to an artist's studio, a workshop, a quirky restaurant, or some oddball boutique. There is little historical significance in these former workers' quarters, but the area is a unique slice of Parisian life. Look for olives in the independent grocery, try some Chilean food, or spend an evening with a glass of wine and charcuterie at any of

the local bars here. Tourists rarely make it this far, stopping instead at the Canal St-Martin. A walk along Rue Sainte-Marthe, however, is a very Parisian experience.

7

Gare de l'Est

L3 **Place du 11 Novembre 1918 75010**
Gare de l'Est

Whether travelling to Germany or just passing through the neighbourhood, visitors should take a moment to marvel at one of Paris's oldest train stations. Opened in 1849, it had doubled in size by 1931 after several renovations. Statues atop the façade represent Strasbourg and Verdun, two of the

HIDDEN GEM
Marché St-Quentin

The 19th-century covered market Marché St-Quentin on Boulevard de Magenta makes a handy stop for last-minute cheese and wine before you board a train from the Gare de l'Est or Gare du Nord.

original destinations served by the station. In 1883, the very first Orient Express departed from Gare de l'Est for Istanbul. Inside the main hall, a massive painting by American artist Albert Herter depicts French troops leaving the station for the Front during World War I in 1914. German forces transformed an underground air-raid shelter into a wartime bunker during World War II, which is still preserved under the station, though it is not open to visitors.

← Statues adorning the imposing façade of the Gare du Nord station

Gare du Nord

🚇 L2 🏠 18 Rue de Dunkerque 75010 Ⓜ Gare du Nord

Opened in 1864, this train station is best known today as the hub for the Eurostar to London, as well as services to Brussels and Amsterdam. This massive station is Europe's busiest, with over 200 million passengers per year. The imposing façade is dotted with sculptures representing other European capitals, including Berlin and London. The soaring iron structure inside creates a romantic departure hall, and has been used as a film location for several movies. Inside the station, a new wave of cafés and restaurants is reinventing the travelling experience, as well as the surrounding neighbourhood. The station is undergoing further refurbishments in preparation for the 2024 Olympic Games.

⑨ Portes St-Denis et St-Martin

🚇 K4, L4 🏠 Blvds St-Denis & St-Martin 75010 Ⓜ Strasbourg-St-Denis

These imposing gates give access to the two ancient and important thoroughfares whose names they bear, running across Paris in a north–south direction. They once marked the entrance to the city. The Porte St-Denis is 23 m (76 ft) high and was built in 1672 by François Blondel. It is decorated with figures by Louis XIV's sculptor, François Girardon. The gates commemorate the victories of the king's armies in Flanders and the Rhine that year. Porte St-Martin is 17 m (56 ft) tall and was built in 1674 by Pierre Bullet, a student of Blondel. It celebrates the capture of Besançon and the defeat of the Triple Alliance of Spain, Holland and Germany.

EAT & DRINK

Le Plomb du Cantal

A local establishment serving well-prepared, no-frills, traditional French food.

🚇 L4 🏠 4 Bvld St-Denis 75010 🕐 Tue 🌐 leplombducantal.com

€€€

Pink Flamingo

Unique, delicious pizzas with eclectic ingredients such as figs, chutney and duck.

🚇 M4 🏠 67 Rue Bichat 75010 📞 01 42 02 31 70

€€€

Le Comptoir Général

This quirky venue hosts events and has a bar popular during the evenings and on Sunday afternoons.

🚇 M4 🏠 80 Quai de Jemmapes 75010 🌐 lecomptoir general.com

La Barav

This popular wine bar fills up with locals sharing bottles and cheese plates.

🚇 M5 🏠 6 Rue Charles-François Dupuis 75003 🌐 lebarav.fr

Le Mary Celeste

Go for cocktails, stay for the small plates, and then have more cocktails.

🚇 M6 🏠 1 Rue Commines 75003 🌐 lemaryceleste.com

↓ The impressive interior of Gare de l'Est

BELLEVILLE AND MÉNILMONTANT

Belleville and Ménilmontant are two of the newest districts to have been incorporated into the city. Various religious orders called the area home in the Middle Ages, and the land was cultivated by monks. Belleville was famous as a wine-growing suburb of Paris, with vineyards covering the hilly district. Both districts were beyond the tax reaches of the city, and in the 18th century Ménilmontant became popular with the working classes, who would drink cheaply at watering holes called *guinguettes*. After city planners removed the wall circling Paris in 1860, the two areas were absorbed into the 20 arrondissements, and much of the farmland and vineyards gave way to new homes. The districts became militant hotbeds during the 1871 Paris Commune, when clashes with the army erupted in the streets. Throughout the 20th century, the area attracted immigrants fleeing persecution, including Jewish people from Europe and inhabitants of former French colonies in North Africa. A bustling Chinese community added to the multicultural fabric of the districts, where cheap rent continues to attract many artists and migrants today.

BELLEVILLE AND MÉNILMONTANT

Must See
1 Cimetière du Père Lachaise

Experience More
2 Parc de Belleville
3 Rue de Belleville
4 Rue Dénoyez
5 Marché de Belleville
6 La Maroquinerie
7 Notre-Dame-de-la-Croix
8 La Bellevilloise
9 Église Saint-Jean-Baptiste
10 Jourdain Quartier
11 Regard Saint-Martin

12 La Campagne à Paris

Eat
1 Tin-Tin
2 Guo Xin
3 La Baratin

Drink
4 Aux Folies
5 Le Barbouquin
6 Café Chéri
7 Les Trois 8

Stay
8 Mama Shelter

CIMETIÈRE DU PÈRE LACHAISE

EXPERIENCE Belleville and Ménilmontant

R6 ☑ Blvd de Ménilmontant Ⓜ Père Lachaise, Alexandre Dumas
🚌 26, 60, 61, 64, 69 to Pl Gambetta ⏰ 8am–5:30pm daily (from 8:30am
Sat, 9am Sun; mid-Mar–early Nov: to 6pm)

This is the most visited cemetery in the world. It contains over
70,000 graves, including the tombs of numerous famous figures,
such as the writer Honoré de Balzac, the composer Frédéric
Chopin, the singer Jim Morrison and the actor Yves Montand.

Paris's most prestigious cemetery is set on a wooded
hill overlooking the city. The land was once owned by
Père de la Chaise, Louis XIV's confessor, but it was
bought in 1803 by order of Napoleon to create a new
cemetery. Père Lachaise, the first cemetery in France
with a crematorium, became so popular that it was
expanded six times during the 19th century.

Today the cemetery is a place of pilgrimage for
rock fans, who come from around the world to see
the grave of Jim Morrison of The Doors. With its moss-
grown tombs and ancient trees, as well as striking
funerary sculpture, Père Lachaise is an atmospheric
and rather romantic place for a stroll.

Did You Know?

The remains of Molière
were transferred here
in 1817 to add historic
glamour to the new
cemetery.

→
A visitor exploring the
funerary art among the lanes
of Père Lachaise

← Théodore Géricault's tomb, with a depiction of *The Raft of the Medusa*

MUR DES FÉDÉRÉS

Following France's defeat in the Franco-Prussian War in 1871, a left-wing group revolted, setting up the Paris Commune. After 72 days, government troops marched on the city and in a week of brutal street fighting, much of the city was burned and thousands were killed. Mur des Fédérés in Père Lachaise is where the last Communard rebels were shot by government forces.

Notable Residents

Allan Kardec

▶ Kardec was the founder of a 19th-century spiritual cult, which still has a strong following. His tomb is perpetually covered in pilgrims' flowers.

George Rodenbach

The monument to this 19th-century poet depicts him rising out of his tomb with a rose in the hand of his outstretched arm.

Oscar Wilde

◀ The Irish dramatist, aesthete and great wit was exiled from virtuous Britain to die of drink and dissipation in Paris in 1900. American-British artist Jacob Epstein sculpted his tomb.

Marcel Proust

The French novelist brilliantly chronicled the belle époque in *Remembrance of Things Past*.

Sarah Bernhardt

▶ The great French tragedienne, who died in 1923 aged 78, was once the most famous actress in the world.

Edith Piaf

Known as the "Little Sparrow" because of her size, Piaf was the 20th century's greatest French popular singer. In her tragic voice, she sang of the sorrows and woes of the Paris working class.

Jim Morrison

▶ The Doors' lead singer died in Paris in 1971. The circumstances of his death are still a mystery.

EXPERIENCE MORE

2

Parc de Belleville

🅠 Q4 🅐 47 Rue des Couronnes 75020
Ⓜ Couronnes, Belleville
🕒 8am-9:30pm (to 7pm in winter)

It has less of the manicured appeal of some of Paris's other parks, but the Parc de Belleville has views that no other green space can boast. This steep garden offers unparalleled panoramas of Paris, including the Eiffel Tower and Notre-Dame. The hill was originally settled by religious orders, who purchased parcels of land and planted vines. *Guinguettes* popped up in the Middle Ages, the outdoor pubs or beer gardens of their day. It was here that Parisians drank "*piquette*", a young wine from the area, which today is also French slang for bad wine. Eventually windmills dominated the landscape, owing to the park's altitude.

The park is a welcome green space in densely populated east Paris. Between the patches of exquisitely maintained flowerbeds are stairs and pathways crisscrossed by waterways and trestles. There is even a waterfall that trickles 100 m (328 ft) from the top of the grounds to the bottom. In a throwback to Belleville's winemaking past, 140 grapevines grow on the slopes, and the grapes are harvested each year.

3

Rue de Belleville

🅟 P4 🅐 75020
Ⓜ Belleville, Pyrénées, Jourdain

The main street of the former Belleville village, Rue de Belleville cuts through the district from Belleville Metro station. The street used to be the location of the old wall that separated Paris from its suburbs. Belleville gets its name from a deformation of the French words *belle vue*, or "beautiful view" – the reason for which becomes apparent when you look downhill from the street towards where the Eiffel Tower rises up in the distance. The stretch between the Metro stations Belleville and Pyrénées is the most interesting. At No 72, a plaque commemorates the birth in 1915 of Edith Piaf, who, according to popular legend, was born here on the steps. Over the past decades, many ethnic restaurants and East Asian shops have sprung up along the street as immigrants have moved into the area, and all sorts of exotic and inexpensive food items can be found here. Restaurants serve a variety of dumplings, pork-filled *bao* and *banh mi* sandwiches that are worth the hike up the hilly street. Cafés are far from fussy affairs, serving inexpensive wine and beer in the old working-class Belleville tradition.

Did You Know?

At 108 m (354 ft), Parc de Belleville is the highest park in Paris.

→ The streets of Belleville, with stalls selling fresh produce *(above)*

→ The "open-air art gallery" of Belleville's Rue Dénoyez

Rue Dénoyez

📍 P4 🏠 75020
Ⓜ Belleville

Throughout Paris, street artists take advantage of any surface they can. In Rue Dénoyez, however, it seems as if the city actively encourages it. This narrow street, tucked away off Rue de Belleville and formerly rather run down, is essentially an outdoor contemporary art gallery where street artists constantly leave their mark. It is named after a local family who ran a popular dance hall in the 1830s, but today it is all about street art, reflecting the lively, bohemian spirit of the neighbourhood. On any given day, someone will be out there, spray-painting their newest mural on one of the walls. The buildings are mostly artists' studios – some will let you in if you are lucky – but the real draw is the colourful and daring works on the walls. In recent years, some of the studios have been replaced by more modern social housing, but the artistic spirit of Rue Dénoyez remains. Parisians still gather at the end of the street at Aux Folies, a bar known for its cheap drinks and a sea of plastic chairs spilling onto the sidewalk, while at the other end of the street Le Barbouquin is a great place to relax with a drink and a book from one of its groaning shelves.

DRINK

Aux Folies

Plastic chairs all over the terrace give this a homey feel, reinforced by cheap drinks and loud locals.

📍 P4 🏠 8 Rue de Belleville 75020
🌐 aux-folies-belleville.fr

Le Barbouquin

This cosy café – part coffee shop, part bar and part bookshop/library – is an ideal chill-out spot. It also hosts regular music nights.

📍 P4 🏠 1 Rue Dénoyez 75020 📞 09 84 32 13 21

Café Chéri

An edgy dive bar, attracting a hip local crowd. Regular live music includes electro, rock, hip-hop, funk and indie.

📍 N3 🏠 44 Boulevard de la Villette 75019
📞 09 53 05 93 36

Les Trois 8

A wide range of artisan and international beer is the main draw at this trendy local watering hole.

📍 Q5 🏠 11 Rue Victor Letalle 75002
🌐 lestrois8.fr

The ever-popular
La Maroquinerie rock, pop
and world music venue ↑

5

Marché de Belleville

📍 P4 ⊕ Blvd de Belleville
75020 Ⓜ Belleville
🕐 Tues & Fri 7am–2:30pm

Every Tuesday and Friday morning, the Belleville outdoor market comes alive, stretching from the Belleville Metro station to Couronnes. It dates back to the 19th century, when it was just a little market for the independent commune outside Paris's wall, and is still a popular and inexpensive source of fresh produce for eastern Parisians. The stalls follow the seasons, with clementines in the winter, strawberries in the spring, and the best tomatoes in late summer. Some stalls sell odds and ends such as wine openers, French candy bars and bags of olives – it's the place to stock up on anything and everything. Vendors yell out prices, pushing the foods that need to go. By the end of the market, they start selling large piles of produce for a euro, so there are true bargains to be had. The locals pile into the crowded market rain or shine, so be prepared to manoeuvre around caddies and Parisians arguing about bruised apples.

6

La Maroquinerie

📍 R5 ⊕ 23 Rue Boyer
75020 Ⓜ Ménilmontant,
Gambetta 🌐 lamaro
quinerie.fr

True music fans will want to visit this former leather workshop turned concert

Did You Know?

The first ever telegraph was communicated from Ménilmontant in 1793.

venue. It's intimate, with a capacity of about 500, and has hosted some big names before they hit success. Bruno Mars and Mumford & Sons are just some of the acts who have played here. The bohemian-chic venue also has a restaurant with a constantly changing menu of French classics, and a terrace bar for drinking the night away. Book in advance for a wide range of musical productions.

7

Notre-Dame-de-la-Croix

📍 Q5 ⊕ 3 Place
de Ménilmontant
75020 Ⓜ Ménilmontant,
Couronnes 🕐 8am–7:30pm
Tue–Sun, 8:30am–7pm Sun
🌐 notredamedelacroix.com

Consecrated in 1863 under the reign of Napoleon III, this stunning church looms over Ménilmontant, built as the

---

NIGHTLIFE HOTSPOT

Both Belleville and Ménilmontant have historically been popular drinking locations with a reputation for being cheap and rowdy – labels that locals would defend proudly. Their former position just outside the tax wall meant that drinks were cheaper, so Parisians flocked to the *guinguettes* (taverns) that made these districts popular. Today the area is still known as inexpensive, whether it's for cheap Vietnamese food or drinks at Les Trois 8. Nightlife has evolved from *guinguettes* as well, and popular hotspots such as La Bellevilloise and La Maroquinerie keep the neighbourhood lively at night.

population of the area boomed. Its architecture is an odd mix of Romanesque and Gothic elements, with an enormous tower reaching 78 m (256 ft) high. In terms of size, it's actually the third-largest church in Paris after Notre-Dame and St-Sulpice.

This district was particularly caught up by the Paris Commune of 1871, when Parisians rose up against the government, which had been exiled to Versailles by Prussian forces. During this turbulent time the Communards, as the rebels were known, held meetings in Notre-Dame-de-la-Croix. It was here that they decided to execute the Archbishop, Georges Darboy, who had been taken hostage by the Communards, on 24 May at the prison on Rue de la Roquette (p107).

The church does not stir up much of this stormy history, but instead offers a splendid visit devoid of the tourists crushed into other monuments. Look out for the organ, constructed in two separate parts in order to avoid obstructing the rose window overhead. The church also has two significant artworks: *Christ in Limbo* (1819) by Pierre Delorme and *Christ Curing the Sick* (1827) by Jean-Pierre Granger.

EAT

Tin-Tin
A hole-in-the-wall Vietnamese eatery that never fails to produce great pho and bo bun.

📍 P4 🏠 17 Rue Louis Bonnet 75011 📞 01 43 55 50 13 🕐 Wed

Guo Xin
It's all about the dumplings here – cheap and delicious. Eat at tables packed together.

📍 P4 🏠 47 Rue de Belleville 75019 📞 01 42 38 17 53

La Baratin
An institution; go to experience quintessentially meaty French fare.

📍 Q4 🏠 3 Rue Jouye-Rouve 75020 📞 01 43 49 39 70 🕐 Sun, Mon

La Bellevilloise

📍 R5 🏠 19 Rue Boyer 75020 Ⓜ Ménilmontant, Gambetta 🌐 labellevilloise.com

Set up in 1877, this community art centre's original aim was to bring cultural education to less affluent Parisians. This spirit lives on in its numerous events, which include concerts – often jazz or Latin – and art exhibits, as well as freelancer fairs, vintage markets and the occasional jazz brunch. A standout feature is the Halle aux Olives, a glass atrium performance area with tables surrounded by an urban jungle of sorts.

→ The Neo-Romanesque façade of Notre-Dame-de-la-Croix

The soaring Neo-Gothic interior of Église St-Jean-Baptiste

Stone carvings, Église St-Jean-Baptiste

⑨ Église St-Jean-Baptiste

📍Q3 🏠139 Rue de Belleville 75019 Ⓜ Jourdain ⏰8:15am-7:45pm daily (Mon 9:30am-8:30pm, Fri to 8:30pm) 🌐sjbb.fr

As far as churches go, the Neo-Gothic St-Jean-Baptiste de Belleville flies under the radar of most people in Paris. Set high above the city in a vibrant district full of shops, it's an exciting find for architecture enthusiasts. Built to replace the original church dating back to the 1600s, the current structure was erected between 1854 and 1859. The architect, Jean-Baptiste Antoine Lassus, was a specialist in medieval architecture. He is largely responsible for bringing back Gothic themes in modern structures and participated heavily in the restorations of Notre-Dame and other monuments. Though a master in his craft, Lassus is often overlooked for the more famous Viollet-le-Duc, who lauded this structure after Lassus' death. It was, in fact, Lassus' final project. This church, with its twin bell towers and vaulted ceilings, evokes the grandeur and traditions of churches such as the Sainte-Chapelle (p74).

⑩ Jourdain Quartier

📍R4 🏠75020 Ⓜ Jourdain

If you are looking to get away from the crowds but still get a taste of Parisian life, an afternoon wandering the Jourdain quarter is a perfect start. Sprawling out from the Neo-Gothic St-Jean-Baptiste church, the area has really come into its own. The central square, full of cafés and quintessentially Parisian shops – cheese here, meat there, pastries everywhere – is little visited by tourists; this is one of the rare districts of Paris that still retains a village feel. It might be towards the edge of the city, but it is a quick and easy trip on line 11 of the Metro from Hôtel de Ville in the centre. The nearby Parc des Buttes-Chaumont (p146) pairs nicely with a visit to Jourdain, as does a detour to Le Plateau on Rue des Alouettes, an industrial-white exhibition space run by Frac (the Fonds régional d'art contemporain, or regional collection of contemporary art). It displays modern art – including paintings, photography and everything in between – from its 1,600-piece collection. There's also occasional performance art.

Regard St-Martin

◉ R4 🅐 42 Rue des Cascades 75020 Ⓜ Jourdain, Pyrénées

This curious little stone building on Rue des Cascades was once vital to ensuring medieval Parisians had clean drinking water. Known as a *regard* – or, essentially, a manhole – it was part of a system to collect rainwater from the hilly area of Belleville and channel it to the fountains of Paris below. The water of the Seine was infamously dirty, polluted by the mix of sewage and chemicals from tanneries flowing into it. These stone structures provided fresh water before the canals were constructed in the 19th-century. Renovated in the 17th century (as a plaque in Latin on the building testifies), but dating from the 12th century, the Regard St-Martin still functions, except that nowadays the water makes it no further than the sewers.

La Campagne à Paris

◉ T5 🅐 Rue du Père-Prosper-Enfantin, Rue Irénée Blanc, Rue Mondonville, Rue Jules Siegfried 75020 Ⓜ Porte de Bagnolet

This former housing estate is one of the most picturesque parts of Paris, with stone-fronted houses lining the

ARTISTS OF BELLEVILLE

In the late 1990s, artists flocked to Belleville for cheap rents, ample space and the bohemian lifestyle that many still associate with Paris today. Their galleries, like those along Rue Dénoyez *(p133)*, have become permanent fixtures. Each year for four days at the end of May, artists all over Belleville open up their workshops, welcoming thousands of visitors into around 120 studios producing painting, photography, sculpture and ceramics. The Portes Ouvertes, literally "open doors", has been running since 1990. More information can be found online at ateliers-artistes-belleville.fr.

cobbled streets. La Campagne, literally "the countryside", feels exactly like that. A pastor, Sully Lombard, conceived of the development in 1907 for lower-income Parisians. Built on top of an old gypsum quarry and completed well after World War I, the 90-odd houses stood out from the rest of Paris's architecture. Brick façades, creeping ivy and wisteria, and tiny gated gardens full of roses and clematis adorn the two-storey houses. These provincial-looking cobbled streets offer some splendid photo opportunities and are a wonderful oasis of calm away from the bustle of urban Paris.

One of the village-like streets that make up La Campagne à Paris ↑

LA VILLETTE

A Gallo-Roman town once stood in this area, which subsequently became home to religious workers at a nearby leper colony. It remained an agricultural hamlet beyond the city wall for many years, but gained attention when Napoleon began his canal project here. The district formally joined Paris in 1859. La Villette is best known for its large 19th-century slaughterhouses, constructed under Napoleon III. The giant halls replaced those in five other locations in Paris, centralizing the city's meat industry. By the 1970s, the slaughterhouses had ceased operations and the mayor decided to revive the area with a new park. Designed in the 1980s, Paris's third-largest green space evokes post-modern and deconstructive concepts, with standout cultural centres including Europe's largest science museum and the Philharmonie de Paris, designed by Jean Nouvel. Outside the park there are theatres and art centres to explore, as well as another of Paris's most iconic green spaces, the Buttes Chaumont.

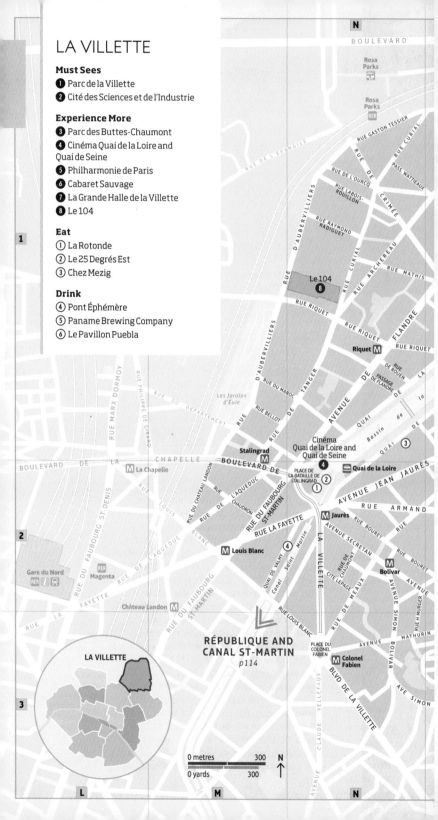

LA VILLETTE

Must Sees

1 Parc de la Villette
2 Cité des Sciences et de l'Industrie

Experience More

3 Parc des Buttes-Chaumont
4 Cinéma Quai de la Loire and Quai de Seine
5 Philharmonie de Paris
6 Cabaret Sauvage
7 La Grande Halle de la Villette
8 Le 104

Eat

1 La Rotonde
2 Le 25 Degrés Est
3 Chez Mezig

Drink

4 Pont Éphémère
5 Paname Brewing Company
6 Le Pavillon Puebla

PARC DE LA VILLETTE

Q1 **211 Ave Jean Jaurès 75019** **M** Porte de Pantin, Porte de la Villette 75, 139, 150, 152, 375 **T3b** **Public spaces:** 24 hrs daily; gardens: May–Sep: 3–7pm Sat & Sun (Oct–Mar: by reservation only); Jardin des Vents et des Dunes: 10am–8pm daily (Nov–Mar: only Wed, Sat & Sun, plus public and school holidays) **lavillette.com**

This inventive urban park offers an appealing combination of nature and modern architecture, containing gardens, playgrounds and a variety of cultural spaces.

Urban Regeneration

Once home to slaughterhouses and a livestock market, this former industrial area has been transformed into a vibrant urban park. Designed by Bernard Tschumi, its vast facilities cover 55 ha (136 acres) of a previously run-down part of the city. The plan was to revive the tradition of parks for meetings and activities, and to stimulate interest in the arts and sciences. Work began in 1984, and the park has grown to include the Cité des Sciences et de l'Industrie – a high-tech hands-on science museum *(p144)* – a cutting-edge concert hall, an exhibition pavilion, a spherical cinema, a circus and a music centre. Linking them all is the park itself, Paris's third largest, with its follies, walkways, gardens and playgrounds. In the summer, the park holds several festivals, including an open-air film one.

10 million

people visit Parc de la Villette every year.

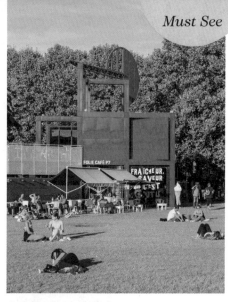

OPEN-AIR FILM FESTIVAL

Each summer the park hosts the free Festival de Cinéma en Plein Air *(p59)*, screening a mix of French and international films in the open air every evening for a month. Deck-chairs and blankets are available for hire, and many people bring their own picnic to make an evening of it.

↑ Taking time out in the sunshine in front of the park's striking red café

The view from the rooftop of the Philharmonie de Paris concert hall *(p147)* ↓

2 🛹 🍴 🖥 🛍

CITÉ DES SCIENCES ET DE L'INDUSTRIE

📍Q1 🏠30 Ave Corentin Cariou 75019 Ⓜ Porte de la Villette
🚌75, 139, 150, 152, 375 🚊T3b ⏰10am-6pm Tue-Sat, 10am-7pm Sun
🚫1 Jan, 1 May, 25 Dec 🌐cite-sciences.fr

Located within the Parc de la Villette, the Cité des Sciences et de l'Industrie is an interactive science and technology museum that is hugely popular with families.

The museum occupies the largest of the old Villette slaughterhouses. Architect Adrien Fainsilber has created an imaginative interplay of light, vegetation and water in the high-tech, five-storey building, which soars 40 m (133 ft) high, stretching over 3 ha (7 acres). At the museum's heart is the Explora exhibit, a fascinating guide to the worlds of science and technology. Visitors can take part in computerized games on space, the earth, transport, energy, design and sound. On other levels, there is a children's science city with machines to play and experiment with, a planetarium, a library and shops.

3

greenhouses on the front of the museum link the building to the park.

Quelles lo⊙
pour l'Uni

Univers – entrée

↑ The Story of the Universe, taking visitors back 13.7 billion years to the creation of the first atom

↑ The museum building, encircled by a moat and joined to the park via raised walkways

LA GÉODE

Fittingly for a building that looks as if its from the set of a sci-fi movie, this Adrien Fainsilber-designed sphere houses a cinema showing IMAX and 3D films. The enormous 1,000-sq-m (11,000-sq-ft) screen provides an immersive experience.

← Youngsters observing plants and insects in the garden of the children's science city

EXPERIENCE MORE

3

Parc des Buttes-Chaumont

📍 Q2 🏠 Rue Manin 75019 (main access from Rue Armand Carrel) Ⓜ Botzaris, Buttes-Chaumont 🕐 7am–8pm daily (open 24 hrs in summer)

For many, this is the most pleasant and unexpected park in the city. The panoramic hilly site was formerly a gallows for the execution of criminals, a lime

---

🔍 HIDDEN GEM
Rosa Bonheur

Named after a 19th-century artist, Rosa Bonheur is a popular *guinguette* in the Parc des Buttes-Chaumont. It's a bucolic spot for a glass of wine and tapas, and on Sunday nights it's a popular LGBT+ venue.

---

quarry and a rubbish dump. It was converted in the mid-1860s, one of Napoleon III's many projects to renovate the city. Baron Haussmann worked with the landscape architect/designer Adolphe Alphand, who organized a vast programme to furnish the new pavement-lined avenues with benches and lampposts. Others involved in the creation of this large park were the engineer Darcel and the landscape gardener Barillet-Deschamps. They created a lake, made an island with real and artificial rocks, gave it a Roman-style classical temple (the Temple de la Sibylle, modelled after the Temple of Sybil in Tivoli, Italy) and also added a waterfall, streams, and two footbridges to connect the island to the park. Today, visitors will also find boating facilities.

→
The romantic Parc des Buttes-Chaumont

4

Cinéma Quai de la Loire and Quai de Seine

📍 N2 🏠 7 Quai de la Loire & 14 Quai de la Seine 75019 Ⓜ Stalingrad, Jaurès 🌐 mk2.com

These two cinemas on opposite banks of the canal basin are popular hangouts during the evenings. Neighbouring cafés and bars fill with cinephiles who are waiting to see the latest release. The cinemas screen a large selection of French and international movies that cater to both art-house and blockbuster crowds, sometimes showing

↑ Views from the Temple in Parc des Buttes-Chaumont

The state-of-the-art interior of the new Paris Philharmonic concert hall ↑

Hollywood pictures before their US release. When buying a ticket, note which cinema your film is in; if it's on the opposite bank, a water shuttle will carry you across the canal. Bear in mind that international films are shown in VO *(version originale)* or VF *(version française)*. If you don't want to watch a film dubbed into French buy tickets for the VO version. Afterwards, you could join a game of *pétanque* along the canal, just next to the cinema, where Parisians while away their evenings.

Philharmonie de Paris

R1 **221 Ave Jean Jaurès 75019** **M** **Porte de Pantin** **Noon-6pm Tue-Sun (from 10am Sat & Sun)** **Mon** **philharmoniedeparis.fr**

Built in 2015, the futuristic Philharmonie, designed by French architect Jean Nouvel, rises above Parc de la Villette like a silver spaceship. The main concert hall seats up to 3,650 people, depending on the configuration and the placement of floating balconies. The idea is that spectators are never further than 32 m (105 ft) from the conductor, creating a more immersive, intimate experience. The building went well over budget – more than double the expected €170 million – causing quite a scandal. Still, the hall's inaugural concert, held in honour of the victims of that year's *Charlie Hebdo* attacks was well attended, with patrons including then-president François Hollande.

The Philharmonie caters mostly to symphonic concerts, but also hosts jazz and world music performances. It houses cultural centres and exhibition halls, as well as smaller concert halls. Visitors can book a concert or just pop into one of its two restaurants for a meal with views over the park. The Philharmonie offers guided tours, with bookings available through their website. Smaller-scale concerts are also held at the neighbouring Cité de la Musique, designed in 1995 by Christian de Portzamparc and now rechristened Philharmonie 2.

> Built in 2015, the futuristic Philharmonie, designed by French architect Jean Nouvel, rises above Parc de la Villette like a silver spaceship.

La Rotonde
Part of Paris's last great peripherary wall, this lovely classical-style rotonda is now a great stop for afternoon or evening drinks.

N2 **6-8 Place de la Bataille de Stalingrad 75019** **grandmarchestalingrad.com**

€€€

Le 25 Degrés Est
With a terrace overlooking the canal, this laid-back bar-restaurant attracts sun-seekers in the summer.

N2 **10 Place de la Bataille de Stalingrad 75019** **01 42 09 66 74**

€€€

Chez Mezig
Located on the canal, this local joint, with adorably mismatched furniture, serves up reliable, standard fare.

N1 **44 bis Quai de la Loire 75019** **09 81 42 98 14**

€€€

The rooftop of Jean Nouvel's Philharmonie de Paris

The Fontaine aux Lions in front of La Grande Halle de la Villette ↑

 6

Cabaret Sauvage

 R1 59 Blvd Macdonald 75019 M Porte de la Villette W cabaret sauvage.com

On the bank of the canal, just before it leaves Paris's city limits, a curious venue stands all by itself in the Parc de la Villette. Opened in 1997, the Cabaret Sauvage is an entertainment venue unlike any other in Paris. Algerian-born Méziane Azaïche created the space, which welcomes all sorts of up-and-coming and little-known artists. Concerts and shows range from contemporary acrobatic and circus displays to dance and West African musical performances, and international artists such as Redman, Mos Def and Noel Gallagher have played here over the years. The structure itself is entirely unassuming on the outside. Once inside the red velour draping, however, spectators cannot help but be drawn into the Cabaret Sauvage's unqiue circus-ring atmosphere. Tickets are available in advance for all the different shows, with 600 seated places and 1,200 spots for events where audiences stand. A night out at the Cabaret Sauvage is sure to be as memorable as it is individual.

7

La Grande Halle de la Villette

Q1 211 Ave Jean Jaurès 75019 M Porte de Pantin W lavillette.com

A former slaughterhouse, this massive hall is one of three that were once in this part of La Villette. In the 19th century, Haussmann decided it would be easier to concentrate all of the meat industry in one spot. Eventually, and perhaps unsurprisingly, the area gained the nickname "City of Blood". In the 1980s, the veal hall was destroyed while the sheep hall was

---

BASSIN DE LA VILLETTE

The Bassin de la Villette hosts activities all year. Join Parisians, both young and old, in a game of *pétanque* on the banks, or try your hand at Mölkky, a Finnish game with wooden pins. The canal is popular with locals for rowing, but visitors can also hit the water by renting a motorboat from the Marin d'Eau Douce. A Paris Plage (beach) is set up here in July and August, and there is swimming and boating. The most popular activity, however, is picnicking. Head here early, especially in the summer, to secure a space along the waterfront.

> **Once inside the red velour draping, however, spectators cannot help but be drawn into the Cabaret Sauvage's unqiue circus-ring atmosphere.**

deconstructed in hopes of rebuilding it elsewhere. President Mitterrand preserved this iron beauty, used for slaughtering cows for beef, and today it houses an event space. Concerts, plays, exhibitions and other events take place regularly. Drop into the café/restaurant for a coffee or meal; it has an inviting garden area for when the weather is fair.

Le 104

📍 **N1** 🏠 **5 Rue Curial 75019** Ⓜ **Riquet, Stalingrad** 🕐 **Noon-7pm daily** 🚫 **Mon** 🌐 **104.fr.**

It might not be obvious upon entering, but this art centre was originally built by the Parisian Archbishop in 1874 for funeral services. It housed a coffin warehouse, stables for horses and shops where individuals could purchase decorations for tombs. Eventually

the hearses of the 20th century disappeared when the public sector lost its monopoly on conducting funeral services. The space, however, underwent a renaissance. The vast hall, with iron beams and a glass roof, was slowly transformed into Le 104 (or Le Centquatre), an artists' residence and exhibition space. The centre is an excellent example of urban renewal in a city skilled at repurposing its historic structures. The mayor inaugurated the space in 2008, and the city still funds the majority of its costs. Today there are performances, concerts and art shows year-round, open to the public. Visitors can see artists at work experimenting with different media. Le Centquatre is quickly becoming a major player on the art scene among local and international artists: it has hosted exhibitions dedicated to well-known contemporary artists such as Keith Haring and Krijn de Koning.

DRINK

Point Éphémère
Part concert hall, part drinking venue. There are often special nights with food trucks or other pop-ups.

📍 **N2** 🏠 **200 Quai de Valmy 75010** 🌐 **pointephemere.org.**

Paname Brewing Company
Perched on the canal in an old warehouse; local craft beers are the favourite here.

📍 **P1** 🏠 **41 bis Quai de la Loire 75019** 🌐 **panamebrewing company.com.**

Le Pavillon Puebla
Nestled in the greenery of Parc des Buttes-Chaumont, this is a peaceful oasis with a mix of Moroccan and modern touches.

📍 **P3** 🏠 **39 Avenue Simon Bolivar 75019** 🌐 **leperchoir.tv**

MONTMARTRE AND PIGALLE

Once a separate village outside Paris, Montmartre was formerly a rural district dotted with windmills and vineyards. Following its incorporation into the city limits in 1860, it swiftly transformed into an urban neighbourhood that was popular with the working classes for its low-cost housing. By the end of the 19th century, this bohemian area had a reputation for decadence and free living, which turned it into a magnet for artists, writers and intellectuals. The still-standing Bateau-Lavoir was a shared studio and home to artists like Matisse, Picasso and Modigliani. Montmartre's reputation for depravity stemmed in large part from its numerous dance halls, among them the infamous Moulin Rouge, said to have been the birthplace of the cancan dance. Although some of the entertainment has taken on a seedier character, Montmartre and Pigalle are still popular nightlife destinations, with numerous lively bars and restaurants.

MONTMARTRE AND PIGALLE

Must See
1. Sacré-Coeur

Experience More
2. St-Pierre de Montmartre
3. Place du Tertre
4. St-Jean l'Evangéliste de Montmartre
5. Place des Abbesses
6. Cimetière de Montmartre
7. Espace Dalí Montmartre
8. Musée de Montmartre
9. Moulin de la Galette
10. Au Lapin Agile
11. Halle St-Pierre
12. Batignolles
13. Moulin Rouge
14. Musée de la Vie Romantique
15. Rue des Martyrs

Eat
1. Un Zèbre à Montmartre
2. Le Pantruche
3. Restaruant Caillebotte

Stay
4. Hôtel Amour
5. Le Pigalle
6. Hôtel Particulier Montmartre

Shop
7. Maison Arnaud Demontel
8. Mesdemoiselles Madeleine
9. Poppelini
10. Henri Le Roux

❶ 🖌️ 🏛️

SACRÉ-COEUR

📍J1 🏠33 Rue du Chevalier-de-la-Barre 75018 Ⓜ Abbesses (then take funicular to the steps of the Sacré-Coeur), Anvers, Barbès-Rochechouart, Lamarck-Caulaincourt 🚌30, 31, 54, 80, 85 🕐6am–10:30pm daily; dome: 9:30am–5pm daily (May–Sep: 9:30am–8pm daily) 🌐sacre-coeur-montmartre.com

Situated atop the hill of Montmartre, the spectacular white basilica of the Sacré-Coeur watches over Paris from the city's highest point. It stands as a memorial to the 58,000 French soldiers killed during the Franco-Prussian War.

At the outbreak of the Franco-Prussian War in 1870, two Catholic businessmen made a private religious vow to build a church dedicated to the Sacred Heart of Christ, should France be spared the impending Prussian onslaught. The two men, Alexandre Legentil and Hubert Rohault de Fleury, lived to see Paris saved from invasion despite the war and a lengthy siege – and were able to witness the start of work on the Sacré-Coeur basilica. The project was taken up by Archbishop Guibert of Paris and construction began in 1875 to Paul Abadie's designs, which were inspired by the Romano-Byzantine church of St-Front in Périgueux. The basilica was completed in 1914, but its consecration was forestalled by World War I until 1919, when France was victorious.

THE SIEGE OF PARIS

Prussia invaded France in 1870. During the four-month siege of Paris, instigated by the Prusso-German statesman Otto von Bismarck, hungry Parisians were forced to eat the city's horses and other animals.

Spiral staircase

Ovoid dome

Bell tower

Statue of Christ

Equestrian statues

Main entrance

↑ The 83-m-
(272-ft-)
high basilica

Crypt vaults

PICTURE PERFECT
**The Basilica
and the City**

The best view of the
Sacré-Coeur is from the
gardens below, but for
a 360-degree panorama
of the city, climb the
300 steps to the top
of the basilica dome.

↑ The beautiful basilica,
crowned by its elegant
ovoid dome

EXPERIENCE MORE

❷ St-Pierre de Montmartre

 J1 2 Rue du Mont-Cenis 75018 Ⓜ Abbesses ⏰ 8am–7pm daily (to 6pm Fri) Ⓦ saintpierrede montmartre.net

Situated in the shadow of the Sacré-Coeur basilica, St-Pierre de Montmartre is all that remains of the great Benedictine Abbey of Montmartre, which was founded in 1133 by Louis VI and his wife, Adelaide of Savoy, who – as its first abbess – is buried here. Inside the church are four marble columns supposedly from a Roman temple which once stood on the site. The vaulted choir dates from

the 12th century, the nave was remodelled in the 15th century and the west front in the 18th. During the Revolution, the abbess was executed by guillotine, and the church fell into disuse. St-Pierre was reconsecrated in 1908. Gothic-style stained-glass windows replace those destroyed by a bomb in World War II. The tiny cemetery opens to the public only once a year, on 1 November.

---

❸ Place du Tertre

🔲 J1 🏠 75018 Ⓜ Abbesses

Tertre means "hillock," or mound, and this picturesque square is the highest point in Paris at 130 m (430 ft).

It was once the site of the abbey gallows but is associated with artists, who began exhibiting paintings here in the 19th century. It is lined with colourful restaurants – La Mère Catherine dates back to 1793. The house at No 21 was formerly the home of the irreverent "Free Commune", founded in 1920 to perpetuate the bohemian spirit of the area. The Old Montmartre information office is now here.

---

❹ St-Jean l'Évangéliste de Montmartre

🔲 H2 🏠 19 Rue des Abbesses 75018 Ⓜ Abbesses ⏰ 9am–7pm Mon–Sat; 9:30am–6pm Sun (to 7pm summer) Ⓦ saintjeandemont martre.com

Designed by Anatole de Baudot and completed in 1904, this church was, controversially, the first to be built from reinforced concrete. The flower motifs on the interior are typical of the Art Nouveau style, while its interlocking arches suggest Islamic architecture. The red-brick facing has earned it the nickname St-Jean-des-Briques.

---

❺ Place des Abbesses

🔲 H2 🏠 75018 Ⓜ Abbesses

This is one of Paris's most picturesque squares. It is sandwiched between the rather dubious attractions of Place Pigalle, with its strip clubs, and Place du Tertre, which is mobbed by hundreds of tourists. Be sure not to miss the Abbesses Metro station with its unusual green wrought-iron arches and

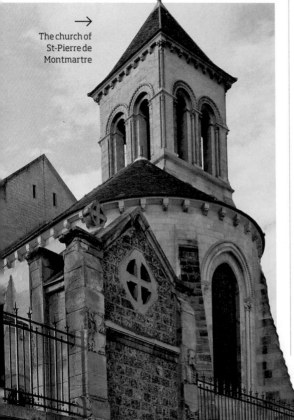

→ The church of St-Pierre de Montmartre

→ The lively Place du Tertre with its many restaurants

amber lights. Designed by the architect Hector Guimard, it is one of the few surviving original Art Nouveau stations.

 6

Cimetière de Montmartre

📍G1 🏠20 Ave Rachel 75018 📞01 53 42 36 30 Ⓜ️Place de Clichy, Blanche 🕐8am–6pm Mon–Fri, 8:30am–6pm Sat, 9am–6pm Sun (to 5:30pm winter)

This has been the resting place for many artistic luminaries since the beginning of the 19th century. The composers Hector Berlioz and Jacques Offenbach (who wrote the famous cancan tune) are buried here, alongside many other celebrities, such as La Goulue (stage name of Louise Weber, the cancan's first star performer and Toulouse-Lautrec's model), the painter Edgar Degas, writer Alexandre Dumas, German poet Heinrich Heine,

Russian dancer Vaslav Nijinsky and film director François Truffaut. Cimetière de Montmartre is an evocative, atmospheric place, conveying some of the heated energy and artistic creativity of the area a century ago.

To the east, close to Square Roland Dorgelès, is the often overlooked **Cimetière St-Vincent**. Here lie more of the great artistic names of the district, including Swiss composer Arthur Honegger and writer Marcel Aymé. Most notable of all is the grave of the great French painter Maurice Utrillo, one of the few famous Montmartre artists actually born in the area and many of whose works afford some of the most enduring, evocative images of the district.

Cimetière St-Vincent

🏠6 Rue Lucien-Gaulard 75018 📞01 46 06 29 78 Ⓜ️Lamarck-Caulaincourt 🕐8am–6pm Mon–Fri, 8:30am–6pm Sat, 9am–6pm Sun (to 5:30pm winter)

> Cimetière de Montmartre is an evocative, atmospheric place, conveying some of the heated energy and artistic creativity of the area a century ago.

EAT

Un Zèbre à Montmartre

This is a great go-to for a lunchtime *croque monsieur* or an evening salmon tartare.

📍H1 🏠38 Rue Lepic 75018 🌐zebreamontmartre.fr

 €€€

Le Pantruche

A handwritten menu is always a good sign; here they serve French classics with fun twists.

📍J2 🏠3 Rue Victor Massé 75009 📞01 48 78 55 60

 €€€

Restaurant Caillebotte

Lunchtime specials are a steal at this little modern bistro, owned by the team behind Le Pantruche *(above)*.

📍J3 🏠8 Rue Hippolyte Lebas 75009 📞01 53 20 88 70 🗓️Sat, Sun

 €€€

The Moulin de la Galette, one of two windmills that can still be seen in Montmartre

STAY

Hôtel Amour

Lively and contemporary, but always with a romantic undertone.

 J2 8 Rue de Navarin 75009
W hotelamourparis.fr

€€€

Le Pigalle

Rooms are decorated with a tasteful play on the former red light district surroundings. Great breakfast and restaurant downstairs.

 H2 23 Rue Frochot 75009 W lepigalle.paris

€€€

Hôtel Particulier Montmartre

Suites in this 19th-century mansion are ideally located for exploring the Montmartre and Pigalle districts.

 H1 23 Ave Junot 75018
W hotel-particulier-montmartre.com

€€€

7

Espace Dalí Montmartre

 J1 11 Rue Poulbot 75018 M Abbesses 10am-6pm daily (to 8:30pm Jul-Aug) W daliparis.com

A permanent exhibition of 330 works by the prolific painter and sculptor Salvador Dalí is displayed here in the heart of Montmartre. Inside, the vast, dark setting reflects the dramatic character of this 20th-century genius, as moving lights grace first one, then another, of his Surrealist works to a soundtrack of Dalí's recorded voice. This fascinating museum also houses a commercial art gallery, a library and a shop selling books, prints and postcards.

8

Musée de Montmartre

 J1 12 Rue Cortot 75018 M Abbesses, Anvers 10am-6pm daily (to 7pm Apr-Sep)
W museedemontmartre.fr

During the 17th century, this charming home belonged to the actor Rose de Rosimond (Claude de la Rose), a member of Molière's theatre company. From 1875, the big white house, undoubtedly the finest in Montmartre, provided living and studio space for artists, including Maurice Utrillo and

his mother Suzanne Valadon, a former acrobat and model who became a talented painter, as well as Raoul Dufy and Auguste Renoir.

The museum recounts the history of Montmartre through artifacts, drawings and photographs. It is particularly rich in memorabilia of bohemian life, and has a reconstruction of the Café de l'Abreuvoir, Utrillo's favourite watering hole. Valdon's studio-apartment was renovated and opened to the public in 2014, as was the Hôtel Demarne, which stages temporary exhibitions on Montmartre themes.

9

Moulin de la Galette

 H1 T-junction at Rue Tholozé and Rue Lepic 75018 M Lamarck-Caulaincourt, Abbesses

Once, some 14 windmills dotted the Montmartre skyline and were used for grinding wheat and pressing grapes. Today, only two remain, both on Rue Lepic: the Radet, now above a restaurant confusingly named Moulin de la Galette, and the reconstructed Moulin de la Galette, originally built in 1622 and formerly known as the Blute-fin. One of its mill owners, Debray, was supposedly crucified on one of the windmill's sails during

EXPERIENCE Montmartre and Pigalle (side)

12 Batignolles

📍 **F1** 🏠 **75007** Ⓜ **Place de Clichy, Rome, Brochant**

Formerly used as a royal hunting ground, this neighbourhood in the 17th arrondissement of northwestern Paris later grew into a small hamlet. Although it officially became part of the city in the second half of the 19th century, it still feels like a small French village inside cosmopolitan Paris. In the 19th century, the area had a lively cultural vibe and counted among its residents the painter Edouard Manet and his fellow artists (who became known as the Groupe des Batignolles), the writer Émile Zola and, later, the Belgian singer Jacques Brel.

The lovely church of Ste-Marie des Batignolles sits in the heart of the neighbourhood. While Batignolles has a calm, community feel, it also has a slightly urban atmosphere, with a good mix of well-frequented bars, stylish boutiques and restaurants. It was one of the first areas in Paris to label its up-and-coming class of residents bobos, a short-hand term for "bourgeois bohemians". Two markets are held in the area: the organic Marché Biologique des Batignolles on Boulevard des Batignolles and covered market on Rue Lemercier, which dates back to 1846. At weekends, families converge on the area's several squares, the two largest being Square des Batignolles

and the Parc Clichy – Martin-Luther-King, which features playgrounds, duck ponds, a skate park and running trails. The district has undergone substantial development in recent years, and there are modern flats, shops and office buildings, including the new Paris law courts.

13 Moulin Rouge

📍 **H2** 🏠 **82 Blvd de Clichy 75018** Ⓜ **Blanche** 🕐 **Dinner: 7pm; shows: 9pm and 11pm daily** 🌐 **moulinrouge.fr**

Built in 1885, the Moulin Rouge was turned into a dance hall as early as 1900. The cancan originated in Montparnasse, in the polka gardens of the Rue de la Grande-Chaumière, but it will always be associated with the Moulin Rouge, where the wild and colourful dance shows were immortalized in the posters and drawings of Henri de Toulouse-Lautrec. The high-kicking routines of famous "Doriss girls" such as Yvette Guilbert and Jane Avril continue

The Moulin Rouge, an iconic symbol of Parisian nightlife

today in a glittering, Las Vegas-style revue that includes sophisticated light shows and displays of magic

14 Musée de la Vie Romantique

📍 **H2** 🏠 **16 Rue Chaptal 75009** Ⓜ **Blanche, Pigall** 🕐 **9am-6pm Tue-Sun** 🌐 **museevieromantique paris.fr**

This quaint, tiny 19th-cent house was once home to Scheffer, the portrait pain of the monarch during th Bourbon Restoration. He the artist welcomed grea cultural icons of the mid-century, including Eugèn Delacroix and Charles Di Now a museum, the hou displays 19th-century p ings, and artifacts that

MONTMARTRE'S WINDMILLS

dmills were common in Montmartre in the late century, when the area was still essentially a ge. As the city began to consume the local farmland, ietors turned their nearly defunct windmills into tainment venues such as the Moulin de la Galette . The most famous windmill, the Moulin Rouge, omage to these parties, though it was never y a functional windmill itself.

Did You Know?

The Pigalle district was dubbed "Pig Alley" by Allied troops after WWII because of its bawdy nightlife.

the 1814 Siege of Paris. He had been trying to repulse the invading Cossacks. At the end of the 19th century, both mills became famous dance halls providing inspiration for many artists, notably Pierre-Auguste Renoir and Vincent van Gogh.

The steep Rue Lepic is a busy shopping area. The Impressionist painter Armand Guillaumin once lived on the first floor of No 54. Van Gogh inhabited its third floor, and painted the view from there.

10 Au Lapin Agile

📍 **J1** 🏠 **22 Rue des Saules 75018** Ⓜ **Lamarck-Caulaincourt** 🕐 **9pm-1am Tue-Sun** 🌐 **au-lapin-agile.com**

The former Cabaret des Assassins derived its current name from a sign painted by the humorist André Gill. His picture of a rabbit escaping from a cooking pot (Le Lapin à Gill) is a pun on his own name. The club enjoyed popularity with intellectuals and artists at the start of the 20th century. Here in 1911,

the novelist Roland Dorgelès and a group of other regulars staged one of the modern art world's most celebrated hoaxes, with the help of the café owner's donkey, Lolo. A paintbrush was tied to Lolo's tail, and the resulting daub was shown to critical acclaim at the Salon des Indépendants, under the enlightening title Sunset over the Adriatic, before the joke was revealed.

In 1903, the premises were bought by the cabaret entrepreneur Aristide Bruand (painted in a series of posters by Toulouse-Lautrec). Years later, the cabaret venue manages to retain much of its original atmosphere.

11 Halle St-Pierre

📍 **J1** 🏠 **2 Rue Ronsard 75018** Ⓜ **Anvers** 🕐 **10am-6pm Mon-Fri, 11am-7pm Sat, noon-6pm Sun** 🔒 **1 Jan, 1 May, 14 July, Aug, 25 Dec** 🌐 **hallesaintpierre.org**

In 1945, the French painter Jean Dubuffet developed the concept of Art Brut (Outsider

INSIDER TIP
Best Baguettes

Many of Montmartre's bakeries are winners of Paris's "Best Baguette" award; look for stickers in the shop windows. Grenier à Pain, at 38 Rue des Abbesses, has achieved the feat of winning the title twice.

or Marginal Art) to describe works created outside the boundaries of "official" culture, often by psychiatric patients, prisoners and children. The Halle St-Pierre, at the foot of the Butte, is a museum and gallery devoted to these "raw" art forms. It also hosts avant-garde theatre and musical productions, holds regular literary evenings and debates and runs children's workshops. In addition to temporary exhibitions, the permanent collection includes more than 500 works of Naïve art collected by the publisher Max Fourny in the 1970s. There is also a specialist bookshop and café.

↑ Suzanne Valadon's studio-apartment at the Musée de Montmartre

161

The stunning view from the Sacré-Coeur in Montmartre

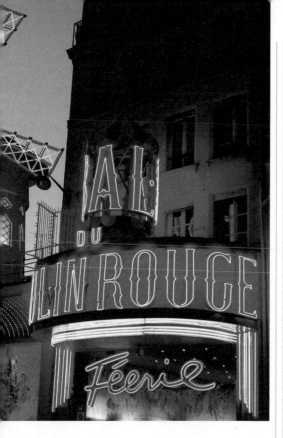

SHOP

Maison Arnaud Demontel

Come for exquisite bread and pastries from this award-winning bakery.

🗺️ J2 🏠 39 Rue des Martyrs 🌐 arnaud-delmontel.com

Mesdemoiselles Madeleine

It's all about multiple varieties of the madeleine here.

🗺️ J3 🏠 37 Rue des Martyrs 🌐 mllesmadeleines.com

Poppelini

Cream-filled choux and nothing else – well, what else is there?

🗺️ J3 🏠 44 Rue des Martyrs 🌐 popelini.com

Henri Le Roux

Salted-butter caramels and chocolate fill this boutique.

🗺️ J3 🏠 24 Rue des Martyrs 🌐 chocolatleroux.com

belonged to celebrated author George Sand, as well as her lover Frédéric Chopin. Sand was a prolific writer and critic of the populist uprising known as the Commune. She also famously wore men's clothes in public and smoked tobacco, unlike most women of the time. The museum has a lovely garden café.

---

⑮ 🍴 🍹 🛍️

Rue des Martyrs

🗺️ J2 🏠 75009
Ⓜ️ Pigalle

This quintessentially Parisian street owes its name to Saint Denis, who was martyred nearby. Rue des Martyrs retains much of the local, market-street vibe that has been lost in many similar locations in Paris. The street is full of tried-and-tested destinations adored by Parisians and visitors alike: pastry shops, restaurants, cafés, and even a boutique dedicated to salted-butter caramel. A few recognizable brands pop up here and there, but overall the street is one of the most individual and fashionable in Paris.

The pretty garden café at the Musée de la Vie Romantique ↑

A SHORT WALK
MONTMARTRE

Distance 1.5 km (1 mile) **Nearest Metro** Abbesses
Time 20 minutes

The steep hill of Montmartre has proved a draw for Parisians and visitors for centuries. Artists Théodore Géricault and Camille Corot came here at the start of the 19th century, and in the 20th century Maurice Utrillo immortalized the streets in his works. Today, this picturesque district, which in places still preserves the atmosphere of pre-War Paris, is a perfect place to wander. A stop at the Place du Tertre is recommended: admire the works of street artists and relax with a coffee and pastry before heading back down the hill.

Au Lapin Agile, a rustic café and cabaret, was a popular meeting point for artists including Picasso (p161).

Musée de Montmartre (p160) features the work of artists who lived in the area. Look out for the Portrait of a Woman (1918), by the Italian painter and sculptor Amedeo Modigliani.

Clos Montmartre is one of the last surviving vineyards in Paris. The grape harvest is celebrated on the first Saturday in October.

Metro Lamarck Caulaincourt

RUE ST VINCENT
RUE DE L'ABREUVOIR
RUE DES SAULES
RUE CORTOT
RUE ST-RUSTIQUE
RUE NORVINS
RUE LEPIC
PL J B CLEMENT
RUE POULBOT
RUE DE LA MIRE
RUE RAVIGNAN
RUE GABRIELLE
RUE BERTHE
RUE DREVET
RUE DES TROIS FRÈRES

The Espace Dalí Montmartre is France's only permanent collection of the Surrealist master's sculptures, paintings and graphic works (p160).

The bustling Place du Tertre is the tourist centre of Montmartre and is full of portraitists and other easel artists (p158). Cafés and bars surround the square.

↑ Admiring the works of street artists in the lively Place du Tertre

| 0 metres | 100 |
| 0 yards | 100 |

N ↑

La Mère Catherine was a favourite eating place of Russian Cossacks in 1814. They would bang on the table and shout "Bistro!" (Russian for "quick") – hence the Paris bistro was born.

St-Pierre de Montmartre was transformed into a "Temple of Reason" during the Revolution (p158).

Locator Map
For more detail see p154

MONTMARTRE AND PIGALLE

↑ The beautiful Sacré-Coeur, illuminated at sunrise

The Romano-Byzantine Sacré-Coeur, started in the 1870s and completed in 1914, is a highlight of the area (p156).

Halle St-Pierre hosts exhibitions of Art Brut and Naïve Art (p161).

RUE DU MONT CENIS
RUE DU CHEVALIER
RUE DU CARDINAL GUIBERT
RUE AZAÏS
RUE ST-ELEUTHÈRE
RUE LAMARCK
RUE PAUL ALBERT
PL DU PARVIS DU SACRÉ-COEUR
RUE DU CARDINAL DUBOIS
SQ WILLETTE
RUE CH NODIER
RUE CHAPPE
PL ST-PIERRE
RUE TARDIEU
RUE DE STEINKERQUE
START
FINISH

Did You Know?

Montmartre's name is ascribed to local martyrs tortured in around AD 250: *mons martyrium*.

The funiculaire, or cable railway, at the end of Rue Foyatier, takes you to the foot of the basilica of Sacré-Coeur. Metro tickets are valid on it.

Square Willette lies below the parvis (forecourt) of Sacré-Coeur. It is laid out on the side of the hill in a series of descending terraces with lawns, shrubs, trees and flower beds.

OPÉRA AND GRANDS BOULEVARDS

Known for its elegant avenues and the Opéra Garnier, this area was an important focus of Baron Haussmann's renovation of Paris in the 19th century. The crowded streets of the medieval city were demolished to make way for a series of Grands Boulevards – Madeleine, Capucines, Italiens and Montmartre – wide avenues flanked by imposing stone buildings with intricate wrought-iron balconies. Many glass-roofed shopping arcades were also constructed around this time, followed by the Printemps and Galeries Lafayette department stores, which firmly established the area's reputation as a major shopping destination. It also became a popular entertainment district, with venues including the dazzling Opéra National de Paris Garnier, and in 1895 the Lumière brothers held the world's first public film show at the Grand Café on Boulevard de Capucines. Today the area is more of a business hub, but night-time revellers will still find a host of clubs and theatres to enjoy.

OPÉRA AND GRANDS BOULEVARDS

Must See

1 Opéra National de Paris Garnier

Experience More

2 La Madeleine
3 Place de la Madeleine
4 Église Ste-Trinité
5 Théâtre Mogador
6 Galeries Lafayette
7 Chapelle Expiatoire
8 Église St-Augustin
9 Gare St-Lazare
10 Printemps
11 Musée Grevin
12 Le Grand Rex

Eat & Drink

① Pascade
② Chartier
③ Harry's New York Bar

Stay

④ W Hôtel
⑤ Hôtel Chopin
⑥ Hôtel Parister

1

OPÉRA NATIONAL DE PARIS GARNIER

H4 **Pl de l'Opéra 75009** **Opéra** **10am–4:30pm daily (1pm on matinée days); mid-Jul–late Aug: 10am–5:30pm** **1 Jan, 1 May** **operadeparis.fr**

Sometimes compared to a giant wedding cake, this palatial opera house with its ornate interior is a sumptuous setting in which to enjoy a ballet or opera.

The building was designed by Charles Garnier for Napoleon III; construction started in 1862 and finished in 1875 after interruptions from the Prussian War and 1871 uprising. Its unique appearance is due to a mixture of materials (including stone, marble and bronze) and styles, ranging from classical to Baroque, with a number of columns, friezes and sculptures on the exterior.

Behind the flat-topped foyer, the cupola sits above the auditorium, while the triangular pediment that rises up behind the cupola marks the front of the stage. Don't miss the magnificent Grand Staircase, made of white marble with a balustrade of red and green marble, and the Grand Foyer, its domed ceiling covered with mosaics. The five-tiered auditorium is a riot of red velvet, plaster cherubs and gold leaf. The false ceiling was painted by Marc Chagall in 1964.

Operas are performed both here and at the Opéra National de Paris Bastille (p106), but the ballet predominantly remains here.

> **The five-tiered auditorium is a riot of red velvet, plaster cherubs and gold leaf.**

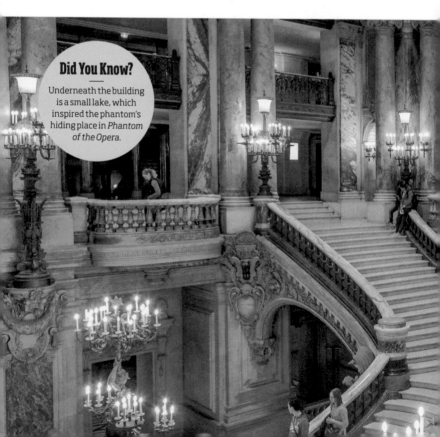

Did You Know?

Underneath the building is a small lake, which inspired the phantom's hiding place in *Phantom of the Opera*.

① With nearly 480,000 visitors each year, the Opéra is one of Paris's most-visited sights.

② The auditorium, which can accommodate 2,054 spectators, was designed so that the audience can see and be seen.

③ The ceiling of the Grand Foyer is decorated with paintings by Paul Baudry.

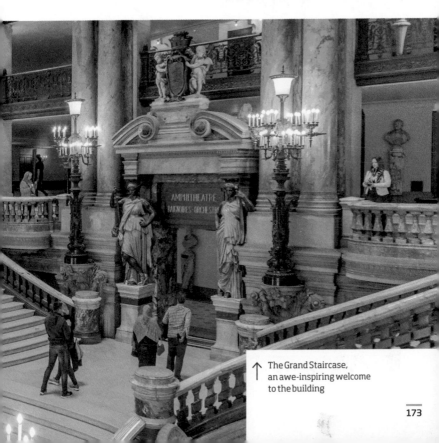

↑ The Grand Staircase, an awe-inspiring welcome to the building

EXPERIENCE MORE

La Madeleine

G4 **Pl de la Madeleine 75008** **M Madeleine** **9:30am–7pm daily** **w eglise-lamadeleine.com**

This church, dedicated to Mary Magdalene, is one of the best-known buildings in Paris because of its prominent location and great size. It stands facing south to Place de la Concorde and is the architectural counterpoint of the Palais Bourbon (home of the French Parliament) across the river. It was started in 1764 but construction halted with the onset of the Revolution in 1789. After the battle of Jena (Iéna) in 1806, Napoleon decided to build a temple dedicated to military glory and he commissioned Pierre Vignon to design it. The church was finished in 1842.

A colonnade of Corinthian columns encircles the building and supports a sculptured frieze. The bas-reliefs on the bronze doors by Henri de Triqueti show the Ten Commandments. The interior is decorated with marble and gilt, and has some fine sculpture, notably François Rude's *Baptism of Christ*. The church has a rich musical tradition; Gabriel Fauré and Camille Saint-Saëns were both organists here. Concerts, especially choral and organ recitals, take place regularly.

Since the funeral of French music icon Johnny Hallyday was held here in 2017, the church has become a shrine to his fans.

Did You Know?

The flower market at Place de la Madeleine has sold colourful bouquets since the early 1800s.

Place de la Madeleine

F4 **75008** **M Madeleine** **Flower market: 8am– 7:30pm Mon–Sat**

The Place de la Madeleine was created at the same time as the Madeleine church. It is a food lover's paradise, with many shops specializing in truffles,

Inside the Église Ste-Trinité, each chapel reveals rich paintings and decorations celebrating saints.

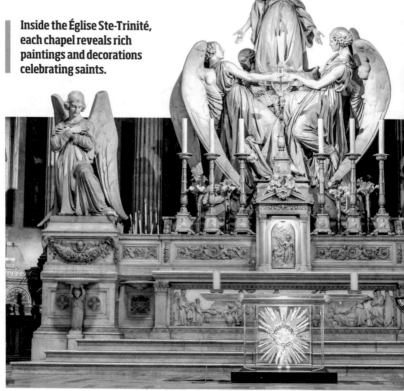

champagne, caviar and handmade chocolates. Fauchon, the luxury supermarket, is situated at No 26. The large house at No 9 is where Marcel Proust spent his childhood. To the east of La Madeleine are a small flower market and some excellently preserved 19th-century Art Nouveau public toilets.

④
Église Ste-Trinité

📍G3 🏛Place d'Estienne d'Orves 75009 Ⓜ Trinité-d'Estienne d'Orves ⏰7:15am-7:45pm Mon-Fri, 10am-7:30pm Sat, 9:30am-8:15pm Sun 🌐latriniteparis.com

Inspired by Renaissance-era Italian churches, this 19th-century masterpiece was consecrated in 1913. The church, often referred to simply as La Trinité, is the monumental centrepiece of the busy Place d'Estienne d'Orves intersection, created by Baron Haussmann. As part of his grand project to redesign Paris, Haussmann

moved the church a few hundred metres from its original location. The chuch is beautifully decorated with a large belfry. Inside, each chapel reveals a rich series of paintings and decorations celebrating saints such as local favourites Geneviève and Vincent de Paul.

⑤
Théâtre Mogador

📍G3 🏛25 Rue de Mogador 75009 📞01 53 32 32 32 Ⓜ Trinité-d'Estienne d'Orves

The Théâtre Mogador was built by London theatre mogul Alfred Butt. It was inaugurated in 1919 by future American president Franklin Delano Roosevelt. Numerous politicians were in town to negotiate the Treaty of Versailles after World War I, so taking in a show must have seemed like a good idea. It once hosted operettas and Sergei Diaghilev's Ballets Russes, but has also staged classic musicals such as *Hello, Dolly!* and *Les Misérables*. Now, this majestic three-tier theatre produces mostly big-budget Broadway shows in French, such as *Phantom of the Opera* and *Grease*.

⑥
Galeries Lafayette

📍H4 🏛40 Blvd Haussmann 75009 Ⓜ Chaussée d'Antin-Lafayette ⏰9:30am-8:30pm daily (Sun 11am-7pm) 🌐haussmann.galerieslafayette.com

Dating back to 1893, this store is a Parisian icon and an essential stop on any visit

The ornate high altar of the Église de la Madeleine

to the city. The massive complex includes men's and women's fashion, a homewares department and a gourmet food hall. At Christmas, a massive tree fills the Art Nouveau cupola, while the windows tell whimsical holiday stories popular with kids. Anyone can take the escalator to the rooftop terrace, where spectacular views of the city await. The store can become a madhouse during the biannual sales, the *soldes*, but it's all part of the Galeries Lafayette experience.

EAT & DRINK

Pascade
The chef offers an innovative take on a sort of crêpe-like dish filled with gourmet ingredients.

📍G4 🏛14 Rue Daunou 75002 ⏰ Sun, Mon 🌐pascade.com

€€€

Chartier
This old workers' canteen is still a budget favourite for French classics.

📍J4 🏛7 Rue du Faubourg Montmartre 75009 🌐bouillon-chartier.com.

€€€

Harry's New York Bar
Birthplace of the Bloody Mary - and other cocktails - it's tradition to make a stop here.

📍H4 🏛5 Rue Daunou 75002 🌐harrysbar.fr

THE VICTIMS OF THE GUILLOTINE

Along with Louis XVI and Marie-Antoinette, numerous other famous figures were buried where the Chapelle Expiatoire now stands. Among them were Murat's murderer Charlotte Corday, writer and feminist Olympe de Gouges, Louis XV's mistress Jeanne du Barry and Madame Roland.

⑦ Chapelle Expiatoire

📍 F4 🏛 29 Rue Pasquier 75008 Ⓜ Madeleine
📞 01 42 65 35 80 🕐 Apr-Sep: 10am-12:30pm & 1:30-6:30pm Tue-Sat; Oct-Mar: 10am-12:30pm & 1:30-5pm

King Louis XVIII dedicated this chapel in 1816 to the memory of his brother King Louis XVI and sister-in-law Marie-Antoinette. The pair were buried in a cemetery here after being guillotined nearby at Place de la Concorde (p224). The mass grave, known as the Madeleine Cemetery, was one of four to hold the remains of guillotine victims. Marie-Antoinette and Louis XVI were moved to the Basilica of St-Denis (p305) in the 19th century. The chapel merely hints at this turbulent history with a modest Neo-Classical memorial. The tiny garden contains cenotaphs to those who were buried here, including victims of the fireworks disaster at Marie and Louis's wedding in 1770.

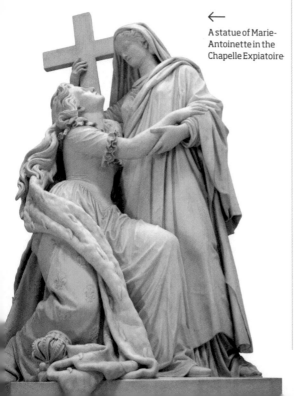

← A statue of Marie-Antoinette in the Chapelle Expiatoire

⑧ Église St-Augustin

📍 F3 🏛 8 Ave César Caire 75008 Ⓜ St-Augustin
🕐 10am-4:30pm Mon-Fri, 10am-noon Sat
🌐 saintaugustin.net

This church is located in one of Paris's most exclusive neighbourhoods. Designed by Victor Baltard, the architect of Les Halles, and completed in 1868 at the intersection of sweeping new boulevards, the building initially drew criticism for its oversized dome and curious red turret. Large quantities of metal were used in the church's construction, and its cast iron framework provides a decorative feature of the interior, complete with iron angels at the tops of the pillars.

⑨ Gare St-Lazare

📍 G3 🏛 13 Rue d'Amsterdam 75008 Ⓜ Gare Saint-Lazare

Europe's second-busiest train station after the Gare du Nord, the Gare St-Lazare is probably the most celebrated in art. Opened in 1837, it sends trains to the station closest to Giverny, where Claude Monet painted his famous water lilies. The artist was just one of many 19th-century painters to immortalize the Saint-Lazare station in his canvases. Renowned painters Caillebotte and Manet also lived near the station, and their depictions of it hang in galleries around the world. The station has recently undergone major renovations, with new shopping and dining areas.

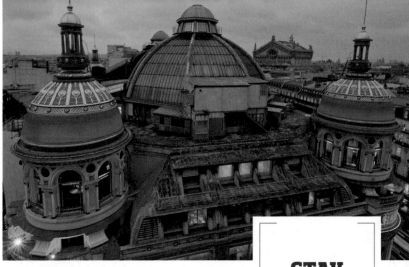

↑ A rooftop view of the Art Nouveau Printemps department store

Printemps

☉ G4 **☖** 64 Blvd Haussmann 75009 **Ⓜ** Havre Caumartin **◷** 9:35am-8pm Mon-Sat (to 8:45pm Thu), 11am-7pm Sun **Ⓦ** printemps.com

A stunning Art Nouveau palace dedicated to shopping, the Printemps department store dates back to 1865. High fashion fills the floors, and it feels slightly more elegant and refined than neighbouring Galeries Lafayette. The brasserie under the massive stained-glass dome is a resplendent spot for lunch, while the rooftop café offers great views of the Sacré-Coeur.

Musée Grévin

☉ J4 **☖** 10 Blvd Montmartre 75009 **Ⓜ** Grands Boulevards **◷** 9am-7pm daily (times can vary, check website) **Ⓦ** grevin-paris.com

This waxworks museum was founded in 1882 and is now a Paris landmark, on a par with Madame Tussauds in London. It contains tableaux of vivid historical scenes (such as the arrest of Louis XVI), the Palais des Mirages (a giant walk-in kaleidoscope) and the Cabinet Fantastique, which features regular conjuring shows given by a live magician. Famous figures from the worlds of art, sport and politics are also on show, with new celebrities constantly replacing faded and forgotten stars.

Le Grand Rex

☉ K4 **☖** 1 Blvd Poissonnière 75002 **Ⓜ** Bonne Nouvelle **Ⓦ** legrandrex.com

A national monument, as well as an innovative example of Art Deco architecture, Le Grand Rex, built in 1932, was long touted as Europe's most opulent cinema, hosting many red-carpet events. One of the largest of its kind in Europe, the Grand Rex is a fading but beautiful symbol of the history of cinema. The auditorium has a starred ceiling, 2,800 seats and an enormous screen. Every December, the cinema hosts the Féerie des Eaux, a family-film event featuring an on-stage water show.

STAY

W Hôtel

Chic and modern, the W brand's stylish hotel overlooking the Opéra National de Paris Garnier doesn't disappoint.

☉ H4 **☖** 4 Rue Meyerbeer 75009 **Ⓦ** marriott.fr

€€€

Hôtel Chopin

Hidden away in a 19th-century covered *passage*, this well-located hotel has charm in spades.

☉ J4 **☖** 46 Passage Jouffroy 75009 **Ⓦ** hotelchopin-paris-opera.com

€€€

Hôtel Parister

Quiet and calm with contemporary décor, this is a wonderful retreat, with its own swimming pool, and very reasonably priced.

☉ J3 **☖** 19 Rue Saulnier 75009 **Ⓦ** hotelparister.com

€€€

A SHORT WALK
OPÉRA

Distance 1.5 km (1 mile) **Nearest Metro** Madeleine
Time 15 minutes

It has been said that if you sit for long enough at the Café de la Paix (opposite the Opéra National de Paris Garnier) the whole world will pass by. During the day, the area is a mixture of commerce – France's top three banks are based here – and tourism.

A profusion of shops, ranging from the chic, exclusive and expensive to popular department stores, draws the crowds. In the evening, the theatres and cinemas attract a totally different clientele, and the cafés along Boulevard des Capucines throb with life.

← The exquisite high altar of La Madeleine

On the north side of Place de la Madeleine the windows of the Fauchon shop are filled with exquisite delicacies.

RUE TRONCHET

RUE VIGNON

RUE GODOT DE MAUROY

RUE CAUMARTIN

RUE EDOUARD

PL DE LA MADELEINE

BLVD DE LA MADELEINE   BLVD DES

Ⓜ **START**

Metro Madeleine

The church of La Madeleine is dedicated to Mary Magdalene and is one of the best-known in Paris (p174).

Did You Know?

George Gershwin is said to have composed *An American in Paris* at Harry's New York Bar.

← The opulent Opéra National de Paris Garnier, sometimes described as an enormous wedding cake

OPÉRA AND GRANDS BOULEVARDS

Locator Map
For more detail see p170

With a mixture of styles ranging from classical to Baroque, the Opéra National de Paris Garnier of 1875 has come to symbolize the opulence of the Second Empire (p172).

The world of opera is celebrated at the Bibliothèque-Musée de l'Opéra.

Metro Chaussée d'Antin

The Place de l'Opéra was designed by Baron Haussmann and is one of Paris's busiest intersections.

The Café de la Paix maintains its old-fashioned ways and still has its 19th-century decor, designed by Garnier. Their vanilla slices are legendary.

Metro Opéra

FINISH

At No 14 Boulevard des Capucines, a plaque tells of the world's first public screening of a movie, by the Lumière brothers in 1895; it took place in the Salon Indien, a room in the Grand Café.

Harry's New York Bar was named after Harry MacElhone, a bartender who bought the bar in 1913. Past regulars have included F Scott Fitzgerald and Ernest Hemingway (p175).

0 metres 100
0 yards 100
N ↑

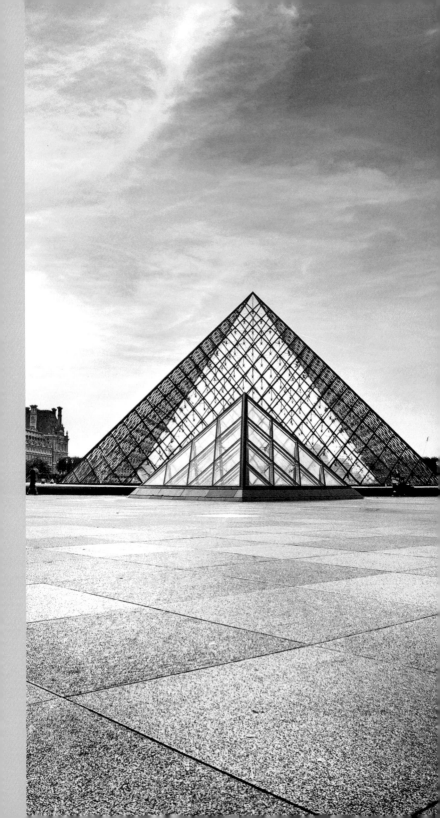

LOUVRE AND LES HALLES

Today the heart of the city, this area lay on the outskirts of Paris in the Middle Ages. Its vulnerable position led Philippe Auguste to build a defensive fortress here in 1190, around which grew up a dense urban district. In 1528, François I took up residence in the Louvre, marking the start of centuries of royal redevelopment and the construction of numerous grand buildings and gardens. The area remained affluent following the downfall of the monarchy in 1789, and is still home to many exclusive shops and luxury hotels.

Les Halles, meanwhile, has much more humble origins. For 800 years, the "Belly of Paris" was the site of the central food market in the city. Housed from the late 19th century in 12 magnificent iron-and-glass pavilions designed by Victor Baltard, the market was demolished in 1971 and transformed into a huge underground mall called the Forum des Halles. Deeply unpopular, it was redeveloped as part of a €1 billion infrastructure project and reopened in 2016.

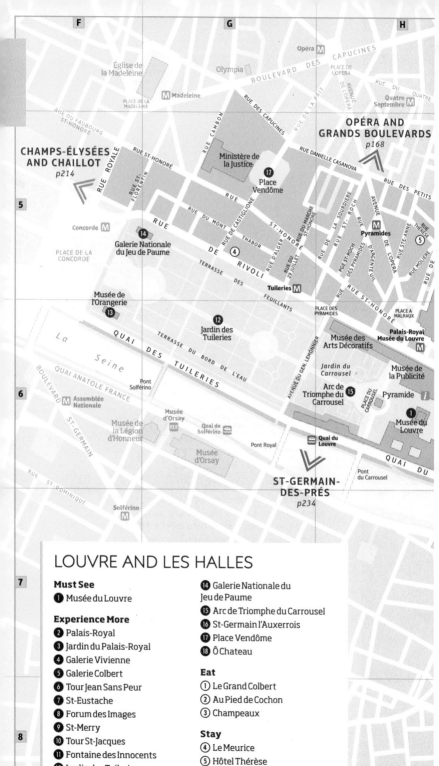

LOUVRE AND LES HALLES

Must See
1 Musée du Louvre

Experience More
2 Palais-Royal
3 Jardin du Palais-Royal
4 Galerie Vivienne
5 Galerie Colbert
6 Tour Jean Sans Peur
7 St-Eustache
8 Forum des Images
9 St-Merry
10 Tour St-Jacques
11 Fontaine des Innocents
12 Jardin des Tuileries
13 Musée de l'Orangerie
14 Galerie Nationale du Jeu de Paume
15 Arc de Triomphe du Carrousel
16 St-Germain l'Auxerrois
17 Place Vendôme
18 Ô Chateau

Eat
1 Le Grand Colbert
2 Au Pied de Cochon
3 Champeaux

Stay
4 Le Meurice
5 Hôtel Thérèse
6 Grand Hôtel du Palais Royal

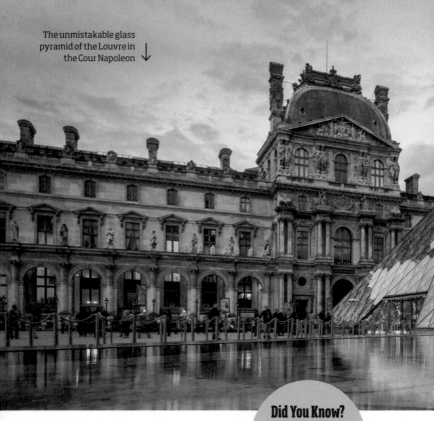

The unmistakable glass pyramid of the Louvre in the Cour Napoleon ↓

Did You Know?
—
Napoleon temporarily renamed the museum after himself and hung the *Mona Lisa* in his bedroom.

MUSÉE DU LOUVRE

Q H6 **A** Pl du Louvre **M** Palais-Royal-Musée du Louvre ⊞ 21, 24, 27, 39, 48, 68, 69, 72, 81, 95 ⊞ Châtelet-Les-Halles ⊙ Louvre ⊙ 9am-6pm Wed-Mon (to 9:45pm Wed & Fri) ⊙ 1 Jan, 1 & 8 May, 25 Dec ⊞ louvre.fr

First opened to the public in 1793 after the Revolution, the Louvre contains one of the most important art collections in the world.

Constructed as a fortress in 1190 by King Philippe-Auguste to protect Paris against Viking raids, the Louvre lost its imposing keep during the reign of François I (1514–47), who replaced it with a Renaissance-style building. Thereafter, four centuries of French kings and emperors improved and enlarged it. A glass pyramid designed by I M Pei was added to the main courtyard in 1989, from which all of the galleries can be reached.

The Louvre's treasures can be traced back to the 16th-century collection of François I, who purchased many Italian paintings, including the *Mona Lisa (La Gioconda)*. At the time of Louis XIV's reign (1643–1715) there were a mere 200 works, but donations and purchases augmented the collection and it has been continually enriched ever since.

GALLERY GUIDE

There are eight departments over four floors: Near Eastern antiquities; Egyptian antiquities; Greek, Etruscan and Roman antiquities; Islamic art; sculptures; decorative arts; paintings; and prints and drawings.

① This sculptural spiral staircase forms part of the modern entrance hall designed by I M Pei.

② The Marly Horses by Guillaume Coustou once stood near the Place de la Concorde.

③ *The Coronation of Napoleon* by Jacques-Louis David is an impressive 6.2 m (20½ ft) high by 9.8 m (32 ft) wide.

↑ *St Bonaventura's Body Lying in State* (c 1629) by Francisco de Zurbarán

EUROPEAN PAINTING: 1200 TO 1850

Painting from northern Europe is well covered, with Flemish, Dutch, German and English works by artists including Jan van Eyck, Vermeer, Hans Holbein and J M W Turner. The Spanish collection tends towards depictions of the tragic side of life, although several portraits by Goya are in a lighter vein.

The large collection of Italian paintings covers the period 1200 to 1800. Key figures of the Renaissance are here, including Giotto and Raphael. Several paintings by Leonardo da Vinci are as enchanting as his *Mona Lisa*.

The French collection ranges from the 14th century to 1848. There are superb works by Jean Fouquet, Georges de la Tour and Jean Watteau, as well as J H Fragonard, master of the Rococo.

MONA LISA: WHY DO WE CARE?

Acquired by King François I, this portrait of a mysterious woman was one of the first paintings displayed in the Louvre when the museum opened. For many years it was simply one da Vinci work among many, but that all changed when the painting was stolen in 1911. The much-publicized theft pushed the artwork into the public eye, with reproductions appearing around the world. Its popularity has not dwindled since.

EUROPEAN SCULPTURE: 1100 TO 1850

Early Flemish and German sculpture in the collection has many masterpieces, including an unusual life-size nude figure of the penitent Mary Magdalene by Gregor Erhart (early 16th century). The French section opens with early Romanesque works, such as a Figure of Christ by a 12th-century Burgundian sculptor and a Head of St Peter. With its eight black-hooded mourners, the Tomb of Philippe Pot is one of the more unusual pieces.

The works of Pierre Puget have been assembled inside the Cour Puget, while the Cour Marly houses the Marly Horses and other master-pieces of French sculpture.

The Italian sculpture collection includes pre-Renaissance works by Duccio and Donatello, and later masterpieces such as Michel-angelo's *Slaves* and Cellini's *Nymph of Fontainebleau*.

←

Saint Mary Magdalene by Gregor Erhart (c 1515–20)

DECORATIVE ARTS

↑ Serpentine stone plate (1st century/ 9th century AD)

The Louvre has well over 8,000 "decorative art" objects, including jewellery, silver and glassware, bronzes, porcelain, snuffboxes and armour. Many of these precious objects are from the Abbey of St-Denis (*p305*), where the kings of France were buried. The treasures include a serpentine stone plate from the 1st century AD with a 9th-century border of gold and precious stones, and the golden sceptre made for King Charles V in about 1380.

The French crown jewels include the coronation crowns of Louis XV and Napoleon, and the Regent, one of the purest diamonds in the world.

The French crown jewels include the coronation crowns of Louis XV and Napoleon, and the Regent, one of the purest diamonds in the world.

The large collection of French furniture ranges from the 16th to the 19th centuries. On display are important pieces by prominent furniture-makers such as André-Charles Boulle, who was cabinet-maker to Louis XIV.

In 2012, the Islamic Art Department opened in the Cour Visconti, with around 18,000 objects on display covering 3,000 years of history from three continents. The museum also recently installed decorative art galleries dedicated to objects from the reign of Louis XIV and the 18th century.

NEAR EASTERN, EGYPTIAN, GREEK, ETRUSCAN AND ROMAN ANTIQUITIES

The range of antiquities is impressive, with objects from the Neolithic period to the fall of the Roman Empire. Important works of Mesopotamian art include the seated figure of Ebih-il, from 2400 BC, while the warlike Assyrians are represented by delicate carvings and a spectacular reconstruction of part of Sargon II's (722–705 BC) palace. A fine example of Persian art is the enamelled brickwork depicting the king of Persia's personal guard of archers (5th century BC).

Most Egyptian art was made for the dead to take to the afterlife. One exquisite example is the tiny carved funeral chapel built for a high official in about 2500 BC. A special crypt dedicated to the god Osiris contains some colossal sarcophagi and mummified animals.

The department of Greek, Roman and Etruscan antiquities contains some exceptional pieces. The two most famous Greek statues in the Louvre, the *Winged Victory of Samothrace* and the *Venus de Milo*, belong to the Hellenistic period (late 3rd to 2nd century BC), when more natural-looking human forms were first produced. The star of the Etruscan collection is the terracotta *Sarcophagus of the Cenestian Couple*, while the Roman section includes a bust of Agrippa and a splendid, powerful bronze head of Emperor Hadrian.

→
Winged Victory of Samothrace (c 190 BC)

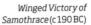

EXPERIENCE MORE

2

Palais-Royal

📍 H6 📍 Pl du Palais-Royal 75001 Ⓜ Palais-Royal 🌐 domaine-palais-royal.fr

This former royal palace, closed to the public, has had a turbulent history. Starting out in the early 17th century as Richelieu's Palais Cardinal, it passed to the Crown on his death and was the childhood home of Louis XIV. Under the control of the 18th-century royal dukes of Orléans, it was the scene of brilliant gatherings, as well as periods of debauchery and gambling. The cardinal's theatre, where Molière had performed, burned down in 1763, but was replaced by the Comédie Française. After the Revolution, the palace became a gambling house. In 1815, it was reclaimed by the future King Louis-Philippe, one of whose librarians was Alexandre Dumas.

After being restored again between 1872 and 1876, the palace reverted to the state, and it now houses the Council of State, the supreme legal body for administrative matters, and the Constitutional Council. Another wing of the palace is occupied by the Ministry of Culture.

3

Jardin du Palais-Royal

📍 H5 📍 6 Rue de Montpensier, Pl du Palais-Royal 75001 Ⓜ Palais-Royal 🕐 Apr–Sep: 8am–10:30pm daily; Oct–Mar: 8am–8:30pm daily 🌐 domaine-palais-royal.fr

The current garden is about one-third smaller than the original one, laid out by the royal gardener for Cardinal Richelieu in the 1630s. This is due to the construction, between 1781 and 1784, of 60 uniform houses bordering three sides of the square. Today, restaurants, art galleries and specialist shops line the square, which has numbered Jean Marais, Jean Cocteau and Colette among its famous former residents.

The courtyard contains the controversial black-and-white striped stone columns that form conceptual artist Daniel Buren's *Les Deux Plateaux.*

The columns were installed in the pedestrianized Palais-Royal courtyard in 1986, despite vociferous opposition about their suitability for the space. Today, they are loved by children and skateboarders alike.

4

Galerie Vivienne

📍 J5 📍 4 Rue des Petits Champs 75002 Ⓜ Bourse, Pyramides 🕐 Generally 8:30am–8:30pm daily 🌐 galerie-vivienne.com

The early 19th century saw the rise of fashionable covered *passages*, reminiscent of the souks explored during Napoleon's conquests in North Africa. At the height of their popularity there were over 100 of them; they were the shopping malls of their day, well before the department stores came of age. Galerie Vivienne, built in 1823, was a particularly sumptuous example of such a covered *passage*. Its lovely décor has been restored, including its atrium ceilings and mosaic floor with

Daniel Buren's columns in the courtyard of the Jardin du Palais-Royal ↑

patterns reminiscent of decorations from Pompeii. It's the perfect all-weather retreat for a glass of wine, a little bit of shopping in the elegant boutiques, or browsing in the Librairie Jousseaume second-hand bookshop.

5

Galerie Colbert

⦿ J5 ⌂ 2 Rue Vivienne 75002 Ⓜ Bourse, Pyramides 🕘 Generally 9am–5pm daily

Unlike nearby Galerie Vivienne, the covered Galerie Colbert, as exquisite as its neighbour and also completed in 1823, is not used for commercial purposes. The two *passages* have historically been in competition to be Paris's favourite. It was in Galerie Colbert that composer Hector Berlioz, famous for *La Symphonie Fantastique*, sang

with crowds at the onset of the July Revolution in 1830. Today, it houses various institutions and parts of the University of Paris, all dedicated to the arts and cultural preservation. The *passage* is usually open to the public and is worth seeing for its lovely glass rotunda, with a statue of Eurydice beneath it. The *passage* can also be viewed from the adjacent brasserie Le Grand Colbert.

6

Tour Jean Sans Peur

⦿ K5 ⌂ 20 Rue Étienne-Marcel 75002 Ⓜ Étienne-Marcel, Sentier 🕘 1:30–6pm Wed–Sun 🌐 tourjeansanspeur.wordpress.com

The Duc de Bourgogne feared reprisals after the Duc d'Orléans was assassinated on his orders in 1408. To protect himself, he had this 27-m (88-ft) tower built onto his home, the Hôtel de Bourgogne, and moved his bedroom up to the fourth floor (reached by a flight of 140 steps). The fine vaulted ceiling is decorated with stone carvings of oak leaves, hawthorn and hops, symbols of the Burgundys.

↑ The lofty, light-filled interior of the elegant Galerie Vivienne

EAT

Le Grand Colbert
This old-world brasserie still charms, and the traditional French food still pleases.

⦿ J5 ⌂ 2 Rue Vivienne 75002 🌐 legrandcolbert.fr

€€€

Au Pied de Cochon
Onion soup is a staple of this Les Halles institution, which is open all night.

⦿ J6 ⌂ 6 Rue Coquillière 75001 🌐 pieddecochon.com

€€€

Champeaux
Alain Ducasse's casual-yet-chic eatery under the new canopy at Forum des Halles serves French classics done just right.

⦿ K6 ⌂ La Canopée, Forum des Halles 75001 🌐 restaurant-champeaux.com

€€€

St-Eustache

📍 J6 🏠 2 Impasse St-Eustache, Pl du Jour 75001 Ⓜ Les Halles 🚉 Châtelet-Les-Halles 🕐 9:30am-7pm Mon-Fri, 10am-7:15pm Sat, 9am-7:15pm Sun 🌐 saint-eustache.org

With its Gothic plan and Renaissance decoration, St-Eustache is one of the most beautiful churches in Paris. Its interior layout is modelled on Notre-Dame (p70), with five naves and side and radial chapels. The 105 years (1532–1637) it took to complete the church saw the flowering of the Renaissance style, which is evident in the arches, pillars and columns. The stained-glass windows in the chancel are created from cartoons by Philippe de Champaigne.

The church has associations with many famous figures: Molière was buried here; and the Marquise de Pompadour, official mistress of Louis XV, was baptized here, as was Cardinal Richelieu. Don't miss a chance to hear the fine organ at one of the regular recitals that take place.

---

⑧

Forum des Images

📍 J6 🏠 2 Rue du Cinéma, Forum des Halles 75001 Ⓜ Les Halles 🚉 Châtelet-Les-Halles 🕐 Opening hours vary; check website for details 🌐 forumdes images.fr

At the Forum des Images, you can choose from thousands of cinema, television and amateur films, many featuring the city of Paris. There is footage on the history of Paris since 1895,

including a remarkable newsreel of General de Gaulle avoiding sniper fire during the Liberation of Paris in 1944. There are countless movies, too, such as François Truffaut's *Baisers Volés*. On Friday evenings the forum hosts "Cours de Cinéma", when classic films are analysed. There are also regular film festivals and screenings.

---

⑨

St-Merry

📍 K7 🏠 76 Rue de la Verrerie 75004 Ⓜ Hôtel de Ville 🕐 Apr-Oct: 3-7pm Mon-Sat; Nov-Mar: 2-6pm Mon-Sat 🌐 saintmerry.org

The site of this church dates back to the 7th century. St Médéric, the abbot of St-Martin d'Autun, was buried here at the beginning of the 8th century; he died while on pilgrimage in Paris. Construction of the church – in the Flamboyant Gothic style – took place in 1500–1550.

The west front is especially rich in decoration, and the northwest turret contains the oldest bell in Paris, dating from 1331. St-Merry was the wealthy parish church of the Lombard moneylenders, who gave their name to the nearby Rue des Lombards. Guided tours usually take place after concerts on the first and third Sundays of the month.

---

⑩ 🔄 🔄

Tour St-Jacques

📍 K7 🏠 Square de la Tour St-Jacques 75004 Ⓜ Châtelet, Hôtel de Ville 🕐 Gardens: year-round; tower: Jun & Sep: 10am-5pm Fri-Sun, Jul-Aug: 10am-5pm Fri-Mon 🌐 Tower: desmotsetdes arts.com

This imposing late-Gothic tower, dating from 1523, is all that remains of an ancient church that was a rendezvous for pilgrims setting out on long journeys. The church was destroyed after the Revolution. Earlier, Blaise Pascal, the 17th-century mathematician, physicist, philosopher and writer, used the tower for experiments. Queen Victoria passed by on her state visit in 1854, giving her name to the nearby Avenue Victoria. The tower can be visited in the summer only; book ahead online.

→ A mild summer evening in the Jardin des Tuileries

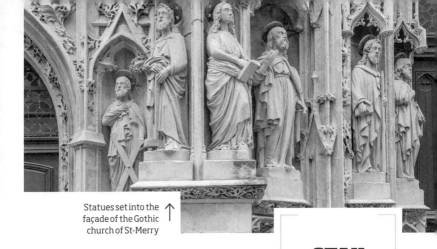

Statues set into the
façade of the Gothic
church of St-Merry

Fontaine des Innocents

 K6 Pl Joachim-du-Bellay 75001 Ⓜ Les Halles
🚇 Châtelet-Les-Halles

This carefully restored Renaissance fountain is a popular meeting place and a Les Halles landmark. It stands in the Place Joachim-du-Bellay, the area's main crossroads. Erected in 1549 on the Rue St-Denis, it was moved to its present location in the 18th century, when the square was constructed on the site of a former graveyard.

Originally set into a wall, the fountain had only three sides so a fourth had to be constructed. It is decorated with mythological figures.

Jardin des Tuileries

G6 Pl de la Concorde 75001 Ⓜ Tuileries, Concorde ⏰ Apr- Sep: 7am-9pm (to 11pm Jun-Aug); Oct-Mar: 7:30am-7:30pm

Once belonging to the old Palais des Tuileries, these gardens form part of the landscaped area between the Louvre and the Champs-Élysées. They were laid out in the 17th century by royal gardener André Le Nôtre, and later filled with striking sculptures. A staggering 125,000 plants are replanted annually.

STAY

Le Meurice
A mighty palace hotel, it has all the amenities a luxury traveller could want, including a Michelin-starred restaurant.

 G5 228 Rue de Rivoli 75001 🌐 dorchester collection.com

€€€

Hôtel Thérèse
A chic boutique-hotel alternative to the big-name hotels in the area, with individually decorated rooms.

 H5 5 Rue Thérèse 75001 🌐 hoteltherese.fr.

€€€

Grand Hôtel du Palais Royal
Tucked behind the Palais-Royal and overlooking its garden, this luxury property is central but has a secluded feel.

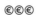 H6 4 Rue de Valois 75001 🌐 grandhoteldupalais royal.com.

€€€

JEU DE PAUME

Nobles used to play a version of handball, *jeu de paume*, in the former royal court that today houses the Galerie Nationale du Jeu de Paume. French players would yell "*tenez*" or "take it" to their opponents. As the game evolved, the word did, too, and the English began to call it tennis, or real tennis, and used rackets instead of their hands. Later, the Jeu de Paume became a storehouse during World War II, where the Nazis stashed stolen art. Those deemed offensive, for example many Picasso and Dalí paintings, were burned in front of it in 1942.

Stained glass at St-Germain l'Auxerrois ↑

Musée de l'Orangerie

📍F6 🏛Jardin des Tuileries, Pl de la Concorde 75001 Ⓜ Concorde 🕐9am–6pm Wed–Mon 🗓1 May, 14 Jul am & 25 Dec 🌐musee-orangerie.fr

Claude Monet's crowning work, the water lily series, or *Nymphéas*, can be found here. The series was painted in his garden at Giverny, near Paris, and presented to the public in 1927. These superb large-scale canvases are complemented well by the outstanding Walter-Guillaume collection of artists of the École de Paris, from the late-Impressionist era to the inter-War period. This is a remarkable concentration of masterpieces, including a room of dramatic works by Soutine and some 14 works by Cézanne – still lifes, portraits (*Madame Cézanne*) and landscapes, such as *Dans le Parc du Château Noir*.

Pierre-Auguste Renoir is represented by 27 canvases, including *Les Fillettes au Piano (Young Girls at the Piano)*. There are early Picassos, works by Henri Rousseau – notably *La Carriole du Père Junier (Old Junier's Cart)* – and Matisse, and a portrait of Paul Guillaume by Modigliani. All are bathed in the natural light that flows through the windows. Temporary exhibitions are shown on the lower ground floor.

Galerie Nationale du Jeu de Paume

📍F5 🏛Jardin des Tuileries, 1 Pl de la Concorde 75008 Ⓜ Concorde 🕐11am–7pm Tue–Sun (to 9pm Tue) 🗓1 Jan, 1 May & 25 Dec and in between exhibitions 🌐jeudepaume.org

The Jeu de Paume – or real tennis court – was built by Napoleon III in 1851. When real (royal) tennis was replaced in popularity by lawn tennis, the court was used to exhibit art. Eventually, an Impressionist museum was founded here. In 1986, the collection moved to the Musée d'Orsay (*p238*). The Jeu de Paume now houses the Centre National de la Photographie, and shows exhibitions of contemporary photography and art from both established and emerging artists.

Arc de Triomphe du Carrousel

📍H6 🏛Pl du Carrousel 75001 Ⓜ Palais-Royal

Built by Napoleon in 1806–8 as an entrance to the former Palais des Tuileries, this vast pink marble arch, inspired by ancient Roman triumphal arches, was originally topped by the so-called Horses of St Mark's from Venice's St Mark's Cathedral. They were returned in 1815 after Napoleon's defeat at Waterloo and replaced by copies.

St-Germain l'Auxerrois

📍J6 🏛2 Pl du Louvre 75001 Ⓜ Louvre, Pont-Neuf 🕐9am–7pm Tue–Sat, 9am–8pm Sun (Jul & Aug: 9:30am–7pm Tue–Sun) 🌐saintgermainauxerrois.fr

This church has been built in a combination of Renaissance and Gothic

Did You Know?

The façade of St-Germain l'Auxerrois is mirrored by the nearby town hall of the 1st arrondissement.

styles. The first church on the site was constructed in the 12th century, of which only the foundations of the bell tower remain. The splendid rose stained-glass windows date from the Renaissance period.

After the Valois Court decamped to the Louvre in the 14th century, this became the favoured church of kings. The church's many historical associations include the horrific St Bartholomew's Day Massacre on 24 August 1572, the eve of the royal wedding of Henri of Navarre and Marguerite de Valois. Thousands of Huguenots who had been lured to Paris for the wedding were murdered as the church bell tolled. Later, after the Revolution, the church was used as a barn and as a police station. Despite many restorations, it is a jewel of Gothic architecture. Check the website for details of the regular concerts held here.

___

17

Place Vendôme

G5 **75001** **M** Tuileries

Perhaps the best example of 18th-century elegance in the city, the architect Jules Hardouin-Mansart's stately square was begun in 1698. The original plan was to house academies and embassies behind the arcaded façades. However, bankers moved in and created opulent homes. Miraculously, the square has remained virtually intact, and is home to jewellers and bankers. Among the famous, Frédéric Chopin died here in 1848 at No 12, and César Ritz established his luxury hotel at the turn of the 20th century at No 15.

18

Ô Chateau

J5 **68 Rue Jean-Jacques Rousseau 75001** **M** Louvre-Rivoli, Étienne Marcel **4pm–midnight Mon-Sat** **o-chateau.com**

With 50 wines served by the glass, this wine-tasting bar in the heart of Les Halles is one of the best places to learn about your soon-to-be favourite vintages (p53). You can stop in for a few drinks, or take a class or even a trip. They can organize outings to Champagne for tastings or prepare a multi-course meal served in one of their vaulted dining rooms. A sommelier pairs each dish with wine, explaining the particularities of French viticulture. English-speakers are catered for, so there's no chance of losing anything in translation.

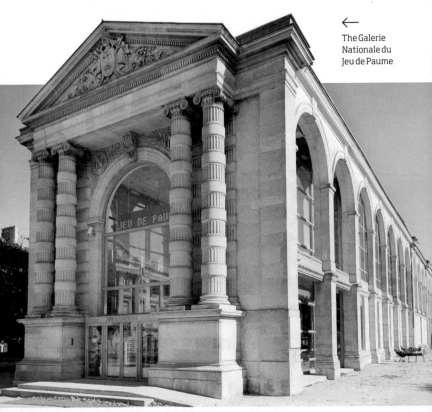

← The Galerie Nationale du Jeu de Paume

A SHORT WALK
TUILERIES QUARTER

Distance 2 km (1.25 miles) **Nearest Metro** Pyramides
Time 20 minutes

Elegant squares, formal gardens, street arcades and courtyards give this part of Paris its special character. Monuments to monarchy and the arts coexist with contemporary luxury: sumptuous hotels, world-famous restaurants, fashion emporiums and jewellers of international renown. Combine a walk around the area with a visit to the world-famous Louvre, and end the day with a well-deserved sit-down in the Jardin des Tuileries.

Metro
Pyramides

START

St-Roch is a remarkably long 17th-century church, unusually set on a north-south axis, and a treasure house of religious art.

The Normandy is an elegant hotel in the belle époque style, a form of graceful living that prevailed in Paris at the turn of the 20th century.

In Place des Pyramides is Frémiet's gilded statue of Joan of Arc, a focus of pilgrimage for royalists.

A highlight of the Musée des Arts Décoratifs' displays of art and design is the Art Nouveau collection.

The formal Jardin des Tuileries were designed by royal gardener André Le Nôtre in the 17th century.

RUE DES PYRAMIDES

RUE ST-HONORE

RUE DE L'ECHELLE

RUE DE

AVE DU GL LEMONNIER

FINISH

| 0 metres | 100 |
| 0 yards | 100 |

N ↑

←
Taking a break in the sunshine at the verdant Jardin des Tuileries

The elegant interior of
the renowned restaurant
Le Grand Véfour

The 18th-century
décor makes Le
Grand Véfour one
of the most beautiful
restaurants in Paris.
Napoleon and Victor
Hugo were two
of the many
famous people
who dined here.

Locator Map
For more detail see p182

LOUVRE AND
LES HALLES

With a fountain pool and
benches, the Jardin du
Palais-Royal is a city
haven, bordered by
arcades housing
restaurants, art galleries
and shops (p188).

France's national theatre,
the Comédie Française is the
setting for the works of great
dramatists, such as Molière.

In the 18th century, the
Palais-Royal was a setting
for brilliant gatherings,
debauchery and gambling.
Today, modern sculptures
grace its square (p188).

Three floors of a former
department store house the
Louvre des Antiquaires, a chic
art and antiques supermarket
for the rich collector.

*Metro Palais-Royal,
Musée du Louvre*

Home to French kings for
almost four centuries, the
Musée du Louvre is now host to
one of the world's greatest art
collections (p184).

EIFFEL TOWER AND INVALIDES

On the Left Bank of the Seine, this quarter in the 7th arrondissement is monumental in scale. The construction of the Hôtel des Invalides in the late 17th century brought with it the urbanization of the surrounding area, and the neighbourhood quickly became popular with the city's nobles, who wanted more space for their palaces. Many wealthy residents of the Marais moved here in the early 18th century, building the aristocratic town houses that line the Rue de Varenne and Rue de Grenelle. Some of these were destroyed during the Revolution, while others were subsequently converted into national institutions, such as the Assemblée Nationale Palais-Bourbon, or embassies.

The quarter has long had a strong military connection as the home of the École Militaire. In 1889, the school's former parade ground, the Champ-de-Mars, was chosen as the site of an Exposition Universelle to commemorate the 100th anniversary of the Revolution. The centre-piece of that exhibition, the Eiffel Tower, is today the main draw for most visitors to the area.

Alma-Marceau Ⓜ
PLACE DE L'ALMA
Port de la Conférence
Berges de Seine 🚌 ⑬

M Trocadéro

CHAMPS-ÉLYSÉES AND CHAILLOT
p214

Pont de l'Alma

Passerelle Debilly

Pont de l'Alma RER ⑫ Musée des Égouts

Palais de Chaillot

Jardins du Trocadero

QUAI BRANLY

QUAI   D'ORSAY

PLACE DE LA RESISTANCE

RUE COGNACQ JAY

RUE MALAR

Seine
PORT DE LA BOURDONNAIS

RUE DE L'UNIVERSITÉ

Musée du Quai Branly-Jacques Chirac ②

CITE DE L'ALMA

AVE FRANCO RUSSE

RUE DE

PASSAGE LANDRIEU

RUE PIERRE VILLEY

Port de la Bourdonnais 🚌

RUE DE MONTESSUY

RUE E VALENTIN

RUE DUPONT DES LOGES

ST-

Pont d'Iéna

ALLEE PAUL DESCHANEL

AVE S DE SACY

RUE DU GENT CAMOU

RUE SEDILLOT

RUE CLER

Port de Suffren 🚌

Eiffel Tower ①

AVE S AVE ELISEE RECLUS

RUE DU MAL DU'HARISPE

RUE DE L'EXPOSITION

Rue Cler ⑪

Champ de Mars - Tour Eiffel RER

AVE GUSTAVE EIFFEL

PLACE DU GENERAL GOURAUD

RUE AUGEREAU

RUE VALDON ⑥

AVE OCTAVE GREARD

AVENUE

Parc du Champ-de-Mars

BOUVARD

ADRIENNE

AVE EMILE

RUE DU CHAMP

RUE DE MARS

RUE BOSQUET

ALLEE

PLACE JACQUES RUEFF

ANATOLE

PIERRE

AVE CHARLES RISLER

RUE DE BELGRADE

LECOURBE

AVE DESCHANEL

PASS DE LA VIERGE

AVENUE J

Champ-de-Mars ⑯

THOMY

FRANCE

LOTI

AVE F LE PLAY

École Militaire Ⓜ

PLACE DE L'ÉCOLE MILITAIRE

AVE DU GEN DETRIE

THIERRY

PLACE JOFFRE

École Militaire ⑨

RUE DUPLEIX

AVE E ACOLLAS

AVENUE DE LA MOTTE PICQUET

AVENUE DE SUFFREN

UNESCO

AVENUE DE LA MOTTE PICQUET

RUE DU LAOS

BLVD DE GRENELLE

La Motte Picquet Grenelle Ⓜ

Square Cambronne

PLACE CAMBRONNE

Cambronne Ⓜ

RUE DU COMMERCE

RUE FREMICOURT

BOULEVARD

RUE MIOLLIS

RUE FRANCOIS BONVIN

RUE DE LA CROIX NIVERT

RUE DE L'AMIRAL ROUSSIN

CAMBRONNE

RUE BLOMET

RUE MADEMOISELLE

Square St-Lambert

RUE LECOURBE

EIFFEL TOWER AND INVALIDES

Must Sees
❶ Eiffel Tower
❷ Musée du Quai Branly-Jacques Chirac
❸ Dôme des Invalides

Experience More
❹ Hôtel des Invalides
❺ Musée de l'Armée
❻ Musée de l'Ordre de la Libération
❼ Musée des Plans-Reliefs
❽ St-Louis-des-Invalides
❾ École Militaire
❿ Musée Rodin
⓫ Rue Cler
⓬ Musée des Egouts
⓭ Berges de Seine
⓮ Assemblée Nationale Palais-Bourbon
⓯ Ste-Clothilde
⓰ Champ-de-Mars

Eat
① Café Christian Constant
② David Toutain
③ Arpège

Stay
④ Hôtel de Varenne
⑤ Hôtel 7 Eiffel
⑥ Hôtel du Cadran

Port des
Champs-Elysées

**LOUVRE AND
LES HALLES**
p180

Pont des
Invalides

Pont
Alexandre III

PLACE DE
FINLANDE

Invalides RER

QUAI D'ORSAY

Pont de la
Concorde

La Seine

6

Pont
Solférino

QUAI ANATOLE FRANCE

RUE ESNAULT
PELTERIE

AVE R
SCHUMAN

AVE SULLY
PRUDHOMME

RUE
DESGENETTES

RUE SURCOUF

RUE FABERT

AVE DU MARECHAL GALLIENI

Assemblée
Nationale
Palais-Bourbon 14

BLVD

RUE ARLAND

DE COURTY

M Assemblée
Nationale

Musée
d'Orsay
RER

L'UNIVERSITÉ

M Invalides

RUE

DE L'UNIVERSITÉ

PLACE DU
PRESIDENT
E HERRIOT

ST-GERMAIN

RUE DE
SOLFÉRINO

RUE DE

L'UNIVERSITÉ

DOMINIQUE

RUE JEAN NICOT

BLVD DE LA TOUR MAUBOURG

2

RUE FABERT

INVALIDES

RUE

PLACE DU
PALAIS
BOURBON

RUE DE
BELLECHASSE

RUE AMÉLIE

RUE DE LA COMETE

Esplanade des
Invalides

RUE DE
CONSTANTINE

RUE

Institut
Géographique
National

RUE DE
BOURGOGNE

ST-DOMINIQUE

PLACE I
BAINVILLE

5

GRENELLE

PLACE DES
INVALIDES

RUE DE MARIGNAN

RUE
LAS
CASES

Solférino
M

15 Ste-
Clothilde

7

RUE DUVIVIER

RUE CLER

AVENUE DE LA MOTTE PICQUET

La Tour-
Maubourg
M

Square
Santiago
du Chili

Hôtel des
Invalides

Square
d'Ajaccio

4

INVALIDES

RUE PERIER

RUE DE GRENELLE

RUE DE VARENNE

Rue du Bac M

Musée de
l'Armée 5

4

M Varenne

BLVD RASPAIL

RUE L CHEVERT

Musée de
l'Ordre de la
Libération

7

Musée des
Plans-Reliefs

3

DES

RUE DE JOUY

**ST-GERMAIN-
DES-PRÉS**
p234

RUE J
GRANIER

RUE L CODET

BLVD DE LA TOUR MAUBOURG

6

8

St-Louis-des-
Invalides

10 Musée
Rodin

CITE VANEAU

VARENNE

3

Dôme des
Invalides

RUE DE VANEAU

AVENUE

DE

TOURVILLE

BOULEVARD

RUE BARBET DE JOUY

AVENUE DUQUESNE

AVENUE
DE LOWENDAL

RUE SEXTIUS MICHEL

RUE DE SÉGUR

PLACE
VAUBAN

AVE DE VILLARS

RUE DE
CHANALEILLES

8

Esplanade
du Souvenir
Francais

RUE D'ESTRÉES

PLACE EL
SALVADOR

RUE DE BABYLONE

RUE DE BABYLONE

Jardin
Catherine
Laboure

Le Bon
Marché

PLACE DE
FONTENOY

AVENUE
DE SAXE

DE

AVENUE DE BRETEUIL

PLACE ANDRE
TARDIEU

St-François
Xavier

RUE MONSIEUR

RUE OUDINOT

RUE DE SÈVRES

RUE DE SÈVRES

PLACE DU
PRESIDENT
MITHOUARD

RUE EBLE

RUE MASSERAN

BOULEVARD DES INVALIDES

RUE PIERRE LEROUX

RUE ROUSSELET

Vaneau
M

RUE DU CHERCHE MIDI

ABBE GREGOIRE

Ségur
M

VILLA DE SAXE

RUE PERIGNON

RUE L VAUDOYER

RUE BOUCHUT

PLACE DE
BRETEUIL

RUE DU GENERAL BERTRAND

AVENUE COQUELIN

AVENUE D LESUEUR

RUE DE LA
SIZERANNE

Duroc
M

PLACE L P
FARGUE

9

AVE DE SUFFREN

AVE DE SUFFREN

RUE R BONHEUR

RUE
BARTHELEMY

RUE DE SÈVRES

Sèvres
Lecourbe M

PLACE HENRI
QUEUILLE

**MONTPARNASSE AND
JARDIN DU LUXEMBOURG**
p278

Falguière M

EIFFEL TOWER
AND INVALIDES

GARIBALDI

RUE LECOURBE

BOULEVARD

DE

PASTEUR

VAUGIRARD

0 metres   250

0 yards   250

N
↑

RUE DES VOLONTAIRES

M Pasteur

M Volontaires

10

EIFFEL TOWER

Q B7 **Q** Quai Branly and Champ-de-Mars **M** Bir Hakeim **🚌** 42, 69, 72, 82, 87 to Champ-de-Mars **🚆** Champ-de-Mars-Tour Eiffel **⏰** Sep-Jun: 9:30am-11:45pm daily (6:30pm for stairs); Jul-Aug: 9am-12:45am **📅** 14 Jul **🌐** toureiffel.paris

An impressive feat of engineering and the most distinctive symbol of Paris, the Eiffel Tower stands 324 m (1,063 ft) tall and offers unrivalled views over the city.

Originally built to impress visitors to the 1889 Exposition Universelle, the Eiffel Tower (Tour Eiffel) was meant to be a temporary addition to the Paris skyline. Built by the engineer Gustave Eiffel, it was fiercely decried by 19th-century aesthetes – the author Guy de Maupassant frequently ate lunch at the tower as it was the only place he could avoid seeing it. The world's tallest structure until 1931, when New York's Empire State Building was completed, the tower is now an icon of Paris and attracts 7 million visitors a year. The glass-floored first level houses a modern visitors' centre and an interactive museum chronicling the history of the tower.

THE TOWER IN FIGURES

276 m (905 ft): the height of the viewing gallery on the third level

1,665: the number of steps to the third level

2.5 million: the number of rivets holding the tower together

7 cm (2.5 in): the maximum amount that the tower ever sways

10,100 tonnes: the tower's total weight

60 tonnes: the amount of paint needed to decorate the ironwork

18 cm (7 in): how far the top can move in a curve under the effect of heat

↑ The view from the tower, ranging up to 72 km (45 miles)

← The Eiffel Tower under construction in April 1888, less than halfway complete

Did You Know?

Franz Reichelt died in 1912 after attempting to fly from the parapet using a modified cape as wings.

↑ A view of the Eiffel Tower from the Jardins du Trocadéro *(p222)*

2 🏛️ 🚫 🍴 🖥️ 🏪

MUSÉE DU QUAI BRANLY-JACQUES CHIRAC

📍C6 🏠37 Quai Branly 🚇Alma-Marceau, Bir-Hakeim, léna
🚌42, 63, 72, 80, 82, 92 🚢Pont de l'Alma ⏰11am-7pm Tue, Wed & Sun,
11am-9pm Thu-Sat 🚫Mon (except during all school hols besides
summer hols), 1 Jan, 1 May, 25 Dec 🌐quaibranly.fr

This rich collection of artifacts from Africa, Asia, Oceania and the Americas resides in a striking building that uses surrounding greenery as a natural backdrop to the art.

Widely regarded as former President Jacques Chirac's legacy to Paris's cultural scene, quai Branly has proved a major tourist pull since it opened in 2006. The stylish Jean Nouvel building displays 3,500 exhibits from the French state's vast non-Western art collection, one of the world's most prolific. Items include an array of African instruments, Gabonese masks, Aztec statues and painted animal hides from North America. Outside, the grounds offer visitors breathing space, and in summer the museum's 500-seat auditorium opens onto an outdoor theatre for music and dance. The rooftop restaurant boasts breathtaking views.

GALLERY GUIDE

Tickets are bought outside the main building. Inside, a ramp around a large glass tower displaying musical instruments leads to the main collection level, where a suggested route passes through four colour-coded zones of Oceania, Asia, Africa and the Americas. Three mezzanine galleries house temporary exhibitions.

↑ The museum's eye-catching exterior, with a glass wall and thickets of trees in the surrounding gardens

HIDDEN GEM
Key Object
The Africa collection houses a striking 1.91 m (6 ft 3 in) androgynous wooden statue from Mali, which combines a regal male head with the breasts of a woman.

→ A sculpted female figure on which tribal men would hang ritual offerings

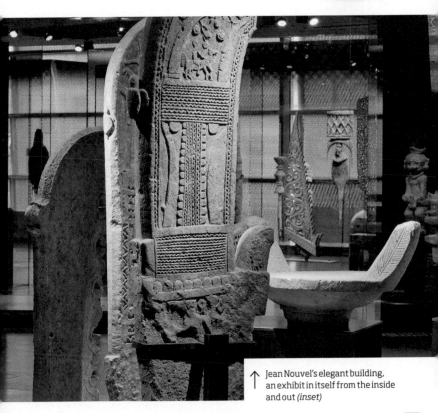

↑ Jean Nouvel's elegant building, an exhibit in itself from the inside and out *(inset)*

3 🏃 Ⓜ 🖥 🛍

DÔME DES INVALIDES

📍E7 🏠6 Blvd des Invalides, Esplanade des Invalides Ⓜ La Tour-Maubourg, Varenne 🚌28, 63, 69, 80, 82, 83, 87, 92, 93 to Les Invalides 🚆Invalides 🚇Tour Eiffel 🕐Hôtel National des Invalides: Apr–Oct: 10am–6pm daily (Jul & Aug: to 7pm; Apr–Sep: to 9pm Tue); Nov–Mar: 10am–5pm daily 🚫1st Mon of month, 1 Jan, 1 May, 25 Dec 🌐musee-armee.fr

Built on the orders of Louis XIV, this church with its magnificent gilded dome is the final resting place of Napoleon Bonaparte and a host of other great French military men.

The Dôme des Invalides was designed in 1676 by Jules Hardouin-Mansart for the exclusive use of Louis XIV and for the location of royal tombs. Slotted among the existing buildings of the Invalides military complex, the resulting masterpiece complements the surrounding structures and is one of the greatest examples of 17th-century French architecture. After Louis XIV's death, plans to bury the royal family in the church were abandoned, and it became a monument to Bourbon glory. In 1840, Louis-Philippe decided to install Napoleon's remains in the crypt, and the addition of the tombs of Vauban, Marshal Foch and other figures of military prominence have since turned this church into a French military memorial.

Charles de la Fosse's circular painting (1692) on the ceiling of the dome, showing the *Glory of Paradise*, with Saint Louis presenting his sword to Christ

NAPOLEON'S RETURN

King Louis-Philippe decided to bring the Emperor Napoleon's body back from St Helena as a gesture of reconciliation to the Republican and Bonapartist parties contesting his regime. The Dôme des Invalides, with its historical and military associations, was an obvious choice for Napoleon's final resting place. His body was encased in six coffins and finally placed in the crypt in 1861, at the culmination of a grand ceremony which was attended by Napoleon III.

Did You Know?

The dome stands 107 m (351 ft) high and was first gilded in 1706.

↑ The church with its glittering dome, which required 12 kg (26 lb) of gold to re-gild it in 1989

EXPERIENCE MORE

4

Hôtel des Invalides

9 E7 **A** Place des Invalides 75007 **M** La Tour-Maubourg, Varenne **RER** Invalides **7** 7:30am-7pm daily (Apr-Sep: to 9pm Tue) **C** Jan, 1 May, 25 Dec **W** musee-armee.fr

Founded by Louis XIV, this was France's first military hospital and became home to French war veterans and disabled soldiers, who had hitherto been reduced to begging. It was designed by Libéral Bruand and completed in 1675.

Today, the classical façade is one of the most impressive sights in Paris, with its four storeys, cannon in the forecourt, garden and tree-lined esplanade stretching to the Seine. Part of the building is still home to veterans. The south side leads to St-Louis-des-Invalides, the soldiers' church, which backs on to the magnificent Dôme des Invalides of Jules Hardouin-Mansart (p204). The dome was regilded in 1989.

5

Musée de l'Armée

9 E7 **A** Hôtel des Invalides, 129 Rue de Grenelle, 75007 **M** La Tour-Maubourg, Varenne **RER** Invalides **7** Apr-Oct: 10am-6pm daily (to 9pm Tue); Nov-Mar: 10am-5pm daily **C** 1st Mon of month (except Jul-Sep), 1 Jan, 1 May, 25 Dec **W** musee-armee.fr

This is one of the world's most comprehensive museums of military history, with exhibits ranging from the Stone Age to the final days of World War II.

Situated in the northeast refectory, the Ancient Armoury department is worth visiting for the collection on display, one of the largest in the world, as much as for the 17th-century murals by Joseph Parrocel adorning the walls. These celebrate Louis XIV's military conquests.

The life of Charles de Gaulle and his role in World War II are documented in the *Historial de Gaulle*, a film and interactive multimedia attraction (closed Mon). The Département Moderne is in two parts: the first (1648–1792) covers the reign of Louis XIV, while the second (1792–1871) displays a collection of Napoleon's mementos. Items include his campaign bed, famous frock coat and felt hats, and his stuffed dog.

6

Musée de l'Ordre de la Libération

9 E7 **A** Hôtel des Invalides, 129 Rue de Grenelle/Place Vauban 75007 **M** La Tour-Maubourg **RER** Invalides **7** Apr-Oct: 10am-6pm daily (to 9pm Tue); Nov-Mar: 10am-5pm daily **C** 1st Mon of month, public hols **W** ordredelaliberation.fr

This museum is devoted to the wartime Free French and their leader, General Charles de Gaulle, as well as to the

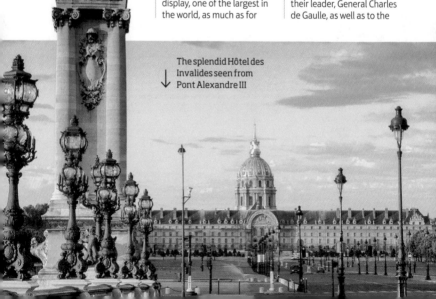

↓ The splendid Hôtel des Invalides seen from Pont Alexandre III

↑ The magnificent organ of St-Louis-des-Invalides, dating from the 17th century

STAY

Hôtel de Varenne

A hotel with a traditional, refined décor and a private garden, in the chic 7th arrondissement.

 F7 44 Rue de Bourgogne 75007 hotelde varenne.com

€€€

Hôtel 7 Eiffel

A modern option near the Eiffel Tower, with a rooftop terrace to boot.

D7 17 bis Rue Amélie 75007 hotel-7eiffel-paris.com

€€€

Hôtel du Cadran

A stylish boutique hotel with contemporary interior design, also featuring a vaulted breakfast room.

D7 10 Rue du Champ de Mars 75007 cadranhotel.com

€€€

Resistance movement within France and the Resistance fighters who were captured and deported.

The Order of Liberation was created by De Gaulle in 1940. It is France's highest honour and was bestowed on those who made an outstanding contribution to the final victory in World War II. Among the recipients of the honour are French civilians and members of the armed forces, plus a number of overseas leaders such as King George VI, Winston Churchill and Dwight Eisenhower.

7
Musée des Plans-Reliefs

 E7 Hôtel des Invalides, 129 Rue de Grenelle 75007 La Tour-Maubourg, Varenne Invalides 10am-6pm daily (Nov-Mar: to 5pm) 1st Mon of month (except Jul, Aug, Sep), 1 Jan, 1 May, 25 Dec museedesplansreliefs. culture.fr

The detailed models of French forts and fortified towns, some dating back to Louis XIV's reign, were considered top secret until the 1950s, when they were put on public display. They were created between the reigns of Louis XIV and Napoléon III in order to plan town defences and plot artillery positions. Out of a total of 260, around 100 of these three-dimensional maps are on display in the museum. The oldest model is that of Perpignan, dating from 1686. It shows the fortifications drawn up by the legendary 17th-century military architect Vauban, who built the defences around several French towns, including Briançon.

8
St-Louis-des-Invalides

 E7 Hôtel des Invalides, 129 Rue de Grenelle 75007 La Tour-Maubourg, Varenne Invalides 10am-6pm daily (Nov-Mar: to 5pm) 1 Jan, 1 May, 25 Dec musee-armee.fr

The "soldiers' church" was built in 1679–1708 by Jules Hardouin-Mansart from original designs by Libéral Bruand. The imposing but stark interior is decorated with banners seized in battle.

The first performance of Berlioz's *Requiem* was given on the fine 17th-century organ in 1837, with an orchestra accompanied by a battery of outside artillery.

 INSIDER TIP
Combined Ticket

Entrance to the Musée de l'Armée, the Musée de l'Ordre de la Libération and the Musée des Plans-Reliefs is all included on one ticket.

9
École Militaire

D8 **1 Pl Joffre 75007** **01 80 50 14 00** **M École Militaire**

Founded in 1751 to educate 500 sons of impoverished officers, the Royal Military Academy was designed by architect Jacques-Ange Gabriel. The central pavilion, a magnificent example of the French classical style, is graced with eight Corinthian pillars and a quadrangular dome. The ornate interior is decorated in Louis XVI style; of main interest are the chapel and a Gabriel-designed wrought-iron banister on the main staircase.

One of the academy's early cadets was Napoleon Bonaparte, whose passing-out report stated that "he could go far if the circumstances are right". Today, the academy is used as a cavalry training ground and isn't generally open to the public.

10
Musée Rodin

E7 **79 Rue de Varenne 75007** **M Varenne** **10am–5:45pm Tue–Sun** **1 Jan, 1 May, 25 Dec** **w musee-rodin.fr**

Auguste Rodin, widely regarded as one of the greatest French sculptors of the 19th century, lived and worked in the elegant 18th-century Hôtel Biron from 1908 until his death in 1917. In return for a state-owned flat and studio, Rodin agreed to leave his work to the nation. Some 300 works from Rodin's collection can now be seen in the museum. The attractive grounds consist of a rose garden, an ornamental garden and a relaxation area with benches, and contain some

EAT

Café Christian Constant
Classic and reasonable French fare near the Eiffel Tower – a rarity.

D7 **139 Rue St-Dominique 75007** **w maisonconstant.com**

€€€

David Toutain
This relaxed one-star Michelin experience is great value. It's worth booking at lunch.

E6 **29 Rue Surcouf 75007** **Sat, Sun** **w davidtoutain.com**

€€€

Arpège
Alain Passard's three-star restaurant, with a focus on fresh produce, is a worthwhile treat.

F7 **84 Rue de Varenne 75007** **Sat, Sun** **w alain-passard.com**

€€€

The grandiose classical façade of the École Militaire ↓

The market street Rue Cler, with its many fine food shops ↑

of Rodin's most celebrated sculptures: *The Thinker*, *The Burghers of Calais*, *The Gates of Hell* and *Balzac*. Spread across 18 rooms, the museum combines a chronology of Rodin's creative development with a thematic exploration of his workshop. It has even re-created a space exactly as it was when Rodin lived and worked here. The outdoor café makes a lovely spot for a drink in warmer weather.

Rue Cler

◉ D7 ⏣ 75007 Ⓜ École Militaire, La Tour-Maubourg ◷ Market: all day Tue–Sat & Sun am

This is the street market of the 7th arrondissement, the richest in Paris. The bulk of senior civil servants, wealthy expatriates, business leaders and many diplomats live in this residential neighbour-hood. The market area occupies a cobblestoned pedestrian precinct stretching south from Rue de Grenelle. Popular with locals, the vibrant market is frequented by the best-dressed shoppers in town. The produce is excellent, especially the patisseries and cheese shops.

→

Auguste Rodin's famed sculpture *The Three Shades* at the Musée Rodin

⑫ ⏣ Ⓜ 🏛

Musée des Égouts

◉ D6 ⏣ Pont Alma, opposite 93 Quai d'Orsay 75007 ☎ 01 53 68 27 81 Ⓜ Alma-Marceau Ⓡ Pont de l'Alma ◷ 11am–5pm Sat–Wed (to 6pm May–Sep) ⏹ 1 Jan, 2 weeks Jan, 25 Dec

One of Baron Haussmann's finest achievements, the majority of Paris's sewers (*égouts*) date from the Second Empire (1852–70). In the 20th century, surprisingly the sewers became a popular attraction. Closed for reno-vations until the start of 2020, the Musée des Égouts allows visitors to tour a small area around the Quai d'Orsay entrance. Display boards explain the history of Paris's water supply and waste management. Guided tours are best reserved in advance.

Did You Know?

If laid end to end, the city's 2,100 km (1,300 miles) of sewers would stretch from Paris to Istanbul.

Berges de Seine

D6 **Quai d'Orsay 75007** **Assemblée Nationale, Invalides**

In 2013, this former busy roadway along the river bank was revamped for pedestrians, turning it into one of Paris's loveliest promenades. As well as offering spectacular views of the Louvre, Jardin des Tuileries and other monuments along the way, the 2.3-km (1½-mile) walkway is studded with activities for children, like mini playgrounds, climbing walls and floating gardens. The promenade also has an athletics track, a fitness course (check out the daily programme of free exercise classes) and Vélib' bikes (p313) for all ages. Cyclists and joggers zigzag between pedestrians taking advantage of a traffic-free stroll. There are cafés and restaurants both on land and aboard boats, especially around Pont Alexandre III. Picnickers and evening revellers often crowd the banks during the summer, making the Berges de Seine one of the liveliest places for evening tipples on the Left Bank.

Assemblée Nationale Palais-Bourbon

F6 **126 Rue de l'Université 75007** **Assemblée Nationale** **Invalides** **assemblee-nationale.fr**

Built in 1722 for the Duchesse de Bourbon, daughter of Louis XIV, the Palais-Bourbon was confiscated during the Revolution. It has been home to the lower house of the French Parliament since 1830. During World War II, the palace became the Nazi administration's seat of government. The grand Neo-Classical façade with its fine columns was added in 1806, partly to mirror the façade of La Madeleine church facing it across the Seine (p174). The adjacent Hôtel de Lassay is the residence of the president of the National Assembly. Group tours can be organized for a maximum of 50 people on the invitation of a member of parliament, with several months' prior notice.

Ste-Clotilde

F7 **23B Rue las Cases 75007** **Solférino, Varenne, Invalides** **9am–7:30pm Mon–Fri, 10am–8pm Sat & Sun. Times vary for Jul & Aug; check website** **Non-religious public hols** **sainte-clotilde.com**

Designed by the German architect François-Christian Gau and the first of its kind

Did You Know?
—
Pont de la Concorde was built using stones from the Bastille fortress destroyed during the French Revolution.

→
The Assemblée Nationale on the Left Bank of the Seine

The pretty Champ-de-Mars gardens at the foot of the Eiffel Tower

> Picnickers and evening revellers crowd the banks during the summer, making the Berges de Seine one of the liveliest places for evening tipples on the Left Bank.

to be built in Paris, this church, in Neo-Gothic style, was inspired by the mid-19th-century enthusiasm for the Middle Ages, made fashionable by such writers as Victor Hugo. The church is noted for its imposing twin towers, visible from across the Seine, and there are sculptures of the Stations of the Cross inside. The composer César Franck was the organist here.

16

Champ-de-Mars

📍 C7 🏠 75007 Ⓜ️ École Militaire 🚉 Champ de Mars-Tour Eiffel

The gardens stretching from the Eiffel Tower to the École Militaire were originally a parade ground for the officer cadets of the École Militaire (*p208*). The area has since been used for horse-racing, hot-air balloon ascents and the mass celebrations for 14 July, the anniversary of the Revolution. The first Bastille Day ceremony was held in 1790 in the presence of a glum, captive Louis XVI. Vast exhibitions were held here in the late 19th century, including the 1889 World Fair for which the Eiffel Tower was erected. *Le Mur de la Paix*, Clara Halter and Jean-Michel Wilmotte's symbolic monument to world peace, stands at one end.

The park is popular with Parisian families and tourists, who come here to relax, walk their dogs (it is one of the few parks in Paris where dogs are allowed) and to participate in the numerous activities for children, which include playgrounds, pony rides, puppet shows and a carousel. There is also an outdoor café.

A SHORT WALK
INVALIDES

Distance 1.5 km (1 mile) **Nearest Metro** La Tour-Maubourg **Time** 15 minutes

This walk concentrates on the imposing Hôtel des Invalides, from which the area takes its name. The hôtel was built from 1671 to 1676 by Louis XIV for his wounded and homeless veterans and as a monument to his own glory. At its centre, the glittering golden roof of the Sun King's Dôme des Invalides marks the final resting place of Napoleon Bonaparte. The emperor's body was brought here from St Helena in 1840, 19 years after he died, and placed inside the majestic sarcophagus, designed by Joachim Visconti, that lies at the centre of the Dôme's circular glass-topped crypt. Just to the east of the hôtel on the corner of the Boulevard des Invalides, the superb Musée Rodin offers artistic relief from the pomp and circumstance of the surrounding area.

After the two World Wars, Louis XIV's Hôtel des Invalides was returned to its original use as a hospital for veterans (p206).

The Invalides gardens were designed by de Cotte in 1704 and are lined by bronze cannons from the 17th and 18th centuries.

Metro La Tour-Maubourg

PL DES

M START

AVE DE LA MOTTE PICQUETTE

The façade of the hôtel is 196 m (645 ft) long and is topped by dormer windows, each decorated in the shape of a different trophy. A head of Hercules sits above the central entrance.

The vast Musée de l'Armée covers military history from the Stone Age to World War II. It contains the third-largest collection of armoury in the world (p206).

The Musée de l'Ordre de la Libération was set up to honour feats of heroism during World War II (p206).

From St-Louis-des-Invalides, the soldier's chapel, it is possible to see into the Dôme (below), which was built as Louis XIV's private chapel.

In the crypt of the Dôme des Invalides lies Napoleon, whose final wish was to have his ashes "rest on the banks of the Seine" (p204).

AVE DE TOURVILLE

AVE DE SÉGUR

Did You Know?

In 1789 rioters stormed the hôtel and seized cannons and muskets to use against the Bastille.

↑ Relaxing in the gardens that surround the Hôtel des Invalides on a sunny afternoon

Locator Map
For more detail see p198

INVALIDES

RUE DE GRENELLE

Metro Varenne

FINISH

BLVD DES INVALIDES

AVE DE VILLARS

The Musées des Plans-Reliefs contains military models of forts and towns, as well as a display on model-making (p207).

The Cour d'Honneur is still used for military parades. Seurre's statue of Napoleon, known as the Little Corporal, stands above the south side.

Auguste Rodin's key works, including The Thinker (c 1880), are on display at the Musée Rodin (p208).

0 metres   100
0 yards   100
N ↑

↑ Visitors exploring fine sculpture at the excellent Musée Rodin

CHAMPS-ÉLYSÉES AND CHAILLOT

This area radiates wealth and power, but it was once little more than open fields lying on the outskirts of Paris. In 1616, Marie de Medici, wife of Henri IV, commissioned a tree-lined approach road through here to the Tuileries Palace, which was expanded in the late 17th century by Louis XIV's landscape designer, André Le Nôtre. The avenue was christened Champs-Élysées in the 18th century, and became a fashionable location for the nobility to build grand town houses.

The nearby Chaillot quarter, however, remained just a village before becoming absorbed into the city of Paris in the 19th century. Subsequently bestowed with similarly wide avenues and grand mansions, it became one of the city's most elegant neighbourhoods. The districts' allure has not faded, and today they are home to numerous embassies and *haute couture* fashion houses, as well as five-star hotels and fine restaurants.

CHAMPS-ÉLYSÉES AND CHAILLOT

A

RUE D'ARMAILLE

AVENUE DES TERNES

AVENUE D'ARMAILLE

AVE DE LA GRANDE ARMÉE

AVENUE FOCH

RUE DE LA PompE

B

AVENUE DE WAGRAM

RUE DE TILSITT

Place Charles de Gaulle (L'Étoile) **9**

Arc de Triomphe **1**

RUE LAURISTON

AVENUE VICTOR HUGO

Kléber **M**

6

RUE PAUL VALERY

RUE DE DÔME

RUE DE LA POMPE

PLACE VICTOR HUGO **M** Victor Hugo

RUE COPERNIC

RUE DE BELLOY

RUE CIMAROSA

RUE GALILÉE

RUE LAURISTON

AVENUE RAYMOND POINCARÉ

RUE BOISSIÈRE

RUE LÉO DELIBES

M Boissière

RUE ST-DIDIER

RUE ST-DIDIER

AVENUE KLÉBER

RUE HAMELIN

RUE BOISSIÈRE

RUE DE LONGCHAMP

Musée National des Arts Asiatiques Guimet

RUE DE LUBECK

PLACE D'IÉNA

M Iéna

CHAILLOT

AVENUE DU PRÉSIDENT

Trocadéro **M**

Cité de l'Architecture et du Patrimoine **3**

AVENUE DU

PLACE DU TROCADÉRO ET DU 11 NOVEMBRE

Aquarium de Paris - Cinéaqua **7**

Cimetière de Passy **19**

Musée National de la Marine **5**

Palais de Chaillot **2**

Musée de l'Homme **4**

Jardins du Trocadéro **6**

AVE GEORGES MANDEL

AVE PAUL DOUMER

RUE FRANKLIN

RUE LE TASSE

AVE DES NATIONS UNIES

PLACE DE VARSOVIE

PLACE DE COSTA RICA

BLVD DELESSERT

RUE DE PASSY

SQUARE L'ALBONI

RUE L'ALBONI

RUE RAYNOUARD

Passy **M**

AVE RENÉ BOYLESVE

Parc de Passy

AVENUE DU PRÉSIDENT KENNEDY

PORT DE PASSY

1

La Seine

Pont de Bir-Hakeim

Port d'Iéna

QUAI BRANLY

M Bir Hakeim

QUAI DE GRENELLE

C

M Courcelles

BLVD DE COURCELLES

RUE DARU

Ternes **M**

RUE DU FAUBOURG ST-HONORÉ

RUE HOCHE

PLACE G GUILLAUMIN

RUE BALZAC

AVENUE DE FRIEDLAND

Charles de Gaulle-Étoile **M RER**

RUE LORD BYRON

RUE BALZAC

2

AVENUE DES

RUE LAMENNAIS

RUE WASHINGTON

RUE DE PRESBOURG

RUE VERNET

RUE GALILÉE

Avenue des Champs-Élysées

George V **M**

8

CHAMPS-

AVENUE GEORGE V

RUE LINCOLN

RUE PIERRE CHARRON

RUE DE BASSANO

RUE QUENTIN

4

10

RUE FRANÇOIS

RUE KEPLER

RUE JEAN GIRAUDOUX

5

RUE MARBEUF

3

PLACE DES ÉTATS UNIS

PLACE AMIRAL DE GRASSE

RUE DE BASSANO

RUE DE CHAILLOT

Galerie-Musée Baccarat

Cathédrale Américaine

RUE DE SERBIE

AVE PIERRE 1er

RUE GOETHE

RUE FRESNEL

Musée Galliera

Théâtre des Champs-Élysées

WILSON

Alma-Marceau **M**

PLACE DE LA REINE ASTRID

PLACE DE L'ALMA

Palais de Tokyo **21**

Musée d'Art Moderne de la Ville de Paris **20**

Pont de l'Alma

RUE DE LA MANUTENTION

AVENUE DE NEW YORK

RUE FRESNEL

AVE ALBERT DE MUN

Passerelle Debilly

Pont de l'Alma **RER**

QUAI

PLACE DE LA RÉSISTANCE

EIFFEL TOWER AND INVALIDES
p196

Musée du Quai Branly-Jacques Chirac

PORT DEBILLY

AVENUE DE NATIONS UNIES

Port de la Bourdonnais

Port de Suffren

Eiffel Tower

Champ de Mars - Tour Eiffel **RER**

Parc du Champ-de-Mars

AVENUE DE SUFFREN

AVENUE DE LA BOURDONNAIS

AVENUE RAPP

AVENUE BOSQUET

0 metres 300
0 yards 300

N ↑

CHAMPS-ÉLYSÉES AND CHAILLOT

Must Sees

1. Arc de Triomphe
2. Palais de Chaillot

Experience More

3. Cité de l'Architecture et du Patrimoine
4. Musée de l'Homme
5. Musée National de la Marine
6. Jardins du Trocadéro
7. Aquarium de Paris – Cinéaqua
8. Avenue des Champs-Élysées
9. Place Charles de Gaulle (L'Étoile)
10. Place de la Concorde
11. Grand Palais
12. Petit Palais
13. Pont Alexandre III
14. Palais de la Découverte
15. Avenue Montaigne
16. Parc Monceau
17. Musée Jacquemart-André
18. Palais de l'Élysée
19. Cimetière de Passy
20. Musée d'Art Moderne de la Ville de Paris
21. Palais de Tokyo

Eat

1. L'Astrance
2. Pierre Gagnaire
3. Relais de l'Entrecôte

Drink

4. Le Bar at the Four Seasons Hotel George V
5. Bar de l'Hôtel Belmont
6. Bar Kléber at the Peninsula
7. Le Bar Botaniste at the Shangri-La
8. Le Bar du Bristol

Stay

9. Hôtel Barrière Le Fouquet's
10. Four Seasons Hotel George V
11. Shangri-La

OPÉRA AND GRANDS BOULEVARDS p168

LOUVRE AND LES HALLES p180

30

shields just below the Arc's roof each bear the name of a victorious Napoleonic battle.

The golden tones of the arch's stonework, highlighted by the sunset ↑

❶ 🏃 🕍 🏛

ARC DE TRIOMPHE

📍 C4 🚇 Pl Charles de Gaulle Ⓜ/🚋 Charles de Gaulle-Étoile 🚌 22, 30, 31, 52, 73, 92
to Pl Charles de Gaulle ⏰ Apr-Sep: 10am-11pm daily; Oct-Mar: 10am-10:30pm daily
🔒 am only 8 May, 14 Jul, 11 Nov; all day 1 Jan, 1 May, 25 Dec 🌐 paris-arc-de-triomphe.fr

Situated at the heart of Place Charles de Gaulle, overlooking the Champs-Élysées, the Arc de Triomphe was commissioned by Napoleon to celebrate France's military might. The exterior is adorned with sculptures depicting various battles, while the viewing platform at the top affords one of the best views in Paris.

After his greatest victory, the Battle of Austerlitz in 1805, Napoleon promised his men, "You shall go home beneath triumphal arches." The first stone of what was to become the world's most famous triumphal arch was laid the following year, but disruptions to architect Jean Chalgrin's plans and the demise of Napoleonic power delayed the completion of this monumental building until 1836. Standing 50 m (164 ft) high, the Arc is now the customary starting point for victory celebrations and parades.

← The twelve avenues radiating from Place Charles de Gaulle

→ The symbolic torch at the Tomb of the Unknown Soldier

NUPTIAL PARADE

Napoleon divorced Josephine in 1809 because she was unable to bear him children. A diplomatic marriage was arranged in 1810 with Marie-Louise, daughter of the Austrian emperor. Napoleon was determined to impress his bride by passing through the Arc on their way to the wedding, but work had barely started, so Chalgrin built a full-scale mock-up of the arch on the site for the couple to go through.

Timeline

1806

▼ Napoleon commissions Chalgrin to build the triumphal Arc following the Battle of Austerlitz in the previous year

1815

Napoleon abdicates after defeat at the Battle of Waterloo, causing work on the Arc to cease

1919

Victory parade of Allied armies through the Arc to celebrate the end of World War I

1836

King Louis-Philippe completes the Arc during the Bourbon Restoration

1944

▲ De Gaulle leads the crowd from the Arc following the liberation of Paris

2 🖵 🛍

PALAIS DE CHAILLOT

📍 B6 🏠 Pl du Trocadéro 75016 Ⓜ Trocadéro

The Palais, with its huge, curved colonnaded wings each culminating in an immense pavilion, was designed in Neo-Classical style for the 1937 Paris Exhibition by Léon Azéma, Louis-Hippolyte Boileau and Jacques Carlu. Today it houses three major museums: the Cité de l'Architecture et du Patrimoine, the Musée de l'Homme and the Musée National de la Marine.

The present Palais replaced the Trocadéro palace built for the World Fair of 1878. It is adorned with sculptures and bas-reliefs, and on the walls of the pavilions are gold inscriptions by the poet and essayist Paul Valéry. The *parvis*, or square, situated between the two pavilions is decorated with large bronze sculptures and ornamental pools. On the terrace in front of the *parvis* stand two bronzes, *Apollo* by Henri Bouchard and *Hercules* by Albert Pommier. Stairways lead from the terrace to the Théâtre National de Chaillot, which, since World War II, has enjoyed huge fame for its avant-garde productions.

↑ One of the galleries in the Cité de l'Architecture et du Patrimoine *(p222)*

← View of the Palais de Chaillot from the Eiffel Tower

THÉÂTRE NATIONAL DE CHAILLOT

In addition to being a prestigious performance venue, the Théâtre National de Chaillot has also played an important role in world history. It was here that the Universal Declaration of Human Rights was signed in 1948.

Exhibits from the anthropology and ethnology collection of the Musée de l'Homme *(p222)* ↑

 PICTURE PERFECT
Eiffel Tower

The palace's terrace boasts magnificent views of the Eiffel Tower. Head here to get a panoramic shot of the Iron Lady.

← The bronze *Hercules* statue on the terrace

EXPERIENCE MORE

 3

Cité de l'Architecture et du Patrimoine

📍 B6 🏛 Palais de Chaillot, Pl du Trocadéro 75016 Ⓜ Trocadéro 🕐 11am-7pm Wed-Mon (to 9pm Thu) 🚫 1 Jan, 1 May, 25 Dec 🌐 citedelarchitecture.fr

In the east wing of the Palais de Chaillot, this museum charts the development of French architecture through the ages. Among the unmiss-able displays is the Galerie des Moulages, which covers the period from the Middle Ages to the Renaissance. Here, you will find three-dimensional models of great French cathedrals, such as Chartres. Also worth a look is the Galerie Moderne et Contem-poraine, with a reconstruction of an apartment designed by Le Corbusier.

 4

Musée de l'Homme

📍 A6 🏛 Palais de Chaillot, Pl du Trocadéro 75016 Ⓜ Trocadéro 🕐 10am-6pm Wed-Mon 🚫 1 Jan, 1 May, 25 Dec 🌐 museedelhomme.fr

Situated in the west wing of the Chaillot palace, this museum traces the process of human evolution, from prehistoric times to the present, through anthropological exhibits from around the world. Reopened in 2015 after five years of renovations, it houses one of the world's most comprehensive prehistoric collections. Displays show how humans have adapted to the environment, and there is also a focus on the development of language and culture.

 5

Musée National de la Marine

📍 B6 🏛 Palais de Chaillot, Pl du Trocadéro 75016 Ⓜ Trocadéro 🌐 musee-marine.fr

Closed for renovation until 2021, this museum recounts French maritime history from the days of the royal wooden warships to today's aircraft carriers and nuclear subma-rines through wonderfully exact scale models (most of them two centuries old), mementos of naval heroes, paintings and navigational instruments. The museum was set up by Charles X in 1827, and was moved to the Chaillot palace in 1943. Exhibits include Napoleon's barge and models of the fleet he assembled at Boulogne-sur-Mer in 1805 for his planned invasion of Britain.

↑ Henri Bouchard's *Apollo* statue outside the Musée de l'Homme

 6

Jardins du Trocadéro

📍 B6 🏛 75016 Ⓜ Trocadéro

These charming gardens were created for the Exposition Universelle in 1937, at the same time as the Palais de Chaillot (p220). Their centre-piece is a long rectangular ornamental pool, bordered by stone and bronze-gilt statues, which look spectacular at night when the fountains are illuminated. The statues include *Man* by Pierre Traverse and *Woman* by Georges Braque, *Bull* by Paul Jouve and *Horse* by Georges Guyot. On either side of the pool, the slopes of the Chaillot hill lead down to the Seine and the Pont d'Iéna. The 10-ha (25-acre) park is laid out with flowering trees, small streams and bridges, and

WORLD FAIR

In 1889, the World Fair (or Exposition Universelle) saw the construction of the Eiffel Tower (p200). The 1937 edition initiated the building of the Palais de Chaillot (p220), which replaced the exotic-looking Palais du Troacadéro, itself erected for the 1878 World Fair. Numerous other temporary struc-tures dotted the area around the Champs de Mars, but today, only the Iron Lady remains. If it weren't for the fact that the Eiffel Tower proved useful as a radio tower, it, too, would have been dismantled.

PICTURE PERFECT
Eiffel Tower

Visit the Eiffel Tower by taking the Metro to the Trocadéro stop, on line 6 or 9. This allows for postcard-perfect photographs from the terrace at the Palais de Chaillot looking across the river with Paris's most iconic landmark in the background.

is a romantic place for a stroll. There is an aquarium in the northeast corner of the gardens, and in December a lovely Christmas market takes place.

7

Aquarium de Paris - Cinéaqua

B6 **5 Ave Albert de Mun 75016** **Trocadéro, Iéna** **10am–7pm daily** **14 Jul** **cineaqua.com**

Originally built in 1878 for the Exposition Universelle, this is now a state-of-the-art aquarium which is home to over 500 species of sea creatures from around the world, including seahorses, clownfish, stonefish and some spectacular sharks and rays.

The building is located in a former quarry and has been designed to blend in entirely with the Chaillot hillside. Cinema screens showing cartoons and animal documentaries are interspersed with the aquariums, and there are art exhibitions and shows for children in the theatre. The aquarium regularly runs special late night openings; check the website for details.

$\rightarrow$

The Eiffel Tower seen from the Jardins du Trocadéro

One of the ornamental fountains in the huge Place de la Concorde ↑

⑧ Avenue des Champs-Élysées

📍 D4 🏠 75008
Ⓜ Franklin D. Roosevelt, George V

Paris's most famous and popular thoroughfare had its beginnings in about 1667, when the royal landscape garden designer André Le Nôtre extended the royal view from the Tuileries by creating a tree-lined avenue which eventually became known as the Champs-Élysées (Elysian Fields). It has been France's national "triumphal way" ever since the homecoming of Napoleon's body from St Helena in 1840. With the addition of cafés and restaurants in the second half of the 19th century, the Champs-Élysées became the place in which to see and be seen. The Rond-Point des Champs-Élysées is the prettiest part, with chestnut trees and flower beds. A number of major brands, such as H&M and Abercrombie & Fitch, have their flagship stores here, while fast-food cafés jostle for space with more upmarket establishments such as Fouquet's Brasserie. In July, the avenue is the setting for the exhilarating sprint finish of the annual Tour de France cycle race.

> One of Europe's most magnificent and historic squares, Place de la Concorde covers more than 8 ha (20 acres) in the middle of Paris.

⑨ Place Charles de Gaulle (l'Étoile)

📍 C4 🏠 75008 Ⓜ Charles de Gaulle-Étoile

Known as the Place de l'Étoile until the death of Charles de Gaulle in 1969, the area is still referred to simply as l'Étoile, "the star". The present *place* was laid out in accordance with Baron Haussmann's plans of 1854 (*p55*). For motorists, it is the ultimate challenge.

⑩ Place de la Concorde

📍 F5 🏠 75008
Ⓜ Concorde

One of Europe's most magnificent and historic squares, Place de la Concorde covers more than 8 ha (20 acres) in the middle of Paris. Starting out as Place Louis XV, displaying a statue of the eponymous king, it was built in the mid-18th century by architect Jacques-Ange Gabriel, who chose to make it an open octagon with only the north side containing mansions. In the square's next incarnation, as the Place de la Révolution, the statue was replaced by the guillotine. The death toll in the square in two and a half years was 1,119, and victims included Louis XVI, Marie-Antoinette (who died in view of the secret apartment she kept at No 2 Rue Royale) and the Revolutionary leaders Danton and Robespierre.

In the spirit of reconciliation, the square was then renamed Concorde (originally by chastened Revolutionaries). Its grandeur was enhanced in the 19th century by the arrival of the 3,200-year-old Luxor obelisk – a gift from Egypt, 23-m (75-ft) tall and covered in hieroglyphics – as well as two fountains and eight statues personifying French cities. It has become the culminating point of triumphal parades down the Champs-Élysées each 14 July, most notably on the memorable Bastille Day of 1989 when the Revolution's bicentenary was celebrated by a million people, including many world leaders.

Grand Palais

⑪E5 **🚪Porte A, Ave Général Eisenhower 75008** **Ⓜ Champs-Élysées-Clemenceau** **🕐1 May, 25 Dec** **🌐grandpalais.fr**

Built at the same time as the Petit Palais and the Pont Alexandre III, the exterior of this massive palace combines an imposing classical stone façade with a riot of Art Nouveau ironwork. The enormous glass roof (15,000 sq m/ 160,000 sq ft) has Récipon's colossal bronze statues of flying horses and chariots at its four corners. The metal structure supporting the glass weighs 8,500 tonnes, some 500 tonnes more than the Eiffel Tower's. Today, the restored Grand Palais hosts art exhibitions and other events. During the winter, the nave turns into the world's biggest indoor ice rink. Major temporary and touring exhibitions are held at the Galeries Nationales in the same building; these are often very popular and it's worth booking ahead. Check the website for details of what's on.

Petit Palais

⑫E5 **🚪Ave Winston Churchill 75008** **Ⓜ Champs-Élysées-Clemenceau** **🕐10am-6pm Tue-Sun (to 9pm Fri for temporary exhibitions)** **🚫Public hols** **🌐petit palais.paris.fr**

Built for the Exposition Universelle in 1900, this jewel of a building now houses the Musée des Beaux-Arts de la Ville de Paris. Arranged around a pretty courtyard, the palace is similar in style to the Grand Palais, and is graced with Ionic columns, a grand porch and a dome. The wing nearest the river is used for temporary exhibitions, while the Champs-Élysées side of the palace houses the permanent collections: Greek and Roman artifacts; medieval and Renaissance ivories and sculptures; Renaissance clocks and jewellery; and 17th-, 18th-, and 19th-century art and furniture. There are also many works by the Impressionists artists.

↓ The Neo-Classical entrance to the Petit Palais

EAT

L'Astrance
Go for broke at this three-Michelin-star restaurant with epic tasting menus.

⑨B7 **🚪4 Rue Beethoven 75016** **🌐astrance restaurant.com**

€€€

Pierre Gagnaire
One of Paris's best chefs wows diners with a contemporary dining experience.

⑨C4 **🚪6 Rue Balzac 75008** **🌐pierre-gagnaire.com**

€€€

Relais de l'Entrecôte
Steak, chips and nothing else. It's a family favourite; just go early to queue up – it doesn't take long to get a table.

⑨D5 **🚪15 Rue Marbeuf 75008** **🌐relaisentrecote.fr**

€€€

↑ A ceiling painting by Maurice Denis inside the Petit Palais

The Avenue de la Grande Armée, looking towards La Défense

13

Pont Alexandre III

📍 E5 🏠 75008
Ⓜ Champs-Élysées-
Clemenceau

This is Paris's prettiest bridge with its exuberant Art Nouveau decoration of lamps, cherubs, nymphs and winged horses at either end. It was built between 1896 and 1900, in time for the Exposition Universelle, and it was named after Tsar Alexander III of Russia, whose son Nicholas II laid the foundation stone in October 1896.

The style of the bridge reflects that of the Grand Palais, to which it leads on the Right Bank. The construction of the bridge is a marvel of 19th-century engineering, consisting of a 6-m- (18-ft-) high single-span steel arch that stretches across the Seine. The design was subject to strict controls that prevented the bridge from obscuring the view of the Champs-Élysées (p224) or the Dôme des Invalides (p204) so, today, you can still enjoy magnificent views from here.

  14

Palais de la Découverte

📍 E5 🏠 Ave Franklin D Roosevelt 75008
Ⓜ Franklin D. Roosevelt
🕐 9:30am–6pm Tue–Sat, 10am–7pm Sun 🚫 1 Jan, 1 May, 25 Dec 🌐 palais-decouverte.fr

Opened in a wing of the Grand Palais (p225) for the World Fair of 1937, this science museum is a Paris institution. Demonstrations and displays, including a planetarium, cover many subjects and explain such phenomena as electromagnetism.

 15

Avenue Montaigne

📍 D5 🏠 75008
Ⓜ Franklin D. Roosevelt

In the 19th century, this avenue was famous for its dance halls and its Winter Garden, where Parisians went to hear Adolphe Sax play his newly invented saxophone. Today, it is still one of Paris's most fashionable streets, bustling with restaurants, cafés, hotels and designer boutiques. At one end lies the beautiful Art Deco Théâtre de Champs-Élysées, built in 1913.

 16

Parc Monceau

📍 D3 🏠 35 Blvd de Courcelles 75017
Ⓜ Monceau, Courcelles
🕐 7am–8pm daily (to 10pm summer)

This green haven dates back to 1778 when the Duc de Chartres (later Duc d'Orléans) commissioned the painter-writer and amateur landscape designer Louis Carmontelle to create a magnificent garden. Also a theatre designer, Carmontelle created a "garden of dreams", an exotic landscape full of architectural follies in imitation of English and German fashions of the time. In 1783, the Scottish landscape gardener Thomas Blaikie laid out an area of the garden in English style. The park was the scene of the first recorded parachute landing,

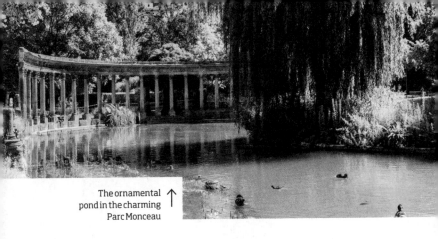

The ornamental pond in the charming Parc Monceau ↑

made by André-Jacques Garnerin on 22 October 1797. Over the years, the park changed hands and in 1852 it was acquired by the state and half the land sold off for property development. The remaining land was made into public gardens. These were restored and new buildings erected by Adolphe Alphand, architect of the Bois de Boulogne *(p292)* and the Bois de Vincennes *(p294)*.

The park, one of the most chic in Paris, has lost many of its early features. A *naumachia* basin – an ornamental version of a Roman pool used for simulating naval battles – remains, flanked by Corinthian columns. Other remaining features include a Renaissance arcade, pyramids, statues, a river and the Pavillon de Chartres, a charming rotunda designed by Nicolas Ledoux which was once used as a tollhouse. Just south of here is a huge red Chinese pagoda, which now houses a gallery devoted to Asian art.

17

Musée Jacquemart-André

E3 **158 Blvd Haussmann 75008** **Miromesnil, St-Philippe-du-Roule** **10am-6pm daily (to 8:30pm Mon)** **musee-jacquemart-andre.com**

This museum is known for its collection of Italian Renaissance and French 18th-century works of art, as well as its beautiful frescoes by Tiepolo. Highlights include works by Mantegna, Uccello's masterpiece *St George and the Dragon* (c 1435), paintings by Boucher and Fragonard, and 18th-century tapestries.

←

Pont Alexandre III, with its flamboyant Art Nouveau decoration

⑱ Palais de l'Élysée

📍E4 🏠55 Rue du Faubourg-St-Honoré 75008 Ⓜ St-Philippe-du-Roule 🚫To the public

Built for the Comte d'Evreux in 1718, the Élysée Palace has been the official residence of the President of the Republic since 1873. From 1805 to 1808, it was occupied by Napoleon's sister, Caroline, and her husband, Joachim Murat. Two rooms have been preserved from this period: the Salon Murat and the Salon d'Argent. General de Gaulle gave press conferences in the Hall of Mirrors. Today, the president's modernized apartments are located on the first floor in the east wing, opposite the Rue de l'Élysée. The palace is open to the public only during the Journées du Patrimoine (p58).

The imposing Art Deco Palais de Tokyo, housing two galleries of modern art

⑲ Cimetière de Passy

📍A6 🏠2 Rue du Commandant-Shloesing 75016 Ⓜ Trocadéro 🕐8am–5:30pm Mon–Sat, 9am–5:30pm Sun (to 6pm 16 Mar–5 Nov)

This small cemetery, opened in 1820, is packed with the graves of eminent Parisians. Figures buried here include the composers Claude Debussy, Gabriel Fauré and Jacques Ibert, and renowned painter Edouard Manet, as well as many politicians and aristocrats, such as Ghislaine Dommanget, Princess of Monaco; Leila Pahlavi, daughter of the Shah of Iran; and Michel Droit, writer and journalist.

← Edouard Manet's gravestone in the Cimetière de Passy

⑳ Musée d'Art Moderne de la Ville de Paris

📍C6 🏠11 Ave du Président-Wilson 75116 Ⓜ Iéna, Alma Marceau 🕐10am–6pm Tue–Sun (to 10pm Thu) 🚫Public hols 🌐mam.paris.fr

This large lively museum houses the city of Paris's own renowned collection of modern art. It has about 10,000 works representing major 20th- and 21st-century artistic movements and artists. Established in 1961, the museum is one of two within the vast Palais de Tokyo, which was built for the 1937 World Fair.

One of the museum's highlights is Raoul Dufy's gigantic mural The Spirit of Electricity, which traces the history of electricity through the ages. It was designed for the Electricity Pavilion in the 1937 fair. One of the largest paintings in the world, measuring 600 sq metres (6,500 sq ft), this curved mural takes up a whole room of the museum. Also notable are the Cubists, Amedeo Modigliani, George Rouault, Duchamp, Klein and the Fauves. This group of avant-garde artists, including Dufy and Derain, was dominated by Matisse, whose celebrated mural *La Danse* is on display here; you can see both the incomplete early version and the finished version. Entry to the permanent exhibition is free, while the frequent temporary exhibitions require a ticket.

Did You Know?
Passy was a small town, integrated into Paris only in 1860.

21 🚴 🚳 🍽 🍺 🏛

Palais de Tokyo

📍 C5 🏛 13 Ave du Président-Wilson 75116 Ⓜ Iéna, Alma Marceau 🕐 Noon–midnight Wed–Mon 🚫 1 Jan, 1 May, 25 Dec, 2 weeks in Dec 🌐 palaisde tokyo.com

This enormous modern art gallery is adjacent to the Musée d'Art Moderne de la Ville de Paris within the imposing 1937 Palais de Tokyo. It presents an innovative, changing programme of contemporary art exhibitions, fashion shows and avant-garde performances. Installations by artists such as Pierre Joseph, Wang Du and Frank Scurti have earned the Palais de Tokyo a reputation as one of the most cutting-edge art houses in Europe. It also has a good bookshop and two restaurants, while club nights regularly take place in its basement space, Yoyo.

DRINK

Here are five of the best hotel bars for enjoying a decadent sundowner around Champs-Élysées.

Le Bar at the Four Seasons Hotel George V
📍 C5 🏛 31 Ave George V 75008 🌐 fourseasons.com

Bar de l'Hôtel Belmont
📍 C5 🏛 30 Rue de Bassano, 75116 🌐 belmont-paris-hotel.com

Bar Kléber at the Peninsula
📍 B4 🏛 19 Ave Kléber 75116 🌐 paris. peninsula.com

Le Bar Botaniste at the Shangri-La
📍 B6 🏛 10 Ave d'Iéna 75116 🌐 shangri-la.com

Le Bar du Bristol
📍 E4 🏛 112 Rue du Faubourg-St-Honoré 75008 🌐 oetkercollection.com

A SHORT WALK
CHAMPS-ÉLYSÉES

Distance 2 km (1.25 miles) **Nearest Metro** Invalides
Time 20 minutes

The formal gardens that line the Champs-Élysées from the Place de la Concorde to the Rond-Point have changed little since they were laid out by the architect Jacques Hittorff in 1838. The Grand Palais and Petit Palais, which were created as showpieces of the Third Republic for the Exposition Universelle of 1900, sit on either side of an impressive vista that stretches from Place Clémenceau across the elegant curve of the Pont Alexandre III to the Invalides.

There are plaques on the back door of the Théâtre du Rond-Point representing Napoleon's campaigns.

Metro Franklin D. Roosevelt Ⓜ

AVE DES CHAMPS

AVE G. EISENHOWER

AVE FRANKLIN D ROOSEVELT

Christian Dior and other haute couture houses are based on chic Avenue Montaigne.

RUE JEAN GOUJON

Designed by Charles Girault, the 19th-century Grand Palais is still used for major exhibitions (p225).

RUE FRANÇOIS PREMIER

The Lasserre restaurant is decorated in the style of a luxurious ocean liner from the 1930s.

Outside the Palais de la Découverte is a pair of equestrian statues (p228).

PL DU CANADA

COURS LA

PONT DES INVALIDES

← The interior of the Palais de la Découverte, a museum of scientific discoveries

Avenue des Champs-Élysées was the setting for the victory parades following the two World Wars, and for the bicentennial parade in 1989 (p224).

Metro Champs-Élysées-Clemenceau

Locator Map
For more detail see p216

CHAMPS-ÉLYSÉES AND CHAILLOT

The Jardins des Champs-Élysées, with their fountains, flower beds, paths and pleasure pavilions, became very popular towards the end of the 19th century. Fashionable Parisians, including Marcel Proust, often came here.

FINISH

AVE GABRIEL

AVE DE MARIGNY

ÉLYSÉES

AVE DES CHAMPS ÉLYSÉES

M

PL CLÉMENCEAU

AVE WINSTON CHURCHILL

REINE

PONT ALEXANDRE III

START

↑ Strolling through the tree-lined Jardins des Champs-Élysées

Lit by natural light, the Petit Palais is as much a work of art as the wide-ranging collections it contains, from antiquity to the belle époque (p225).

Pont Alexandre III's four columns help to anchor the piers that absorb the immense forces generated by such a large single-span structure (p228).

| 0 metres | 100 |
| 0 yards | 100 |

N ↑

ST-GERMAIN-DES-PRÉS

Named after a Benedictine abbey that was founded here in the 6th century, St-Germain-des-Prés came to prominence in the 1950s as the nucleus of the city's intellectual life. Largely working class, the neighbourhood attracted numerous writers and philosophers with its nonconformist atmosphere and profusion of bookshops and publishing houses. Leading figures such as Jean-Paul Sartre and Simone de Beauvoir held court at the district's celebrated cafés, most notably Café de Flore, Les Deux Magots and Le Procope. They and their disciples may have left, but this area is still renowned for its youthful student atmosphere and literary traditions. Since the 1970s, the neighbourhood has become progressively more upmarket, with the emergence of numerous fashionable boutiques. Rue de Seine is lined with charming restaurants and contains many high-end galleries where the smart set purchase their art.

E   F   G

PLACE DE LA CONCORDE

Galerie Nationale du Jeu de Paume

RUE   DE   RIVOLI

Tuileries Ⓜ

Musée de l'Orangerie

Jardin des Tuileries

PLACE DES PYRAMIDES

QUAI   DES   TUILERIES

QUAI ANATOLE FRANCE

6

Palais Bourbon Assemblée Nationale

Ⓜ Assemblée Nationale

Pont Solférino

LOUVRE AND LES HALLES
p180

La

Quai du Louvre

PLACE DU PRÉSIDENT É. HERRIOT

INVALIDES

Institut Géographique National

Musée National de la Légion d'Honneur ❷

PLACE H DE MONTHERLANT

RER Musée d'Orsay

❶ Musée d'Orsay

Quai de Solférino

Pont Royal

Seine

QUAI VOLTAIRE

RUE   ST   DOMINIQUE

Ⓜ Solférino

PLACE J BAINVILLE

RUE DE   BELLECHASSE

RUE DE SOLFÉRINO

RUE DE VILLERSEXEL

RUE   DE   LILLE

RUE DE POITIERS

DE

RUE   DU   BAC

RUE DE BEAUNE

RUE ALLENT

DE LILLE

VERNEUIL

L'UNIVERSITÉ

RUE   DES

7

Ⓜ Varenne

EIFFEL TOWER AND INVALIDES
p196

BOULEVARD

RUE DE BELLECHASSE

RUE DE SAINT-SIMON

RUE P.L. COURIER

Deyrolle ⓰

❾

PLACE ST THOMAS D'AQUIN

Ⓜ Rue du Bac

RUE DU MONTALEM-BERT

RUE DU PRÉ AUX CLERCS

RUE PERRONET

ST-

GERMAIN

RUE DE

Musée Rodin

RUE   DE   VARENNE

RUE   DE   GRENELLE

RUE DE LUNÉS

⓯ Musée Maillol

BOULEVARD

RUE DE GRENELLE

RUE ST GUILLAUME

Hôtel Matignon

RUE   DE   VARENNE

RUE DU BAC

RUE DE COMMAILLE

RASPAIL

RUE DE LA CHAISE

RUE DES SAINTS-PÈRES

RUE DU DRAGON

RUE B PALISSY

RUE DU SABOT

CARREFOUR DE LA CROIX ROUGE

RUE

8

RUE DE BABYLONE

RUE DE BABYLONE

RUE CHOMEL

Sèvres-Babylone Ⓜ

RUE DE SÈVRES

RUE D. VIEUX COLOMBIER

St-Sulpice Ⓜ

Jardin Catherine Labouré

Le Bon Marché ⓬

Square Boucicaut

RUE VELPEAU

RUE   DE   SÈVRES

PLACE LE CORBUSIER

PLACE DEVILLE

RUE DU CHERCHE MIDI

RUE COETLOGON

RENNES

RUE DE MÉZIÈRES

RUE MADAME

RUE VANEAU

⓾

RUE SAINT-PLACIDE

RUE DUPIN

BOULEVARD

RUE DE

RUE D'ASSAS

RUE CASSETTE

RUE MONSIEUR

RUE OUDINOT

Vaneau Ⓜ

RUE DE

RUE DU CHERCHE MIDI

L'ABBÉ GRÉGOIRE

RUE SAINT-PLACIDE

RUE DU CHERCHE MIDI

RUE DU REGARD

RASPAIL

Rennes Ⓜ

9

| 0 metres | 250 |
| 0 yards | 250 |

N ↑

St-Placide Ⓜ

E   F   G

ST-GERMAIN-DES-PRÉS

ST-GERMAIN-DES-PRÉS

Must See

1 Musée d'Orsay

Experience More

2 Musée National de la Légion d'Honneur
3 Académie Française
4 École Nationale Supérieure des Beaux Arts
5 Musée Eugène Delacroix
6 St-Germain-des-Prés
7 Monnaie de Paris
8 Rue St-André-des-Arts
9 Cour du Commerce St-André
10 Le Procope
11 St-Sulpice
12 Le Bon Marché
13 Café de Flore
14 Les Deux Magots
15 Musée Maillol
16 Deyrolle
17 Pont des Arts

Eat

1 Semilla
2 Le Comptoir du Relais
3 Ze Kitchen Galerie

Stay

4 Hôtel d'Aubusson
5 Relais Christine
6 Hôtel Récamier

Shop

7 Rue Lobineau
8 Rue Bonaparte
9 Rue du Bac
10 Rue de Sèvres
11 Rue de Buci

❶ MUSÉE D'ORSAY

📍G6 🏠1 Rue de la Légion d'Honneur Ⓜ Solférino 🚌24, 68, 69, 84 to Quai A France; 73 to Rue Solférino; 63, 83, 84, 94 to Blvd St-Germain 🚆Musée d'Orsay 🕐9:30am–6pm Tue-Sun (to 9:45pm Thu) 🚫1 May, 25 Dec 🌐musee-orsay.fr

The Musée d'Orsay picks up where the Louvre ends, showing a variety of art forms from 1848 to 1914. Its star attraction is a superb collection of Impressionist art, which includes famous works by Monet, Renoir, Manet and Degas, as well as pieces by Georges Seurat, Gaugin and Van Gogh.

In 1986, 47 years after it had closed as a mainline railway station, Victor Laloux's superb late-19th-century building was reopened as the Musée d'Orsay. Originally commissioned by the Orléans railway company to be its Paris terminus, the structure avoided demolition in the 1970s after being classified as a historical monument. During the conversion into a museum, much of the original architecture was retained. The collection was set up to present each of the arts of the period from 1848 to 1914 in the context of contemporary society and other forms of creative activity happening at the time. Renovations to the upper levels have expanded exhibition spaces to improve the display of works.

↑ The light and spacious entrance hall, with curved glass ceiling

GREAT VIEW
City Panorama

Make your way to the rear escalator, ride it all the way up, and head to the small rooftop terrace for a great bird's-eye view of the city.

① The clock face on the fifth floor provides views over the Seine to the Jardin des Tuileries.

② *Le Déjeuner sur l'herbe* (1863) by Manet caused a scandal when it was first exhibited.

③ Monet's *Le Déjeuner sur l'herbe* (1865–6) was a tribute to the work of the same name by Manet.

GALLERY GUIDE

The collection occupies three levels. On the ground floor, there are works from the mid- to late 19th century. The middle level features Art Nouveau decorative art and a range of paintings and sculptures from the second half of the 19th century. The upper level has an outstanding array of Impressionist art, as well as a number of Neo-Impressionist and early-20th-century artworks on display.

 ←

The former railway station, designed by Victor Laloux for the Exposition Universelle of 1900

EXPERIENCE MORE

Musée Nationale de la Légion d'Honneur

⚐ G6 ⌂ 2 Rue de la Légion d'Honneur (Parvis du Musée d'Orsay) 75007 Ⓜ Solférino ⬚ Musée d'Orsay ⌚ 1–6pm Wed– Sun ⌖ 1 Jan, 1 May, 15 Aug, 1 Nov, 25 Dec ⌨ legiondhonneur.fr

Next to the Musée d'Orsay is the truly massive Hôtel de Salm. It was one of the last great mansions to be built in the area (1782). The first owner was a German count, Prince de Salm-Kyrbourg, who was guillotined in 1794.

Today, the building contains a museum where you can learn all about the Legion of Honour, a decoration launched by Napoleon I. Those awarded the honour wear a small red rosette in their buttonhole. The impressive displays of medals and insignia are complemented by paintings. In one of the rooms, Napoleon's Legion of Honour is on display with his sword and breastplate.

The museum also contains examples of decorations from most parts of the world, among them the British Victoria Cross and the American Purple Heart.

Académie Française

⚐ H7 ⌂ 23 Quai de Conti 75006 Ⓜ Pont Neuf, St-Germain-des-Prés ⌨ academie-francaise.fr

This striking Baroque edifice was built as a school for young noblemen in 1688 and given over to the Institut de France in 1805. Its cupola was designed by architect Louis Le Vau to harmonize with the Palais du Louvre.

The Académie Française is the oldest of the five academies of the institute. Founded in 1635 by Cardinal Richelieu, it is charged with regulating the French language by deciding acceptable grammar and vocabulary, and with the compilation of an official

 INSIDER TIP
Macaron Mecca

Sample the city's most innovative macarons, such as jasmine and wild strawberry, at Pierre Hermé's flagship, on Rue Bonaparte.

dictionary of the French language. From the beginning, membership has been limited to 40 scholars, who are entrusted with a lifelong commitment to working on the dictionary. The building is only open to the public during the Journées du Patrimoine (Heritage Days) on the third weekend of September.

4

École Nationale Supérieure des Beaux-Arts

H7 13 Quai Malaquais & 14 Rue Bonaparte 75006 St-Germain-des-Prés beauxartsparis.com

The main French school of fine arts occupies an enviable position at the corner of Rue Bonaparte and the riverside Quai Malaquais. The school is housed in several buildings, the most imposing being the

19th-century Palais des Études. A host of budding French and foreign painters and architects have crossed the large courtyard to study in the ateliers of the school. Young American architects, in particular, have frequented the halls since the late 19th century. Works from its collections can be viewed in regular exhibitions; see website.

5

Musée Eugène Delacroix

H7 6 Rue de Fürstenberg 75006 St-Germain-des-Prés, Mabillon 9:30am-5:30pm Wed-Mon 1 Jan, 1 May, 25 Dec musee-delacroix.fr

The leading nonconformist Romantic painter Eugène Delacroix, known for his passionate and highly coloured canvases, lived and worked here from 1857 to his death in 1863. Here, he painted *The Entombment of Christ* and *The Way to Calvary* (which now hang in the museum). He also created superb murals for the Chapel of the Holy Angels in the nearby St-Sulpice church *(p243)*, which is part of the reason why he moved to this area. The first-floor apartment and garden studio now form a national museum, where regular exhibitions of Delacroix's work are held. The apartment has portraits, studies for future works and artistic memorabilia.

The charm of Delacroix's garden is reflected in the tiny Fürstenberg square. With its pair of rare catalpa trees and old-fashioned street lamps, the square is one of Paris's most romantic corners.

←

The Académie Française, ultimate arbiter of French language and grammar

6

St-Germain-des-Prés

H7 3 Pl St-Germain-des-Prés 75006 St-Germain-des-Prés 9am-8pm Mon, 8:30am-8pm Tue-Sun eglise-saint germaindespres.fr

This is the oldest church in Paris, originating in 543 when King Childebert built a basilica to house holy relics. It became a powerful Benedictine abbey, which was suppressed during the French Revolution, when most of the buildings were destroyed by a fire. The present church dates from about the 11th century and was restored in the 19th century. The interior is a mix of architectural styles, with a number of 6th-century marble columns, Gothic vaulting and Romanesque arches. Famous tombs include that of René Descartes.

TOP 5 **SHOPPING STREETS**

Rue Lobineau
H8
Home of the St-Germain food market.

Rue Bonaparte
H8
Full of swanky shops, including the Pierre Hermé flagship.

Rue du Bac
G7
Full of pastry shops and other confections.

Rue de Sèvres
G8
The location of Le Bon Marché *(p243)*, Paris's first department store.

Rue de Buci
H8
A former market street that today houses cafés and cute shops.

7

Monnaie de Paris

Q H7 **A** 11 Quai de Conti 75006 **M** Pont Neuf, Odéon **O** 11am–7pm daily (to 9pm Wed) **C** 1 Jan, 1 May, 25 Dec **W** monnaiedeparis.fr

In the late 18th century, when Louis XV decided to rehouse the Mint, he launched a design competition for the new building. The Hôtel des Monnaies is the result. It was completed in 1775, and the architect, Jacques Antoine, lived here until his death.

Coins were minted in the mansion until 1973, when the process was moved to Pessac in the Gironde. Until recently only a small part of the building was accessible to the public, but after a major renovation, the whole complex can now be visited, including its interior court-yards and a garden, as well as its revamped museum, the Musée du 11 Conti.

Centred around a tranquil public space and surrounded by artists' workshops, the permanent gallery focuses on the history of coins and minting. Regular exhibitions of contemporary art are also staged here. There are also shops selling work by resident artisans, a gastronomic restaurant run by chef Guy Savoy and a more casual café.

The picturesque Cour du Commerce St-André enchants at twilight

---

Did You Know?

Remnants of the old Paris wall can be found in the chocolate shop on Cour du Commerce St-André.

8

Rue St-André-des-Arts

Q J8 **A** 75006 **M** St-Michel, Odéon

Extending from Place St-André-des-Arts, where the square's namesake church once stood, this little street boasts numerous historical monuments. Dating back to 1179, it once led to the gate of the city in the former Philippe Auguste wall. The mansion at No 27 was owned by Louis XIII's geographer in the 1600s, while grammarian and encyclopaedist Pierre Larousse lived at No 49 in the 19th century. Peeling south off Rue St-André-des-Arts is the cobbled Cour du Commerce.

9

Cour du Commerce St-André

Q J8 **A** 75006 **M** Odéon

No 9 in this historic passage has a particularly grisly past, because it was here that Dr Guillotin is supposed to have perfected his "philanthropic decapitating machine". In fact, although the idea was Guillotin's, it was Dr Antoine Louis, a Parisian surgeon, who was responsible for putting

the "humane" plan into action. When the guillotine was first used for execution in 1792, it was known as a *Louisette*.

10

Le Procope

Q J8 **A** 13 Rue de l'Ancienne-Comédie 75006 **M** Odéon **O** Noon– midnight daily (to 1am Thu–Sat) **W** procope.com

Founded in 1686 by the Sicilian Francesco Procopio dei Coltelli, this claims to be the world's first coffee house. It quickly became popular with the city's political and cultural elite.

Its illustrious patrons have included the philosopher Voltaire – who supposedly drank 40 cups of his favourite mixture of coffee and choco-late every day – and the young Napoleon, who would leave his hat as security while he went searching for the money to pay the bill. Le Procope is now an 18th-century-style restaurant run by the famous Frères Blanc group.

A coin press at the newly revamped Musée du 11 Conti

13

Café de Flore

⦿ H7 🏠 172 Blvd St-Germain 75006 Ⓜ St-Germain-des-Prés 🕒 7:30am-1:30am daily 🌐 cafedeflore.fr

The classic Art Deco interior of this café has changed little since World War II. Like its neighbouring rival Les Deux Magots (p244), Café de Flore has hosted most of the French intellectuals during the post-War years.

EAT

Semilla
Sharing plates and fresh, innovative cooking with local ingredients are on the menu here.

⦿ H7 🏠 54 Rue de Seine 75006 🌐 semillaparis.com

€€€

Le Comptoir du Relais
This bistro is a staple of the area for inventive French cooking at lunch and dinner.

⦿ H8 🏠 9 Carrefour de l'Odéon 75006 🌐 hotel-paris-relais-saint-germain.com

€€€

Ze Kitchen Galerie
French cooking infused with international inspirations; the tasting menu at this former canteen is good value.

⦿ J7 🏠 4 Rue des Grands Augustins 75006 🗓 Sat, Sun 🌐 zekitchengalerie.fr

€€€

11

St-Sulpice

⦿ H8 🏠 2 Rue Palatine, Pl St-Sulpice 75006 Ⓜ St-Sulpice 🕒 7:30am-7:30pm daily 🌐 pss75.fr/saint-sulpice-paris

It took over a century, from 1646, for this imposing church to be built. The result is a simple two-storey west front with two tiers of elegant columns. The overall harmony of the building is marred only by the towers, one at each end, which do not match.

Large arched windows fill the interior with light. By the front door are two huge shells given to François I by the Venetian Republic – they rest on bases sculpted by Jean-Baptiste Pigalle.

In the side chapel to the right of the main door are three magnificent murals by Eugène Delacroix: *Jacob Wrestling with the Angel*, *Heliodorus Driven from the Temple* and *St Michael Killing the Dragon*. If you are lucky, you can catch an organ recital. Regular guided tours of the church take place at 2:30pm every Sunday.

12

Le Bon Marché

⦿ G8 🏠 24 Rue de Sèvres 75007 Ⓜ Sèvres-Babylone 🕒 10am-8pm Mon-Sat (to 9pm Thu), 11am-7:45pm Sun 🌐 24sevres.com

Welcoming as many as 15,000 customers per day, "The Good Market" (or "The Good Deal") is the swankiest department store in Paris, selling luxury goods as well as gourmet foods in its annexe La Grande Épicerie on Rue du Bac. The designer clothing section is well sourced, the high-end accessories are excellent, and the own-brand linen has a good quality-to-price ratio.

Le Bon Marché is also the world's oldest department store, founded in 1852 by Aristide Boucicaut and his wife. The Boucicauts used their keen sense of commerce to introduce innovative practices – fixed prices, sales, home delivery, advertising and guarantees – that became the standard for other *grands magasins*. Designed by Louis-Charles Boileau and Gustave Eiffel, it is an architectural landmark.

14

Les Deux Magots

H7 **6 Pl St-Germain-des-Prés 75006** **M** St-Germain-des-Prés **7:30am–1am daily** **One week in Jan** **lesdeuxmagots.com**

Established in 1914, this café still trades on its reputation as the meeting place of the city's literary and intellectual elite. This derives from the patronage of Surrealist artists and writers, including Ernest Hemingway, in the 1920s and 1930s, and existentialist philosophers and writers in the 1950s.

The present clientele is more likely to consist of publishers or people-watchers than the new Hemingway. The café's name comes from the two wooden statues of Chinese commercial agents *(magots)* that adorn one of the pillars. This is a good place for enjoying an old-fashioned hot chocolate and watching the world go by. On Thursdays, there's a live jazz session between 7:30 and 10pm.

15

Musée Maillol

G7 **59/61 Rue de Grenelle 75007** **M** Sèvres-Babylone, Rue du Bac **10:30am–6:30pm daily (to 9:30pm Fri)** **1 Jan, 25 Dec** **museemaillol.com**

Once the home of novelist Alfred de Musset, this museum was created by Dina Vierny, former model of Aristide Maillol. All aspects of the artist's work are here: drawings, engravings, paintings, sculpture and decorative objects. Also displayed is Vierny's private collection, including works

STAY

Hôtel d'Aubusson
A cosy lobby and refined rooms define this Left Bank favourite.

J7 **33 Rue Dauphine 75006** hoteldaubusson.com

€€€

Relais Christine
This luxury property includes a spa for guests who are after a bit of pampering.

J7 **3 Rue Christine 75006** **relais-christine.com**

€€€

Hôtel Récamier
Elegance and comfort are on order at this tiny property tucked behind St-Sulpice.

H8 **3B Place St-Sulpice 75006** hotelrecamier.com

€€€

At night, illuminated every so often by the Bateaux Mouches cruising underneath, the Pont des Arts is an especially romantic place to walk or picnic in warmer months.

The Pont des Arts with its prime views of the Île de la Cité

casual visitor, however, can simply enjoy the collection of taxidermied animals, from giant elephants and rhinos to the most delicate birds and crustaceans. There is a wide range of insects housed in drawers. Iridescent beetles and colourful butterflies sit alongside terrifying tarantulas and scorpions. Everything is for sale, mostly at decent prices considering the quality.

17

Pont des Arts

🔲 H7 🏠 75006
Ⓜ Louvre-Rivoli

Sometimes referred to as the Passerelle des Arts, this picturesque iron bridge, part of the UNESCO-listed Parisian riverfront, has more often been called the "Love Lock Bridge" in recent years. The nickname refers to the now-forbidden practice of couples fixing padlocks to the bridge to signify their love; the practice had to be stopped because the locks exerted too much weight on the structure and started to destroy it. Now revived and restored – following the removal of almost a million locks weighing 45 tonnes – this pedestrian bridge, built under Napoleon from 1801 to 1804, has been returned to its 19th-century splendour. The first iron bridge in Paris, it links the Institut de France with the Louvre, offering resplendent views of the Île de la Cité from above the river. At night, illuminated every so often by the Bateaux Mouches cruising gently underneath, the Pont des Arts is an especially romantic place to walk or picnic in warmer months.

by Matisse, Picasso and Rodin. The museum stages regular temporary art exhibitions, which are usually on themes and artists associated with Maillol. Note that it is closed in between exhibitions, so it is best to check the website before visiting.

Large allegorical figures of the city of Paris, the River Seine and the four seasons decorate Edme Bouchardon's fountain, *La Fontaine des Quatre Saisons*, built in 1739–45, in front of the house.

16

Deyrolle

🔲 G7 🏠 46 Rue du Bac 75005 Ⓜ Rue du Bac ⏰ 10am-1pm & 2-7pm Mon, 10am-7pm Tue-Sat 🌐 deyrolle.com

A Parisian institution since 1831, Deyrolle is a cabinet of curiosities that continues to delight all who enter its doors. Originally a taxidermy shop, it has evolved over the years, and now part of its mission is to raise awareness about wildlife conservation. The

---

┃ **THE CELEBRATED CAFÉS OF PARIS**

One of the most enduring images of Paris is the café scene. For the visitor, it is the romantic vision of great artists, writers or eminent intellectuals consorting in one of the Left Bank's celebrated cafés. For the Parisian, the café is one of life's constants, an everyday experience, providing people with a place to tryst, drink and meet friends, to conclude business deals, or to simply watch the world go by.

The most famous cafés are on the Left Bank, in St-Germain and Montparnasse. Sartre and his intellectual peers, among them the writers Simone de Beauvoir and Albert Camus, gathered to work and discuss their ideas in Les Deux Magots and Café de Flore.

↑ Les Deux Magots, where the literary and intellectual elite used to gather

A SHORT WALK
ST-GERMAIN-DES-PRÉS

Distance 1.5 km (1 mile) **Nearest Metro** St-Germain-des-Prés
Time 15 minutes

A walk around this area is to follow in the footsteps of some of Paris's most iconic inhabitants. After World War II, St-Germain-des-Prés became synonymous with intellectual life centred on bars and cafés. Philosophers, writers, actors and musicians mingled in the cellar nightspots and brasseries, where existentialist philosophy co-existed with American jazz. The area is now smarter than in the heyday of Jean-Paul Sartre and Simone de Beauvoir, but the writers are still around, enjoying the pleasures of café life.

Descartes and Casimir, King of Poland, are among the notables buried in Paris's oldest church, St-Germain-des-Prés (p241).

In the 1950s, French intellectuals wrestled with new philosophical ideas in the Art Deco interior of the Café de Flore (p243).

Les Deux Magots is famous for its celebrity patrons such as Ernest Hemingway (p244).

Colourful ceramics decorate the famous Brasserie Lipp, once frequented by politicians.

START

BLVD ST-GERMAIN

RUE DU DRAGON

RUE DU SABOT

RUE DE RENNES

RUE BONAPARTE

0 metres 100
0 yards 100

N ↑

RUE DU FOUR

Café terraces, boutiques, cinemas, restaurants and bookshops characterize the central section of the Left Bank's Boulevard St-Germain.

← *Les Deux Magots, on the pleasant Boulevard St-Germain*

↑ Admiring the works of the Romantic painter at the Musée Eugène Delacroix

Locator Map
For more detail see p236

Picasso's sculpture Homage to Apollinaire *is a tribute to the artist's friend, the poet Guillaume Apollinaire. It was erected in 1959, near the Café de Flore.*

The tiny square of Rue de Fürstenberg, with its old-fashioned street lamps, is often used as a film set.

The Musée Eugène Delacroix is dedicated to the life and works of the Romantic painter (p241).

Rue de Buci was once the site of some real tennis courts. It now holds a lively daily market.

Palais Abbatial was the residence of abbots from 1586 till the 1789 Revolution.

Danton's statue (1889), by Auguste Paris, is a tribute to the Revolutionary leader.

Ⓜ *Metro Odéon*

Metro Mabillon

Marché St-Germain is an old covered food market which opened in 1818, taking over the site of a former fairground.

LATIN QUARTER

Located on the Left Bank, the Latin Quarter spreads over the 5th and 6th arrondissements. One of the oldest and best-known areas of Paris (the Rue St-Jacques is probably the oldest street in the city), this lively neighbourhood exudes a bohemian charm. It emerged in the Middle Ages as a student quarter, with the celebrated Sorbonne University attracting scholars from all over Europe. Much of the area's character was established at this time, as it grew up into a maze of tiny cobblestoned streets leading to gardens and churches. The Latin Quarter was at the centre of the riots that erupted out of the student protests and workers strike in May 1968, but since then the Boulevard St-Michel, the area's spine, has turned increasingly to commerce, not demonstrations. Today there are cheap shops and fast-food outlets, and the cobbled streets are now pedestrianized and filled with small cafés, ethnic boutiques and second-hand bookshops.

L · MARAIS · M

RUE DE RIVOLI

RUE DU ROI DE SICILE

St-Paul Ⓜ

7

Maison Européenne
de la Photographie

Mémorial
de la Shoah

RUE CHARLEMAGNE

LATIN
QUARTER

Pont Marie Ⓜ

Pont Louis
Philippe

QUAI DES CELESTINS

RUE DES LIONS ST-PAUL

RUE DU PETIT MUSC

QUAI DE L'HÔTEL DE VILLE

DE L'HÔTEL DE VILLE

RUE DES NONNAINS D'HYÈRES

QUAI DE BOURBON

Pont Marie

BOULEVARD HENRI IV

8

ÎLE DE LA CITÉ
AND ÎLE ST-LOUIS
p66

Île
St-Louis

La

PORT DE LA TOURNELLE

TOURNELLE

Pont de la
Tournelle

QUAI DE BÉTHUNE

Seine

Pont de
Sully

ST- GERMAIN

③

RUE DES CHANTIERS

Institut du
Monde
Arabe

JARDIN DES PLANTES
AND PLACE D'ITALIE
p262

Université
Pierre et
Marie Curie

PLACE
JUSSIEU

Ⓜ Jussieu

RUE CUVIER

Arènes de
Lutèce

Jardin des
Plantes

Muséum National
d'Histoire Naturelle

Grande
Mosquée
de Paris

RUE DAUBENTON

RUE BUFFON

L · M

LATIN QUARTER

Must See
❶ Panthéon

Experience More
❷ Musée de Cluny
❸ Musée de la Préfecture de Police
❹ Collège de France
❺ La Sorbonne
❻ St-Séverin
❼ Place St-Michel
❽ Gibert Jeune Bookshops
❾ St-Julien-le-Pauvre
❿ Marché Maubert
⓫ St-Étienne-du-Mont
⓬ Grand Action Cinéma
⓭ Bibliothèque Ste-Geneviève
⓮ Shakespeare and Company
⓯ Square René Viviani

Eat
① Shakespeare and Co Café
② Chez Gladines
③ La Tour d'Argent

Drink
④ Monk Le Taverne de Cluny
⑤ Le Piano Vache
⑥ Le Bombardier

Stay
⑦ Hôtel Design Sorbonne
⑧ Hôtel des Grands Hommes
⑨ Les Degrés de Notre-Dame

❶ 🚲 🅼

PANTHÉON

📍 J9 🏛 Pl du Panthéon Ⓜ Cardinal Lemoine, Maubert-Mutualité
🚌 84 to Panthéon; 21, 27, 38, 82, 85, 89 to Gare du Luxembourg
🚆 Luxembourg 🕐 10am–6:30pm daily (Oct–Mar: to 6pm)
🚫 1 Jan, 1 May, 25 Dec 🌐 paris-pantheon.fr

Inspired by the Pantheon in Rome, Paris's Panthéon was originally built as a church. Today a public building, it provides a fitting final resting place for the nation's great figures.

When Louis XV recovered from desperate illness in 1744, he was so grateful to be alive that he conceived a magnificent church to honour Sainte Geneviève. The design was entrusted to the French architect Jacques-Germain Soufflot, who planned the church in Neo-Classical style. Work began in 1757 and was completed in 1790, ten years after Soufflot's death, under the supervision of Guillaume Rondelet. But with the Revolution under way, the church was soon turned into a pantheon – a location for the tombs of France's great and good. Napoleon returned it to the Church in 1806, but it was secularized and then desecularized once more before finally being made a civic building in 1885.

←

The colonnade encircling the dome, both decorative and part of an ingenious supporting system

Pediment relief

Entrance

THE PANTHÉON'S ENSHRINED

The first of France's great men to be entombed here (though later removed on the orders of Robespierre) was the popular orator Honoré Mirabeau. Voltaire followed, as did other literary notables, including Jean-Jacques Rousseau, Victor Hugo and Émile Zola. In the 1970s, the remains of the wartime Resistance leader Jean Moulin were reburied here. Pierre and Marie Curie's remains were transferred here in 1995, followed by Alexandre Dumas in 2002. In 2015, four more Resistance fighters - two of them women - took their places in the Panthéon.

↑ The elegant arches linking the four pillars that support the dome

↑ Alphonse Terroir's statue (1925) to the political writer Denis Diderot

Dome lantern

Dome galleries

Colonnade

Did You Know?

The dome was inspired by St Paul's in London and the Dôme des Invalides *(p204)*.

Crypt

Dome arches

↑ The church, designed in the shape of a Greek cross

A collection of exquisitely decorated medieval armour and shields at the Musée de Cluny

Curiosities on show include arrest warrants for figures such as the famous Revolutionary Danton, and a rather sobering display of weapons and tools used by famous criminals. There is also a section on the part that the police played in the Resistance and subsequent liberation of Paris.

EXPERIENCE MORE

2

Musée de Cluny

📍 J8 📍 6 Pl Paul-Painlevé 75005
Ⓜ Cluny-La Sorbonne, Odéon, St-Michel
🌐 musee-moyenage.fr

This museum is housed in the former town house of the abbots of Cluny, the Hôtel de Cluny. Surrounded by imaginatively recreated medieval gardens, it is a unique combination of Gallo-Roman ruins incorporated into a medieval mansion, and contains one of the world's finest collections of medieval art. Highlights include the *Lady with the Unicorn*, an outstanding series of six tapestries, and the Gallery of the Kings, which contains 22 of the 27 stone heads of the Kings of Judah (carved around 1220 and removed from Notre-Dame in the 18th century). The museum is partially closed until 2020 while it undergoes renovation; check the website for details before planning a visit.

3

Musée de la Préfecture de Police

📍 K8 📍 4 Rue de la Montagne Ste-Geneviève 75005 📞 01 44 41 52 50
Ⓜ Maubert-Mutualité
🕐 9:30am-5pm Mon-Fri, 10:30am-5pm 3rd Sat of month 🚫 Sun & public hols

A darker side to Paris's history is exposed in this small, rather old-fashioned museum. Created in 1909, the collection traces the development of the police in Paris from the Middle Ages to the 20th century.

← A statue of Guillaume Budé, Collège de France

4

Collège de France

📍 J9 📍 11 Pl Marcelin-Berthelot 75005
Ⓜ Maubert-Mutualité
🕐 Sep-Jun: 9am-6pm Mon-Fri 🚫 School hols
🌐 college-de-france.fr

One of Paris's great institutes of research and learning, the college was established in 1530 by François I. Guided by the great humanist Guillaume Budé, the king aimed to counteract the rigidity and traditionalism of the Sorbonne. A statue of Budé stands in the west courtyard, and the unbiased approach to learning is reflected in the inscription on the old college entrance: *docet omnia* (all are taught here). Lectures are free and open to the public, depending on availability.

🔍 HIDDEN GEM
Thermes de Cluny

These Roman baths were built at the end of the 1st century AD. In the 14th century the Cluny monks built their abbey over the ruins and today they can be seen as part of a visit to the Musée de Cluny.

La Sorbonne

Ⓟ J9 **🏠 1 Rue Victor Cousin 75005** **Ⓜ Cluny-La Sorbonne, Maubert-Mutualité** **🆆 sorbonne.fr**

The Sorbonne, seat of the University of Paris, was established in 1253 by Robert de Sorbon, confessor to Louis IX, for 16 poor students to study theology. The college soon became the centre of scholastic theology. In 1469, the rector had three printing machines brought over from Mainz, thereby founding the first printing house in France. The college's opposition to liberal 18th-century philosophy led to its suppression during the Revolution. It was re-established by Napoleon in 1806. The buildings built by Richelieu in the early 17th century were replaced by the ones seen today, with

→

The chapel of La Sorbonne, with its elegant dome

the exception of the chapel. You can book onto a guided tour by emailing ahead.

6

St-Séverin

Ⓟ J8 **🏠 3 Rue des Prêtres-St-Séverin 75005** **Ⓜ St-Michel** **🕐 11am–7:30pm Mon-Sat, 9am–8pm Sun** **🆆 saint-severin.com**

One of the most beautiful churches in Paris and a popular venue for concerts, St-Séverin, named after a 6th-century hermit who lived in the area, is a perfect example of the Flamboyant Gothic style. Construction finished during the early 16th century and included a remarkable double ambulatory circling the chancel. In 1684, the Grande Mademoiselle, cousin to Louis XIV, adopted St-Séverin after breaking with St-Sulpice and had the church's chancel modernized.

EAT

Shakespeare and Co Café

Sip coffee and nibble cakes outside the iconic bookshop (p258).

Ⓟ K8 **🏠 37 Rue de la Bûcherie 75005** **🆆 shakespeareand company.com**

Chez Gladines

Hearty and affordable no-frills French meals.

Ⓟ K8 **🏠 44 Blvd St-Germain 75005** **🆆 chezgladines-saintgermain.fr**

La Tour d'Argent

Dine where French royalty first used a fork. Try the legendary duck.

Ⓟ L8 **🏠 17 Quai de la Tournelle 75005** **🔒 Sun, Mon** **🆆 tourdargent.com**

€€€

7

Place St-Michel

📍 J8 🏠 75005
Ⓜ St-Michel

This square at a busy intersection is a popular meeting place for Parisians and tour groups. Created in 1855, it's defined by the statue of Saint Michael the archangel slaying Satan, part of the monumental fountain built into the side of an adjacent building. The mix of colours and motifs earned it some criticism initially, and it was the last monumental wall fountain to be built in the city, ending the Renaissance-era trend brought to Paris by Catherine de Medici. Originally the fountain was meant to honour Napoleon Bonaparte, but the city council thought better of it and opted not to ruffle the feathers of anti-Bonaparte reactionaries. Nowadays, the fountain is a memorable welcome to the Latin Quarter for visitors entering the district from Île St-Louis. It is surrounded by cafés and bookshops which are popular with local university students.

8

Gibert Jeune Bookshops

📍 J8 🏠 Multiple locations, Place St-Michel 75005
Ⓜ St-Michel 🕐 9:30am–7:30pm Mon–Sat
🌐 gibertjeune.fr

A former professor, Joseph Gibert opened his first shop in 1886. He sold books on the Quai St-Michel along with the other *bouquinistes* (used-book sellers who ply their wares out of green boxes along the Seine). Gibert's sons continued the family business, opening separate outposts under the name. Gibert Jeune is the original bookshop, while Gibert Joseph is a newer space, with a number of other outlets all dotted around the Place St-Michel, a stone's throw from the Sorbonne. Inside, customers will find academic books, maps

300,000

books are held in the green boxes of the *bouquinistes* along the river.

of Paris, novels, travel guides and much else. At No 10 there is a large collection of travel- and tourism-related books.

9

St-Julien-le-Pauvre

📍 K8 🏠 79 Rue Galande 75005 Ⓜ St-Michel
🚆 St-Michel-Notre-Dame
🕐 9:30am–1:30pm, 3–6:30pm daily
🌐 sjlpmelkites.fr

At least three saints can claim to be patron of this church, but the most likely is St Julian the Hospitaller. The church, together with St-Germain-des-Prés, is one of the oldest in Paris, dating from between 1165 and 1220. The university held its official meetings in

→
The monumental fountain in Place St-Michel

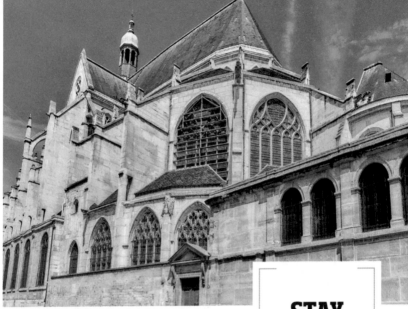

↑ The Gothic-Renaissance church of St-Étienne-du-Mont

the church until 1524, when a student protest created so much damage that meetings were barred from the church by parliament. Since 1889, it has belonged to the Melchite sect of the Greek Orthodox Church, and it is now the setting for chamber and religious music concerts.

Marché Maubert

📍K8 🏠Place Maubert 75005 🕐7am–2:30pm Tue & Thu, 7am–3pm Sat Ⓜ Maubert-Mutualité

Popular with locals, this is one of the city's oldest outdoor markets, dating back to 1547. In earlier times the square was a place where carriage drivers emptied their waste, creating a truly gut-wrenching stench that drove out many inhabitants. Eventually the city cleaned up the mess and repurposed the square as a place for public executions, installing breaking wheels and gibbets here in the 16th century. By the 19th century

the square had returned to commercial use, and included a unique market where beggars would sell unused tobacco that they collected from the streets. Today the market is entirely wholesome, and you can browse stalls selling organic strawberries, cheese and dried hams.

St-Étienne-du-Mont

📍K9 🏠30 Rue Descartes, Pl Ste-Geneviève 75005 Ⓜ Cardinal Lemoine 🕐Opening hours vary; check website for details 🌐saintetiennedumont.fr

This remarkable church houses the shrine of Sainte Geneviève, patron saint of Paris, as well as the remains of the great literary figures Racine and Pascal. Some parts are in the Gothic style and others date from the Renaissance, including a magnificent rood screen that crosses the nave like a bridge. The stained-glass windows are also of note.

STAY

Hôtel Design Sorbonne
Stylish and central, this boutique hotel is a good deal given its location.

📍J9 🏠6 Rue Victor Cousin 75005 🌐hotelsorbonne.com

€€€

Hôtel des Grands Hommes
Sleep in 19th-century grandeur at this tasteful property.

📍J9 🏠17 Place du Panthéon 75005 🌐hoteldesgrands hommes.com

€€€

Les Degrés de Notre-Dame
Good-value simplicity in central Paris, right across from Notre-Dame.

📍K8 🏠10 Rue des Grands Degrés 75005 🌐les-degrés-de-notre-dame.com

€€€

12

Grand Action Cinéma

📍K9 📍5 Rue des Écoles 75005 Ⓜ Cardinal Lemoine, Jussieu Ⓦ legrandaction.com

Located in the heart of the Latin Quarter, this tiny independent operation is one of the most exciting cinematic experiences in Paris. The site has been a handball court, a Revolutionaries' meeting place and a dance hall over the years. Today it welcomes all sorts of films and retrospectives, ranging from niche independent films to Oscar-nominated pictures. The director and local student clubs regularly host industry professionals for talks to the public on themes such as science-fiction movies or Russian films. There are just two theatres with rows of red-cushioned seats, but the Grand Action perseveres even as multiplexes have risen in popularity.

13

Bibliothèque Ste-Geneviève

📍J9 📍10 Place du Panthéon 75005 Ⓜ Maubert-Mutualité 🕐10am–10pm Mon–Sat Ⓦ bsg.univ-paris3.fr

This massive, sober-looking library houses some two million documents salvaged from the nearby abbey of Ste-Geneviève. Visitors to the neighbourhood may completely overlook it, as the enormous dome of the Panthéon tends to command more attention. It was, however, the first French library that was built without any connection to a palace or school building. It opened to the public in 1851, and architect Henri Labrouste incorporated a soaring glass-and-iron ceiling into the main reading room. There is usually a queue to enter the library, and visitors may be required to register at the front desk, but it is worth it to work in such a grand setting.

14

Shakespeare and Company

📍K8 📍37 Rue de la Bûcherie 75005 🕐10am–10pm daily Ⓜ St-Michel, Maubert-Mutualité Ⓦ shakespeareand company.com

George Whitman opened this now-iconic shop in 1951. Originally called Le Mistral, it was renamed Shakespeare and Company in 1964 after the renowned bookshop run by Sylvia Beach on nearby Rue de l'Odéon, which closed in 1941 during the Occupation. Whitman sought to emulate the spirit of Beach's shop, attracting expat writers like Henry Miller and Anaïs Nin. Over the years, the owner

Did You Know?
—
This district was the scene of violent clashes between angry students and police in the riots of May 1968.

The legendary American-run English-language bookshop Shakespeare and Company

allowed young writers to sleep in the shop for free, asking them only to read, pitch in at the shop and write a page-long autobiography. The shop continues Whitman's traditions, and his daughter Sylvia – named after Beach – maintains the ethos. There are always literary events taking place, some featuring big names like David Sedaris. The shop is tiny, but well stocked with contemporary literature, Paris-themed books and a healthy selection of English travel books. Next door is a coffee shop *(p255)*, where you can settle down with a book at one of the outdoor tables facing Notre-Dame.

15

Square René Viviani

🚇 K8 🏠 25 Quai de Montebello 75005 Ⓜ St-Michel, Maubert-Mutualité 🕐 8am–5pm Mon–Fri, 9am–5pm Sat–Sun (to 8:30pm in summer)

One of many little green oases in Paris, Square René Viviani has views of Notre-Dame that beat all others. The park was once a graveyard belonging to the 6th-century basilica that formerly stood here. Now, the church St-Julien-le-Pauvre *(p256)*, begun in the 12th century, sits adjacent to the park. Its most notable

feature is a black locust tree *(Robinia pseudoacacia)*, allegedly planted in 1601. Held up by a couple of concrete stilts, it is generally accepted to be the oldest tree in Paris, having survived shell damage during World War I. The square owes its name to France's first Labour Minister, René Viviani, who once spoke out in support of women's suffrage – albeit, in a limited fashion.

DRINK

Monk le Taverne de Cluny
Craft beer has infiltrated the Parisian scene, and this is the place for it on the Left Bank.

🚇 J8 🏠 51 Rue de la Harpe 75005 🌐 latavernede cluny.com

€€€

–––––––––––

Le Piano Vache
Students and locals hit the bar at this rowdy watering hole.

🚇 K9 🏠 8 Rue Laplace 75005 📅 Sun 🌐 lepianovache.com

€€€

–––––––––––

Le Bombardier
Paris has a few pubs worthy of the name, but this one has earned its stripes.

🚇 K9 🏠 2 Place du Panthéon 75005 🌐 bombardierpub.fr

€€€

← Square René Viviani, a perfect retreat from the bustle of the city

A SHORT WALK
LATIN QUARTER

Distance 2 km (1.25 miles) **Nearest Metro** Cluny - La Sorbonne
Time 20 minutes

This riverside quarter, dating back to Roman times, acquired its name from early Latin-speaking students. The area is generally associated with artists, intellectuals and the bohemian way of life, but it also has a history of political unrest. In 1871, Place St-Michel became the centre of the Paris Commune, and in May 1968, it was the site of the student uprisings. Though now sufficiently chic to contain the homes of some of the establishment, the quarter is still full of bookshops and cafés, perfect for an afternoon of browsing.

Place St-Michel contains a fountain by Davioud. The bronze statue by Duret shows St Michael fighting the devil.

Metro St-Michel

QUAI ST-

RUE DE LA HARPE

No 22 Rue St-Séverin is the narrowest house in Paris and used to be the residence of Abbé Prévost, author of Manon Lescaut.

BLVD ST-MICHEL

The northern end of the Boulevard St-Michel is a lively mélange of cafés, bars, bookshops and clothes stores.

Begun in the 13th century, the beautiful St-Séverin took three centuries to build and is a fine example of the Flamboyant Gothic style (p255).

Metro Cluny – La Sorbonne

RUE DU

RUE ST-JACQUES

RUE DES ÉCOLES

RUE DU

RUE THENARD

START

One of the finest collections of medieval art in the world is kept at the superb Musée de Cluny (p254).

↑ Davioud's decorative fountain, found in Place St-Michel

The iconic Shakespeare and Company bookshop and accompanying café

Locator Map
For more detail see p250

Rue du Chat qui Pêche translates as "street of the fishing cat".

Little Athens is a lively place in the evenings, especially at the weekend, when the Greek restaurants situated in the touristy streets around St-Séverin are at their busiest.

Shakespeare and Company at No 37 Rue de la Bûcherie is a delightful, if chaotic, bookshop. Any books purchased here are stamped with Shakespeare & Co Kilomètre Zéro Paris (p258).

Did You Know?

Rue du Chat qui Pêche is the narrowest street in Paris at just 1.8 m (6 ft) wide.

One of the oldest churches in Paris, St-Julien-le-Pauvre has 13th-century Romanesque architecture. The vault was added in the 17th century (p256).

Rue du Fouarre used to host lectures in the Middle Ages. The students sat on straw (fouarre) in the street.

FINISH

Metro – Maubert Mutualité

Rue Galande was home to the rich and the chic in the 17th century, but subsequently became notorious for its taverns.

0 metres 100
0 yards 100

N

JARDIN DES PLANTES AND PLACE D'ITALIE

This is one of the oldest areas in Paris, with a history dating back to ancient times. Part of the Roman settlement of Lutetia, it housed the large Arènes de Lutèce amphitheatre. The Rue Mouffetard was also established during the Roman era, and remained an important market street throughout the ensuing centuries. In 1626, Louis XIII founded the Jardin des Plantes as the royal medicinal plant gardens, and it soon became a scientific laboratory and botanical research centre – in the 18th centry it was the stomping ground of naturalists Georges Louis Leclerc, Comte de Buffon and Jean-Baptiste Lamarck, whose research eventually influenced Charles Darwin and his *On the Origin of Species*. In more recent years, the area has become home to a sizable Muslim community, focused on the Grande Mosquée de Paris and the Institut du Monde Arabe cultural centre.

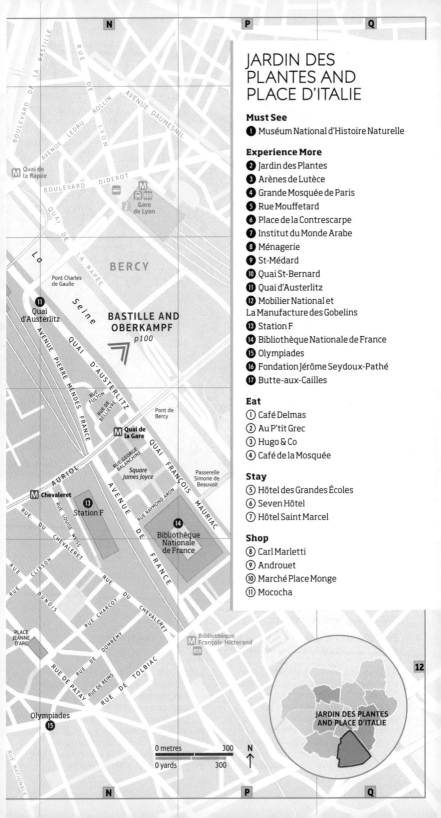

JARDIN DES PLANTES AND PLACE D'ITALIE

Must See
❶ Muséum National d'Histoire Naturelle

Experience More
❷ Jardin des Plantes
❸ Arènes de Lutèce
❹ Grande Mosquée de Paris
❺ Rue Mouffetard
❻ Place de la Contrescarpe
❼ Institut du Monde Arabe
❽ Ménagerie
❾ St-Médard
❿ Quai St-Bernard
⓫ Quai d'Austerlitz
⓬ Mobilier National et La Manufacture des Gobelins
⓭ Station F
⓮ Bibliothèque Nationale de France
⓯ Olympiades
⓰ Fondation Jérôme Seydoux-Pathé
⓱ Butte-aux-Cailles

Eat
① Café Delmas
② Au P'tit Grec
③ Hugo & Co
④ Café de la Mosquée

Stay
⑤ Hôtel des Grandes Écoles
⑥ Seven Hôtel
⑦ Hôtel Saint Marcel

Shop
⑧ Carl Marletti
⑨ Androuet
⑩ Marché Place Monge
⑪ Mococha

BASTILLE AND OBERKAMPF
p100

JARDIN DES PLANTES AND PLACE D'ITALIE

The spectacular ↑
Grande Galerie
de l'Évolution

❶ 🖊️ 🖥️ 🛍️

MUSÉUM NATIONAL D'HISTOIRE NATURELLE

📍L10 🏠2 Rue Buffon 75005 Ⓜ️Jussieu, Austerlitz
🕐10am-6pm Wed-Mon 📅1 Jan, 1 May, 25 Dec 🌐mnhn.fr

This collection of galleries in the Jardin des Plantes houses an impressive display of natural history specimens tracing the evolution of life on Earth.

Originally a botany research centre in the 17th century, the museum was founded in 1793 to include the study of animals. It has three galleries in the Jardin des Plantes: the Galerie de Minéralogie et de Géologie, with its crystals, gems and meteorites; the Galeries d'Anatomie Comparée et de Paléontologie, housing dinosaur skeletons and fossils; and the Grande Galerie de l'Évolution, featuring stuffed tigers and elephants. With more than 62 million specimens, the museum has the third-largest research collection in the world. The Galerie des Enfants (Children's Gallery), in the Grande Galerie de l'Évolution, is a hands-on exhibition focusing on the environment.

The museum also encompasses several other sites in the Jardin des Plantes, including the greenhouses and the zoo *(p270)*.

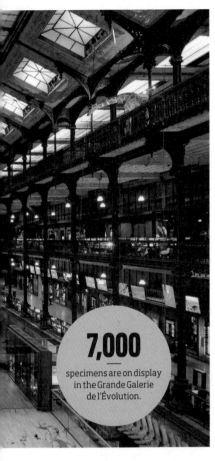

7,000
—
specimens are on display in the Grande Galerie de l'Évolution.

GALERIES D'ANATOMIE COMPARÉE ET DE PALÉONTOLOGIE

Built in 1898 for the Exposition Universelle of 1900, the Galeries d'Anatomie Comparée et de Paléontologie mesmerize young visitors with their collection of dinosaur skeletons, including a Triceratops and a Tyrannosaurus rex. Beginning in the Paleozoic Era, the exhibition takes visitors on a 540-million-year journey through each stage in the development of animal life. Keep a special eye out for the skeleton of Louis XV's rhino; one of the museum's longest-held specimens, it once lived at Versailles.

TYRANNOSAURUS
REX SKULL

① A wide range of flora is on show in the greenhouses.

② The museum sits amid the glorious Jardin des Plantes.

③ The zoo is famed for its orangutans.

EXPERIENCE MORE

Jardin des Plantes

📍 L9 📍 57 Rue Cuvier/
2 Rue Buffon 75005
Ⓜ Jussieu, Austerlitz
🕐 8am–6:30pm daily
(to 5:30pm winter)
🌐 jardindesplantes.net

A treasure to locals in the 5th arrondissement, the Jardin des Plantes comprises a museum, a zoo, botanical gardens, a science lab and a university research centre. Previously known as the Jardin du Roi, it started life as a medicinal herb garden created by Guy de la Brosse and Jean Hérouard, King Louis XIII's physicians, in 1626. After opening to the public in 1640 and offering a free school of botany, chemistry and anatomy, it quickly attracted renowned scientists, such as the Comte de Buffon, whose studies were to shape Darwin's views on evolution.

Today, this popular botanical garden is home to three galleries of the Muséum National d'Histoire Naturelle (p266). It includes a small zoo (p270), rose garden and a labyrinth that kids adore. As well as beautiful vistas and walkways flanked by ancient trees and punctuated with statues, the park features a remarkable alpine garden with plants from the Alps, the Himalayas, Corsica and Morocco, and an unrivalled display of herbaceous and wild plants. It also has the first cedar of Lebanon planted in France, originally from Britain's Kew Gardens.

Arènes de Lutèce

📍 K9 📍 49–59 Rue Monge/
4 Rue des Arènes 75005
📞 01 45 35 02 56 Ⓜ Jussieu, Cardinal Lemoine 🕐 8/9am–6/7:30/8:30pm, depending on the time of year

The remains of this vast Roman arena (Lutetia was the Roman name for Paris) date from the late 1st century AD. Its destruction began towards the end of the 3rd century at the hands of the Barbarians, and later, parts of it were used to build the walls of the Île de la Cité. The arena was then gradually buried and its exact location preserved only in old documents and the local name Clos des Arènes.

It was rediscovered in 1869 during the construction of Rue Monge and the allocation of building plots nearby. Action towards its restoration began with the campaigning of Victor Hugo (among others) in the 19th century, but work did not get underway until 1918.

With a seating capacity of 15,000, arranged in 35 tiers, the original arena was used both for theatrical performances and as an amphitheatre for gladiator fights. This type of combined use was peculiar to Gaul (France), and the arena is similar to the other ones in Nîmes and Arles.

Grande Mosquée de Paris

📍 L10 📍 2 bis Pl du Puits de l'Ermite 75005 (Turkish baths/tearoom: 39 Rue Geoffroy St-Hilaire)
Ⓜ Place Monge 🕐 9am–noon & 2–6pm Sat–Thu; baths: 10am–9pm Wed–Mon 🚫 Muslim hols
🌐 mosqueedeparis.net

Built in the 1920s in the Hispano-Moorish style, this

←

People enjoying a stroll on a spring day in the Jardin des Plantes complex is the spiritual centre of Paris's Muslim community and the home of the Grand Imam. It comprises religious, educational and commercial sections; and at its heart is a mosque. Each of the mosque's domes is decorated in a different style, and the minaret stands nearly 33 m (100 ft) high. Inside is a grand patio with mosaics on the walls and tracery on the arches.

Once used only by scholars, the mosque's place in Parisian life has grown over the years. The Turkish baths are strictly for women only. A tearoom and restaurant set in a peaceful tree-shaded courtyard serve Moorish specialities and make a lovely spot for a glass of mint tea and sticky cakes.

Rue Mouffetard

K10 75005 Censier Daubenton, Place Monge Market Place Maubert: 7am– 2:30pm Tue, Thu, Sat (to 3pm Sat); Place Monge: 7am-2:30pm Wed, Fri, Sun (to 3pm Sun)

A major thoroughfare since Roman times, when it linked Lutetia (Paris) and Rome, this street is one of the oldest in the city. In the 17th and 18th centuries, it was known as the Grande Rue du Faubourg St-Marcel, and many of its buildings date from that time. Some of the small shops still have ancient painted signs, and some houses have mansard roofs.

↑ The tranquil, tiled gardens of the Grande Mosquée de Paris

Did You Know?

Ernest Hemingway lived in the area in the 1920s, at 74 Rue du Cardinal Lemoine.

No 125 has an attractive, restored Louis XIII façade, and the entire front of No 134 is beautifully decorated with wild beasts, flowers and plants. No 69 sports an old shop sign featuring a carved oak tree, while at No 60, the *Fontaine de Pot-de-Fer* is a small fountain dating from Roman times. Later on, it was connected to an aqueduct used by Marie de Médici to take water to the Palais du Luxembourg and its gardens (p286).

The area is known for its open-air markets, especially those in Place Maubert, Place Monge (set around the Monge fountain) and Rue Daubenton, a side street where a lively African market takes place.

At night, the street bustles with people enjoying the Greek, Italian, Argentinian and other cuisines on offer at the many small restaurants.

6

Place de la Contrescarpe

K9 75005
Place Monge

At one time, this site lay outside the city walls. It gets its name from the backfilling of the moat that ran along Philippe Auguste's wall. The present square was laid out in 1852, but the fountain was added in 1994. At No 1, there is a memorial to the old "pine-cone club"; here, a group of writers known as *La Pléiade* used to meet in the 16th century. Four hundred years later, authors such as Ernest Hemingway, James Joyce and George Orwell also found the streets of this historically working-class neighbourhood a great source of inspiration.

The area has always been used for meetings and festivals. Today, it still embodies old Paris, with its narrow cobblestoned streets and charming cafés, and is very lively at weekends.

7

Institut du Monde Arabe

L9 1 Rue des Fossés St-Bernard, Pl Mohammed V 75005 Jussieu, Cardinal Lemoine Museum & temp exhibs: 10am–6pm Tue, Wed & Fri, 10am–7pm Thu, Sat & Sun imarabe.org

This cultural institute was founded in 1980 by France and 20 Arab countries with the intention of fostering cultural links between the Arab world and the West. It is housed in a magnificent building designed by Jean Nouvel (who was also responsible for the Musée du quai Branly and the Philharmonie), combining modern materials with the spirit of traditional Arab architecture. The white marble book tower, which can be seen through the glass of the west wall, spirals upwards, bringing to mind the minaret of a mosque. The emphasis that is traditionally placed on interior space in Arab architecture has been used here to create an enclosed courtyard reached by a narrow gap splitting the building in two.

Flamingos in the Ménagerie, France's oldest public zoo ↑

From floors four to seven, there's a fascinating display of Islamic works of art from the 9th to the 19th centuries, including ceramics, sculpture, carpets and astrolabes. The centre also houses a library and media archive, and puts on a lively programme of lectures and concerts.

8

Ménagerie

L9 57 Rue Cuvier/ Rue Buffon 75005 Jussieu, Austerlitz 9am–5:30pm daily (to 5pm winter) zoo dujardindesplantes.fr

France's oldest public zoo is situated in the pleasant surroundings of the Jardin des Plantes (p268). The Ménagerie was set up during the Revolution to house the survivors from the royal menagerie at Versailles – all four of them. The state

←

St-Médard and a Rue Mouffetard street market

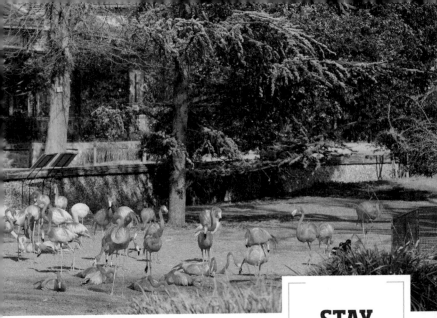

Did You Know?

The old wall of Paris can be seen along Rue Clovis, by the prestigious Henri IV school.

then expanded the collection with animals rounded up from circuses and exotic creatures sent from abroad. Tragically, during the Prussian siege of Paris (1870–71), most of the animals were slaughtered in order to feed the hungry citizens.

The zoo specializes in small mammals, insects, birds, primates and reptiles. It is a great favourite with children as it allows them to get quite close to the animals, and feeding times are especially popular. The big cat house contains panthers from China, and other attractions include a large monkey house, a waterfowl aviary, and wild sheep and goats. The displays in the vivarium (enclosures of live animals in their natural habitat) are changed at regular intervals, and there is a permanent exhibition of micro-arthropods (also known as creepy-crawlies).

St-Médard

🇶K10 🏠141 Rue Mouffetard 75005
Ⓜ Censier-Daubenton
🕐 8am-12:30pm & 2:30-7:30pm Tue-Sat, 9am-12:30pm & 4-8:30pm Sun
🅦 saintmedard.org

The origins of this church go back to the 9th century. St Médard, counsellor to the Merovingian kings, was known for giving a wreath of white roses to young girls noted for their virtue. The churchyard became notorious in the 18th century as the centre of the cult of the Convulsionnaires, whose hysterical fits were brought on by the contemplation of miracle cures. The interior has many fine paintings, including the 17th-century *St Joseph Walking with the Christ Child* by Francisco de Zurbarán, and the organ loft is adorned with Renaissance statues.

STAY

Hôtel des Grandes Écoles

A garden terrace and old-world feel make this a perpetual favourite.

🇶K9 🏠75 Rue du Cardinal Lemoine 75005 🅦 hotel-grandes-ecoles.com

---

Seven Hôtel

Swanky décor sets this modern hotel apart from most in the area.

🇶J10 🏠20 Rue Berthollet 75005 🅦 sevenhotel paris.com

Hôtel Saint Marcel

A great location and amenities such as a wine bar stocked with the family's own wine make this hotel a real bargain.

🇶L11 🏠43 Blvd St-Marcel 75013 🅦 hotel-saint-marcel-paris.com

10

Quai St-Bernard

 M9 🏠 75005
Ⓜ Gare d'Austerlitz

Running along the river from the Pont de Sully as far as the Pont d'Austerlitz is the peaceful Quai St-Bernard. Not always so sedate, Quai St-Bernard was famous during the 17th century as a spot for nude bathing, until scandalized public opinion made it illegal. The quay is studded with contemporary sculptures, but its main draw is the green space known as the Jardin Tino-Rossi, named for the Coriscan singer who recorded "Petit Papa Noël" in 1946, one of France's best-selling songs ever. The park is alive with music in the summer, from French folk to salsa and tango. Dancers of all levels meet here at night, turning the park into an outdoor dance hall.

Butting up to the left-hand corner of the Institut du Monde Arabe, the Pont de Sully links the Île St-Louis with both banks of the Seine. Opened in 1877 and built of cast iron, the Pont de Sully is not an especially beautiful structure. Despite this, it is well worth pausing for a moment on the bridge for a fabulous view of Notre-Dame rising dramatically behind the graceful Pont de la Tournelle.

11

Quai d'Austerlitz

Ⓜ M10 🏠 97013
Ⓜ Gare d'Austerlitz
Ⓦ citemodedesign.fr

Stretching along the Left Bank from Gare d'Austerlitz towards the Bibliothèque, this riverfront promenade is a little-known part of town. It's closed to traffic and offers a pleasant stroll with views of the Seine. Several boats host cafés serving coffee and wine. The impressive contemporary cultural centre known as Les Docks, Cité de la Mode et du Design, perches over the Seine, with its green undulating façade looking northwards. Housed in a former industrial warehouse, it is home to an assortment of bars, cafés and restaurants, as well as a fashion institute, and hosts regular exhibitions. Further south is the Port de la Gare where, in the summer, outdoor restaurants and cafés line the riverfront. The Batofar, a floating nightclub, and the Piscine Josephine Baker, a floating public pool, also moor here year-round.

Did You Know?

The Batofar at Quai d'Austerlitz was one of the first floating clubs in Paris.

12

Mobilier National et La Manufacture des Gobelins

📍 K11 🏠 42 Ave des Gobelins 75013 Ⓜ Gobelins
🕐 11am–6pm Tue–Sun (temporary exhibitions)
📅 1 Jan, 1 May, 25 Dec
Ⓦ mobiliernational.culture.gouv.fr

Originally a dyeing workshop set up in about 1440 by the Gobelin brothers, the building became a tapestry factory

---

→

The striking façade of Les Docks, Cité de la Mode et du Design early in the 17th century. Louis XIV took it over in 1662 and gathered together the greatest craftsmen of the day – carpet-weavers, cabinet-makers and silversmiths – to furnish his new palace at Versailles (p296). Working under the direction of court painter Charles Le Brun, 250 Flemish weavers laid the foundations for the factory's international reputation. Today, weavers continue to work in the traditional way but with modern designs, including those of Picasso and Matisse. Guided tours on Saturday afternoons can be booked via the website.

Station F

📍 N11 🏠 5 Parvis Alan Turing 75013
Ⓜ Chevaleret 🌐 stationf.co

This converted train station, which opened in 2017, houses Paris's burgeoning innovation scene. The world's largest "start-up campus", Station F is as long as the Eiffel Tower is high. The venue hosts a variety of events about business and technology, with registration available on its website. Visitors can take a tour of the new ventures or cosy up with entrepreneurs at the public café. A restaurant area featuring refurbished train cars is open 24 hours for any late-night revellers looking for a place to dine. It features four kitchens, a bar, and an enormous terrace that can seat up to 1,000.

SHOP

Carl Marletti
Daring confectionaries fill Marletti's celebrated patisserie, with ephemeral favourites like the *fraisier* popping up each year.

📍 K10 🏠 51 Rue Censier 75005 🌐 carlmarletti.com

Androuet
Expert artisan cheeses from here have pleased Parisians since 1909, including classics such as Camembert.

📍 K10 🏠 134 Rue Mouffetard 75005 🌐 androuet.com

Marché Place Monge
Vendors stock fresh produce that changes with the seasons at this outdoor market with a focus on quality over quantity.

📍 K10 🏠 1 Place Monge 75005 🕐 7am-2:30pm Wed, Fri & Sun

Mococha
Surprising combinations deck the shelves of this boutique, run by a team of inspired chocolatiers.

📍 K10 🏠 89 Rue Mouffetard 75005 🌐 chocolatsmococha.com

14

Bibliothèque Nationale de France

📍N11 🏛Quai François Mauriac 75013
Ⓜ Bibliothèque François-Mitterrand ⏰10am–8pm Tue-Sat, 1-7pm Sun
🚫Public hols 🌐bnf.fr

The national library collection dates back to the 1300s, when King Charles V began a library at the Louvre. Royals added to the shelves, even involuntarily, as Revolutionaries confiscated thousands of volumes from aristocrats during the French Revolution. Nowadays, the symbol of the BNF is the ultra-modern building rising over the Quai François Mauriac. The structure looks like four giant glass books opening onto a courtyard, and is largely used by scholars. Commissioned by President Mitterrand and completed in 1996, it houses the world's largest selection of medieval manuscripts and boasts over 14 million books in total. Temporary exhibitions take place throughout the year, as well as in the other BNF sites located around the city.

15 🍴🏛

Olympiades

📍N12 🏛75013
Ⓜ Olympiades

This curious, modern corner of Paris is part of the city's larger vision of urban development. It is marked by the Olympiades towers, an innovative housing complex where each tower is named after a different Olympic host city. Today, the area is largely known as Paris's largest Chinatown, where the annual Chinese New Year parade takes place in February. Parisians head here for delicious Chinese and Vietnamese food, including some of the best *bo bun* in the entire city. Its affordable fare and exotic grocery stores, like Tang Frères, are huge draws for anyone interested in a break from *steak-frites* and cheese. The district is bordered on the south by the tramline that stretches around southern Paris.

16

Fondation Jérôme Seydoux-Pathé

📍L11 🏛73 Ave des Gobelins 75013 Ⓜ Place d'Italie, Les Gobelins
🏛Salle Charles Pathé & Exhibitions: 1-8pm Tue, 1-7pm Wed-Fri, 11:30am-7pm Sat; research centre: by appt only 🚫1 Jan, 25 Dec 🌐fondation-jerome seydoux-pathe.com

The headquarters of the Fondation Jérôme Seydoux-Pathé sits on the site of a mid-19th-century theatre that was transformed into one of Paris's first cinemas in the early 1900s. Pathé, a major French film production and distribution company, is the second-oldest operating film company in the world. The foundation is dedicated to the preservation of its legacy and to promoting cinematography. The building has a 68-seat screening room for silent films, plus temporary and permanent collections of films, cameras, projectors, programmes and posters dating back to 1896. It is a treasure trove for film enthusiasts and researchers. Guided tours are held on Saturdays at noon.

17 🍴🖥🏛

Butte-aux-Cailles

📍K12 🏛75013
Ⓜ Place d'Italie, Corvisart

Named after landowner Pierre Caille who grew grapes here in the 1500s, this little hill was once an important area for tanneries and other industry. The La Bièvre river, which now runs underground, used to run right through it. Limestone quarries

↑ Dominique Perrault's modern Bibliothèque Nationale de France

Did You Know?

The Bibliothèque Nationale de France is one of the oldest libraries in the world.

→ A water fountain in Chinatown

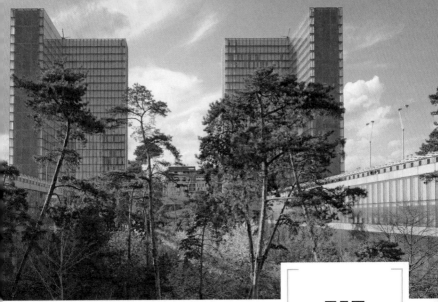

underground made the land unsuitable for Haussmann's large construction projects, and as a result the area has more of a village feel than most parts of Paris – the Rue des Cinq-Diamants is a great example of this. Interestingly, it was in this area, in 1783, that the first official hot-air balloon trip landed successfully. Today the district is full of local character in its bars and cafés; they are relatively cheap, making the area especially popular among young university types. The area is also an excellent place to discover some great street art, with lots of examples of the work of tagger Miss.Tic.

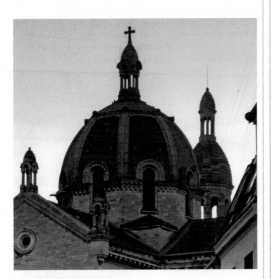

↑ The dome of Ste-Anne-de-la-Buttes-aux-Cailles church in the picturesque Butte-aux-Cailles district

EAT

Café Delmas
Traditional French café overlooking a square.

 K9 🏠 2 Place de la Contrescarpe 75005 🌐 cafedelmas.com

€€€

Au P'tit Grec
A popular spot serving huge take-away crêpes.

K10 🏠 68 Rue Mouffetard 75005 🌐 auptitgrec.com

€€€

Hugo & Co
Convivial restaurant serving chic dishes.

 K9 🏠 48 Rue Monge, 75005 🚫 Sat & Sun 🌐 tomygousset.com/hugo-and-co

€€€

Café de la Mosquée
A lovely tea room attached to the mosque.

 L10 🏠 2 bis Place du Puits de l'Ermite 75005

€€€

A SHORT WALK
JARDIN DES PLANTES QUARTER

Distance 2.5km (1.5 miles) **Nearest Metro** Cardinal Lemoine
Time 25 minutes

A well-to-do residential patchwork of 19th- and early-20th-century buildings, this area also has one or two surprises up its sleeve, including a Roman amphitheatre and a Hispano-Moorish mosque. The area began life in 1626 as a royal medicinal herb garden, the work of two physicians to Louis XIII, Jean Hérouard and Guy de la Brosse. The herb garden and gardens of various religious houses gave the region a rural character. In the 19th century, the population and thus the area expanded and it became more built up, transforming into the area you see today.

Metro Cardinal Lemoine

START

Place de la Contrescarpe is a village-like square filled with restaurants and cafés (p270).

Locals flock to the market street of Rue Mouffetard, one of the oldest in the city, where vendors' displays spill onto the cobblestones in a colourful spread of fresh produce, pastries and wine (p269).

Pot-de-Fer fountain is one of 14 that Marie de Médici had built on the Left Bank in 1624 as a source of water for her palace. The fountain was rebuilt in 1671.

Metro Place Monge

The Passage des Postes is an alley opened in 1830 to link Rue Mouffetard with Rue Lhomond.

The church of St-Médard dates to the mid-1400s. In 1784, the choir was revamped and the nave's windows replaced with contemporary stained glass (p271).

↑ Taking time out on the cobbled square of Place de la Contrescarpe

The Arènes de Lutèce, a Roman amphitheatre, was used for burials in the 4th century (p268).

Rue des Arènes is round the corner from the Arènes de Lutèce. No 5 is an interesting Gothic Revival house in which the writer Jean Paulhan lived from 1940.

Locator Map
For more detail see p264

The Cuvier Fountain is a memorial to naturalist Georges Cuvier. It was erected in 1840 by P Vigouroux, with figure carving by Jean-Jacques Feuchère.

FINISH

↑ The Hispano-Moorish Grande Mosquée de Paris and its garden

Did You Know?

The Grande Mosquée honours Muslims who died on French battlefields during World War I.

The Grande Mosquée de Paris, the centre of Paris's Muslim community, includes within its walls a Turkish bath, a Moorish café and restaurant, and a souk-style bazaar (p268).

Metro Censier-Daubenton

0 metres   100
0 yards   100

N ↑

MONTPARNASSE AND JARDIN DU LUXEMBOURG

Montparnasse takes its name from the Mount Parnassus of Ancient Greece, the home of Apollo, god of poetry and music. In the first three decades of the 20th century, Montparnasse was a thriving artistic literary centre. Many modern painters and sculptors, new novelists and poets were drawn to this bohemian area, where they would frequent cafés such as La Closerie des Lilas and La Coupole. The great epoch ended with World War II, and change continued with the destruction of many ateliers and the construction of the soaring Tour Montparnasse, Paris's tallest office tower, which heralded the more modern quarter.

The Jardin du Luxembourg was initiated by Marie de Médici in 1612, inspired by the Boboli Gardens of her native Florence. Baron Haussmann redeveloped the area around the park in the 19th century; his changes were deeply unpopular with the public for encroaching on the gardens and reducing their size. Nonetheless, the area has retained its own unique charm of winding streets, beautiful buildings, bookshops and art galleries.

MONTPARNASSE AND JARDIN DU LUXEMBOURG

Must See

1 Cimetière du Montparnasse

Experience More

2 Tour Montparnasse
3 Notre-Dame-du-Travail
4 Institut Pasteur
5 Catacombes de Paris
6 Fondation Cartier
7 Musée Antoine Bourdelle

8 Palais du Luxembourg
9 Musée du Luxembourg
10 Jardin du Luxembourg
11 Musée Zadkine

Eat & Drink

1 La Coupole
2 Closerie de Lilas
3 Les Papilles

ST-GERMAIN-
DES-PRÉS
p234

J

Musée
de Cluny

BLVD ST- GERMAIN

K

8

RUE DE TOURNON

PLACE DE
L'ODÉON

Odéon-Théatre
de l'Europe

RUE DE VAUGIRARD

PLACE PAUL
CLAUDEL

RUE DE MÉDICIS

La
Sorbonne

RUE DES ECOLES

8 Palais du
Luxembourg

Collège
de France

9 Musée du
Luxembourg

Fontaine
Médicis

PLACE
EDMOND
ROSTAND

RUE SOUFFLOT

RUE SAINT-JACQUES

LATIN
QUARTER
p248

Alliance
Française

10 Jardin du
Luxembourg

RUE ROYER
COLLARD

PLACE DE
L'ESTRAPADE

RUE DE L'ESTRAPADE

9

M Notre-Dame-
des-Champs

RER Luxembourg

RUE PIERRE ET
MARIE CURIE

RUE TOURNEFORT

RUE AUGUSTE COMTE

PLACE A
HONNORAT

3

RUE GAY-LUSSAC

RUE D'ULM

RUE DESCARTES

RUE DE L'ABBE
DE L'EPEE

RUE DES
URSULINES

RUE L.
THUILLIER

RUE MOUFFETARD

Musée
Zadkine **11**

RUE JOSEPH BARA

RUE
MICHELET

BARBUSSE

RUE ERASME

RUE P.
BROSSOLETTE

Vavin
M

Jardin
Marco Polo

RUE DU VAL DE GRÂCE

RUE DES
FEUILLANTINES

PLACE P
LAMPUE

RUE RATAUD

RUE VAUQUELIN

10

Fontaine de
l'Observatoire

PLACE E
DENIS

RUE HENRI

RUE PIERRE NICOLE

PLACE A
LAVERAN

Église du
Val-de-Grâce

RUE CLAUDE BERNARD

2

MONTPARNASSE

Port Royal RER

RUE ST-JACQUES

Hôpital du
Val de Grâce

RUE BERTHOLLET

JARDIN DES
PLANTES AND
PLACE D'ITALIE
p262

BOULEVARD DE PORT-ROYAL

RUE DE LA GLACIÈRE

Raspail M

6 Fondation
Cartier

AVENUE DENFERT-ROCHEREAU

AVE DE L'OBSERVATOIRE

RUE CASSINI

Hôpital
Cochin

11

Petit Cimetière

RUE DU FAUBOURG ST-JACQUES

RUE DE LA SANTÉ

Observatoire
de Paris

RUE MECHAIN

PLACE DENFERT-
ROCHEREAU

BOULEVARD

ARAGO

Catacombes
de Paris **5**

BLVD

RUE LECLERC

RUE JEAN DOLENT

RUE LEON
MAURICE NORDMANN

RUE PASCAL

Denfert-
Rochereau M RER

ST-JACQUES

M St-Jacques

AVE RENÉ COTY

RUE ST-JACQUES

RUE ÉMILE DUBOIS

M Mouton-
Duvernet

RUE DE LA TOMBE ISSOIRE

RUE DAREAU

Glacière
M

RUE VULPIAN

RUE HALLÉ

DUVERNET

12

RUE BEZOUT

RUE BROUSSAIS

ALLÉE PAUL VERLAINE

RUE D'ALESIA

AVENUE RENÉ COTY

RUE D'ALESIA

RUE SARRETTE

0 metres   300
0 yards   300

N
↑

MONTPARNASSE AND
JARDIN DU LUXEMBOURG

H

J

K

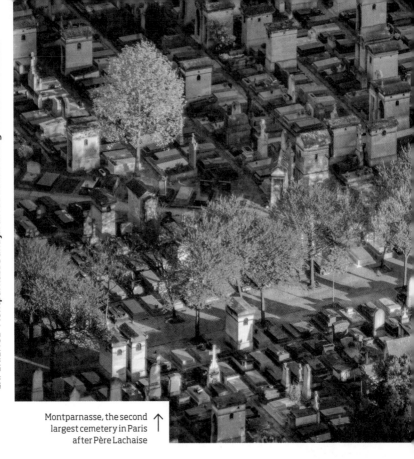

Montparnasse, the second largest cemetery in Paris after Père Lachaise ↑

❶

CIMETIÈRE DU MONTPARNASSE

📍G10 🏠3 Blvd Edgar Quinet Ⓜ Edgar Quinet 🚌28, 58, 68, 82, 83, 88, 91 to Port Royal 🚉Port Royal 🕐Mid-Mar-mid-Nov: 8am-6pm Mon-Fri, 8:30am-6pm Sat, 9am-6pm Sun (mid-Nov-mid-Mar: to 5:30pm)

This cemetery is the resting place of many illustrious Parisians. Sculptures nestle among the funerary art, creating a peaceful haven in the tree-lined grounds.

The Montparnasse Cemetery was planned by Napoleon outside the city walls to replace the numerous, congested, small cemeteries within the old city, viewed as a health hazard at the turn of the 19th century. It was opened in 1824 and contains the graves of many notable, particularly Left Bank, personalities. Like all French cemeteries, it is divided into rigidly aligned paths. The Rue Émile Richard cuts it into two parts, the Grand Cimetière and the Petit Cimetière.

The Kiss by Brancusi, who is buried just off Rue Émile Richard ↑

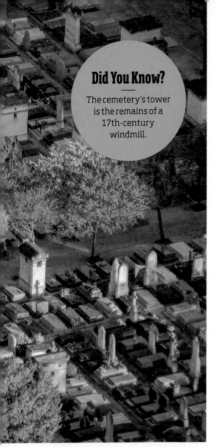

Did You Know?

The cemetery's tower is the remains of a 17th-century windmill.

Notable Residents

Jean-Paul Sartre and Simone de Beauvoir

△ The famous existentialist couple, undisputed leaders of the post-War literary scene, lie here close to their Left Bank haunts.

Jean Seberg

▷ The Hollywood actress, chosen by Jean-Luc Godard as the star of his film *À Bout de Souffle*, was the epitome of American blonde beauty, youth and candour.

Serge Gainsbourg

The French singer, composer and pop icon of the 1970s and 80s is best known for his wistful and irreverent songs. He was married to the actress Jane Birkin.

Samuel Beckett

◁ The great Irish playwright, renowned for *Waiting for Godot*, spent most of his life in Paris. He died in 1989.

Man Ray

The American photographer immortalized the Montparnasse artistic and café scene in the 1920s and 30s.

André Citroën

▷ The engineer and industrialist, who died in 1935, founded the famous French car firm.

CHARLES BAUDELAIRE

The cemetery contains the cenotaph of Charles Baudelaire, the great poet and critic. Baudelaire, who was born and died in Paris, shocked the world with his frank and decadent collection of poems *Les Fleurs Mal*, published in 1857. His work has had a widespread literary influence, and has even inspired rock stars such as Mick Jagger.

EXPERIENCE MORE

②

Tour Montparnasse

📍F10 🏠33 Ave du Maine 75014 Ⓜ️Montparnasse-Bienvenüe 🕐Apr–Sep: 9:30am–11:30pm daily; Oct–Mar: 9:30am–10:30pm daily (to 11pm Fri & Sat) 🅦tourmontparnasse 56.com

This was Europe's largest office block when it was built in 1973. At 210 m (690 ft) high, it totally dominates the area's skyline. A lift takes you up to the observation floor with its panoramic bar. For the best views you'll need to climb up the last three floors to the open-air observatory. The views from here are spectacular – up to 40 km (25 miles) on a clear day. The tower will be closed for major renovations in the run-up to the Olympics from 2020 to 2024.

③

Notre-Dame-du-Travail

📍F11 🏠36 Rue Guilleminot 75014 Ⓜ️Pernety 🕐7:30am–7:45pm Mon–Fri, 9am–7:30pm Sat, 8:30am–7:30pm Sun 🅦notredame dutravail.net

This church dates from 1901 and is made of an unusual mix of materials: stone, rubble and bricks over a riveted steel-and-iron framework. It was the creation of Father Soulange-Boudin, a priest who organized cooperatives and sought to reconcile labour and capitalism. Local parishioners raised the money for its construction, but lack of funds meant that many features, such as the bell towers, were never built. On the façade hangs the Sebastopol Bell,

a trophy from the Crimean War given to the people of the Plaisance district by Napoleon III. The Art Nouveau interior has been restored and features paintings of saints.

---

④

Institut Pasteur

📍E10 🏠25–28 Rue du Docteur Roux 75015 Ⓜ️Pasteur 🅦pasteur.fr

The Institut Pasteur, France's leading medical research centre, was founded by the scientist Louis Pasteur in 1888–9. He discovered the process of milk pasteurization, as well as vaccines against rabies and anthrax. The centre houses a museum that includes a reconstruction of Pasteur's apartment and laboratory. Unfortunately, the museum is currently closed to

→
Tour Montparnasse, as seen from the Eiffel Tower

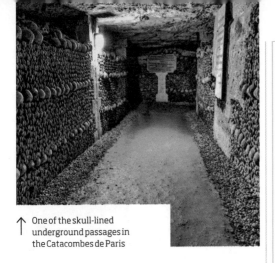

↑ One of the skull-lined underground passages in the Catacombes de Paris

EAT & DRINK

La Coupole
An Art Nouveau brasserie serving up meaty classics.

📍 G10 📍 102 Blvd du Montparnasse 75014
🌐 lacoupole-paris.com

 €€€

Closerie des Lilas
A classic brasserie, once frequented by Hemingway.

📍 H10 📍 171 Blvd du Montparnasse 75006
🌐 closeriedeslilas.fr

 €€€

Les Papilles
Wine bottles line the walls of this friendly local.

📍 J9 📍 30 Rue Gay-Lussac 75005
🕐 Sun, Mon
🌐 lespapillesparis.fr

 €€€

individuals, though groups of ten or more can apply at least three months in advance to visit; check the website for the latest updates. Pasteur's tomb is in a basement crypt built in the style of a small Byzantine chapel. The tomb of Dr Émile Roux, who discovered the treatment for diphtheria, is in the garden. The institute has laboratories for pure and applied research and a hospital established to apply Pasteur's theories. There is also a library – the institute's original building from 1888 – where research into AIDS is carried out, led by pioneering Professor Luc Montagnier, who discovered the HIV virus in 1983.

Catacombes de Paris

📍 H11 📍 1 Ave du Colonel Henri Rol-Tanguy 75014
Ⓜ Denfert-Rochereau
🕐 10am–8:30pm Tue–Sun 🕐 1 Jan, 1 May, 25 Dec
🌐 catacombes.paris.fr

In 1786, a monumental project began here: the removal of the millions of skulls and bones from the unsanitary city cemetery in Les Halles to the quarries at the base of the three "mountains": Montparnasse, Montrouge and Montsouris.

Initially the bones were placed haphazardly, but from the early 19th century they were used to adorn the walls in decorative patterns.

During World War II, the French Resistance set up its headquarters here. Above the door outside are the words "Stop! This is the empire of death." Visiting the catacombs has become very popular, so reserving your ticket in advance is advised. Guided tours in English are held at 3pm on Tuesdays and Fridays.

Fondation Cartier

📍 H11 📍 261 Blvd Raspail 75014 Ⓜ Raspail 🕐 11am–8pm Tue–Sun (to 10pm Tue) 🕐 1 Jan, 25 Dec
🌐 fondationcartier.com

This foundation for contemporary art and architecture is housed in a building designed by architect Jean Nouvel. He has created an air of transparency and light, as well as incorporating a cedar of Lebanon, which was planted in 1823 by François-René de Chateaubriand. The structure complements the nature of the exhibitions of progressive art, which showcase personal, group or thematic displays, often including works by young unknowns.

↑ Equipment on display at the museum at the Institut Pasteur

7

Musée Antoine Bourdelle

📍F10 🏠18 Rue Antoine Bourdelle 75015
Ⓜ Montparnasse-Bienvenüe ⏰10am-6pm Tue-Sun 🚫Public hols
🌐bourdelle.paris.fr

The prolific sculptor Antoine Bourdelle lived and worked in the studio here from 1884 until his death in 1929. The house, studio and garden are now a museum. Among the 900 sculptures on display are the original plaster casts of his monumental works planned for wide public squares. They include the group of sculptures for the relief decoration of the Théâtre des Champs-Élysées. Frequent temporary exhibitions, for which there is an entry fee, complement the free permanent collection.

← One of the many statues in the Musée Antoine Bourdelle

8

Palais du Luxembourg

📍H9 🏠19 Rue de Vaugirard 75006
Ⓜ Odéon ⓇⒺⓇLuxembourg
🌐senat.fr/visite

Now the home of the French Senate, this palace was designed by Salomon de Brosse in the style of Florence's Pitti Palace to remind Marie de Médici, widow of Henri IV, of her native town. By the time it was finished (1631), Marie had been banished, but it remained a royal palace until the Revolution. In World War II, it was the headquarters of the Luftwaffe. Individual visits to the palace are currently suspended (check the website for updates), but the Musée du Luxembourg, in the east gallery, is open.

9

Musée du Luxembourg

📍H9 🏠19 Rue de Vaugirard 75006 Ⓜ St-Sulpice ⓇⒺⓇLuxembourg
⏰Times vary depending on exhibitions; check website 🚫1 May & 25 Dec
🌐museeduluxembourg.fr

Orginally housed in the east wing of the Palais du Luxembourg, France's first public gallery moved to this building, the palace's grand former orangery, in 1886. The collection contained works by renowned artists such as Leonardo da Vinci, Van Dyck and Rembrandt, many of which have since been moved to the Louvre. Following extensive renovations, today the museum hosts impressive temporary exhibitions on leading artists, including Rubens, Cézanne and Pissaro.

10

Jardin du Luxembourg

📍H9 🏠Blvd St-Michel/ Rue de Vaugirard/Rue Guynemer 75006 Ⓜ Odéon
ⓇⒺⓇLuxembourg ⏰Dawn-dusk daily 🌐senat.fr/visite

A green oasis covering 25 ha (60 acres) in the heart of the Left Bank, the Jardin du Luxembourg is one of the most popular parks in Paris. The beautifully landscaped gardens are centred around the Palais du Luxembourg and feature an octagonal basin that is often surrounded by children sailing their wooden toy boats.

The Jardin du Luxembourg was created at the request of Marie de Médici, who had it designed as a fitting reminder of the Boboli Gardens at the Pitti Palace, in her home town of Florence. The original garden measured 8 ha (20 acres); what remains of it today are the large pond, the Fontaine Médicis and 2,000 elm trees.

↑ The stately Palais du Luxembourg in the gorgeous Jardin du Luxembourg

> **A green oasis covering 25 ha (60 acres) in the heart of the Left Bank, the Jardin du Luxembourg is one of the most popular parks in Paris.**

Statues were placed throughout the park in 1848. They include those of the queens of France, famous French women – Sainte Geneviève is an impressive example – and, later, famous writers and artists, too, totalling 106 statues.

The garden is a great space for children, with activities such as a puppet theatre starring the famous character Guignol, a fenced-in playground, a carousel and tennis courts. Adults can play chess or bridge, wander through the open-air photography exhibitions or grab a chair and enjoy a free concert.

Musée Zadkine

📍 H10 🏠 100 bis Rue d'Assas 75116 Ⓜ Notre-Dame-des-Champs 🕐 10am–6pm Tue–Sun ❌ Public hols 🌐 zadkine.paris.fr

The Russian-born sculptor Ossip Zadkine lived here from 1928 until his death in 1967.

The small house, studio and garden contain his works. Here he produced his great commemorative sculpture *Ville Détruite*, commissioned by Rotterdam after World War II, and two monuments to Vincent van Gogh. The museum's works span the development of Zadkine's style, from his Cubist beginnings to Expressionism and Abstractionism.

> ### FONTAINE MÉDICIS
>
> This Baroque fountain in the Jardin du Luxembourg, thought to have been designed by Salomon de Brosse, was built in 1624 in the style of an Italian grotto. It stands at the end of a long pond filled with goldfish. The mythological figures were added much later by Auguste Ottin (1866) and represent Polyphemus discovering the lovers Acis and Galatea.

A SHORT WALK
MONTPARNASSE

Distance 2.5 km (1.5 miles) **Nearest Metro** Gaîté
Time 25 minutes

Renowned for its mix of art and high living (Picasso, Hemingway, Matisse and Modigliani were frequent visitors), Montparnasse is a pleasant mixture of bars, cafés and art galleries. Take a couple of detours on this walk: first, go to the top of the Tour Montparnasse for sweeping views of the city; and second, pay your respects to Parisian icons at the Cimetière du Montparnasse.

Did You Know?

Artists Giacometti and Modigliani were students at the Académie de la Grande-Chaumière.

The Tour Montparnasse, one of Europe's tallest tower blocks, rests on 56 piles that extend 62 m (203 ft) below the surface (p284).

↑ Sculpture at the Cimetière du Montparnasse

Metro Edgar Quinet

The Cimetière du Montparnasse is the final resting place of several Parisian icons (p282).

The Théâtre Montparnasse at No 31 has fully restored original 1880s décor.

START

0 metres 100
0 yards 100
N ↑

BLVD DU

RUE DU DÉPART

RUE D'ODESSA

RUE DU MONTPARNASSE

RUE DE LA GAÎTÉ

BLVD EDGAR

↑ The Art Deco-style interior of the iconic La Coupole

The statue of Balzac by Auguste Rodin was erected in 1939, and stands 3 m (10 ft) tall.

La Coupole, a traditional brasserie-style café, with its large enclosed terrace, opened in 1927 and became a famous meeting place for artists and writers (p285).

Rue Bréa has a variety of shops, restaurants and hotels, all within a 90-m (300-ft) stretch.

The celebrated Académie de la Grande-Chaumière art school was founded at No 14 in 1904.

MONTPARNASSE

RUE BRÉA

RUE J. CHAPLAIN

RUE NOTRE DAME DES CHAMPS

RUE DE LA GDE CHAUMIÈRE

Ⓜ Metro Vavin

SQ DELAMBRE

RUE HUYGHENS

BLVD RASPAIL

RUE LÉOPOLD ROBERT

QUINET

Ⓜ FINISH

Metro Raspail

Must Sees

1 Bois de Boulogne
2 Château and Bois de Vincennes
3 The Palace and Gardens of Versailles
4 Disneyland® Paris

Experience More

5 La Défense
6 Musée Marmottan-Monet
7 Basilique-Cathédrale de St-Denis
8 Potager du Roi
9 Marché aux Puces de St-Ouen
10 Marché aux Puces de la Porte de Vanves

BEYOND THE CENTRE

The area beyond the Périphérique (ring road) once served as a country retreat for the aristocracy, with the medieval Château de Vincennes as the royal residence. It was usurped in the 17th century by Louis XIV's spectacular palace at Versailles, where the excessive displays of opulence were brought to a violent end during the Revolution of 1789. An industrial boom in the 19th century was followed by a number of large-scale construction projects in the 20th century, including blocks of social housing and the Périphérique. Today, the varied neighbourhoods of the suburbs are home to the vast majority of Paris's citizens.

BOIS DE BOULOGNE

🏠75016 Ⓜ Porte Maillot, Porte Dauphine, Porte d'Auteuil, Sablons ⏰24 hrs daily; gardens: 9:30am–dusk daily 🌐Jardin d'Acclimatation: jardindacclimatation.fr; Théâtre de Verdure du Jardin Shakespeare: jardinshakespeare.com; Fondation Louis Vuitton: fondationlouisvuitton.fr

Between the western edges of Paris and the Seine, this 865-ha (2,137-acre) park offers greenery for strolling and a boating lake, plus opportunities for horse-riding, picnicking or a day at the races. It is a favourite outdoor retreat with Parisians, especially on summer weekends.

The remains of a royal hunting ground, the many beautiful areas around the Bois include the Hippodrome de Longchamp racecourse, the Jardin d'Acclimatation amusement park and Roland Garros, home to the French Tennis Open championships. Hidden within its borders is the Théâtre de Verdure, an open-air playhouse that puts on Shakespeare, dance and musical performances in summer. The charming Bagatelle Gardens feature architectural follies and an 18th-century orangery famous for its rose garden. Opened in 2014, Frank Gehry's stunning Fondation Louis Vuitton is a cultural centre dedicated to modern art.

Did You Know?

The orangery was built in 64 days as a bet between the Comte d'Artois and Marie-Antoinette.

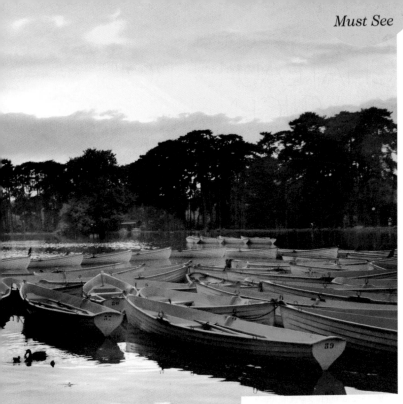

↑ Boats for hire on the Lac Inférieur, the largest of the two lakes in the park

EAT

Le Franck
A high-end restaurant within the Fondation Louis Vuitton.

🏠 8 Ave du Mahatma Gandhi, 75116
🕐 Tue & Sat-Sun lunch
🌐 restaurantlefrank.fr

€€€

 The "sails" of the Fondation Louis Vuitton are made of 3,600 glass panels.

② The Château de Bagatelle was built by Louis XVI's brother, the Comte d' Artois.

③ A statue of French tennis legend Henri Cochet stands outside Roland Garros.

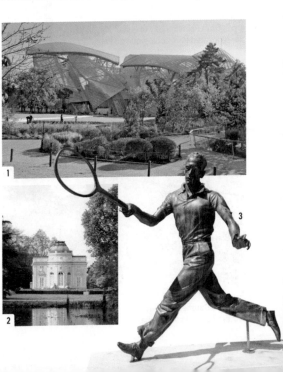

② 🛡 🎨 🍴 ☕ 🛍

CHÂTEAU ET BOIS DE VINCENNES

📍 Ave de Paris, Vincennes 94300 Ⓜ Château de Vincennes 🚉 Vincennes
🕐 Château: mid-May–mid-Sep: 10am–6pm daily (mid-Sep–mid-May: to 5pm daily); Bois de Vincennes: dawn to dusk daily ⊘ Public hols
🌐 chateau-de-vincennes.fr

Guarded by an imposing medieval keep, the sprawling Bois de Vincennes is a verdant wonderland. With boating lakes, formal gardens and numerous walking and cycling trails, it is the perfect playground in which to escape the city.

The Château de Vincennes was once a royal residence; it was here that Henry V of England died of dysentery in 1422. Abandoned when the Palace of Versailles was completed, the château was subsequently converted into an arsenal by Napoleon.

The 14th-century keep is the tallest in Europe and is a fine example of medieval military architecture. It houses the château's museum. The Gothic chapel features beautiful stone rose windows, while two 17th-century pavilions house a fascinating museum of army insignia.

Once a royal hunting ground, the Bois de Vincennes was given to the City of Paris by Napoleon III in 1860. Baron Haussmann's landscape architect added a number of ornamental lakes and cascades. Among the forest's main attractions is the largest funfair in France (open from Palm Sunday to end of May) and the renovated Parc Zoologique de Paris.

> Once a royal hunting ground, the Bois de Vincennes was given to the City of Paris by Napoleon III in 1860.

↑ The château, used as a prison from the 16th to the 19th centuries

↑ Lake Daumesnil, one of four artificial lakes in the park

EAT

Le Château des Vignerons
French dishes with an international twist.

📍 17 Rue des Vignerons, 94300 Vincennes
⊘ Sun 🌐 chateau desvignerons.com

€€€

Did You Know?

Henry V's corpse was boiled in the château's kitchen to prepare it for shipping back to England.

The Amazon-Guyana biozone at the Parc Zoologique de Paris ↑

③

THE PALACE AND GARDENS OF VERSAILLES

📍 Place d'Armes, 78000 Versailles 🚌 Versailles Express from Eiffel Tower 🚆 Versailles-Château-Rive-Gauche, Versailles Chantiers 🕐 Opening hours vary; check website for details 🚫 Mon, 1 Jan, 1 May, 25 Dec 🌐 chateauversailles.fr

This stunning royal residence is overwhelming in its scale and opulence. The spectacular, lavishly decorated palace and vast gardens, complete with fountains, landscaped topiary and even a model farm, make Versailles the top day trip from the centre of Paris.

The Palace

Starting in 1668 with his father's hunting lodge, Louis XIV built the largest palace in Europe, housing up to 20,000 people at a time. Architects Louis Le Vau and Jules Hardouin-Mansart designed the buildings, which grew as a series of "envelopes" around the lodge. The Opera House was added in 1770.

The sumptuous main apartments are on the first floor of the vast château complex. These were richly decorated by Charles Le Brun with coloured marbles, stone and wood carvings, murals, velvet, silver and gilded furniture. The climax is the Hall of Mirrors, where 357 great mirrors face 17 tall arched windows.

TOP 5 TOP FIVE PALACE ROOMS

Salon de Vénus
A statue of Louis XIV stands amid this room's rich marble décor.

Salon d'Apollon
Designed by Le Brun and dedicated to the god Apollo, this was Louis XIV's throne room.

Salon de la Guerre
The room's theme of war is dramatically reinforced by the stuccoed relief of Louis XIV riding to victory.

Hall of Mirrors
This glittering room stretches 73 m (240 ft) along the west façade.

Queen's Bedroom
In this room, the queens of France gave birth to the royal children in full public view.

The palace and gardens of Versailles, the epitome of royal grandeur ↓

① The Marble Courtyard is decorated with marble paving, urns, busts and a gilded balcony.

② Mansart's last great work, the two-storey Baroque Chapelle Royale was Louis XIV's final addition to Versailles.

③ The South Wing's original apartments for great nobles were replaced by Louis-Philippe's museum of French history.

The formal gardens, complete with geometric paths and shrubberies →

The Gardens

The grounds of Versailles are no less impressive than the palace. Designed by the great landscaper André Le Nôtre, the formal gardens are a masterpiece: sculptural fountains and secluded groves sit amid geometric flower beds and hedges. The 1.7-km- (1-mile-) long Grand Canal leads from the gardens to the enormous park, which features wooded areas and agricultural fields delineated by a network of footpaths. The grounds also encompass the Grand Trianon and Petit Trianon palaces, built as private apartments for Louis XIV and Louis V, as well as the Queen's Hamlet – a life-size model village built for Marie-Antoinette that was also a functioning farm.

The formal gardens are a masterpiece: sculptural fountains and secluded groves sit amid geometric flower beds and hedges.

↑ The Grand Trianon, built by Louis XIV in 1687 to escape the rigours of court life

EAT

Ore
This Alain Ducasse dining experience in the Pavillon Dufour is as luxurious as the château it occupies.

🄰 Château de Versailles, 78000 Versailles
🅆 ducasse-chateauversailles.com

€€€

Angelina
The iconic tea house has two outposts in Versailles – one in the Pavillon d'Orléans and one at the Petit Trianon – both serving a selection of snacks and delectable pastries.

🄰 Château de Versailles, 78000 Versailles
🅆 angelina-paris.fr

€€€

Did You Know?

One-third of the estate's budget went to the fountains. Today they only go on during the summer months.

1 The cottages in the Queen's Hamlet were inspired by rural French architecture. Although rustic on the exterior, inside they were richly furnished.

2 During the Grands Eaux Nocturnes in the summer, the gardens of Versailles come alive with superb illuminations and installations.

3 Built in 1762 as a retreat for Louis XV, the Petit Trianon became a favourite of Marie-Antoinette.

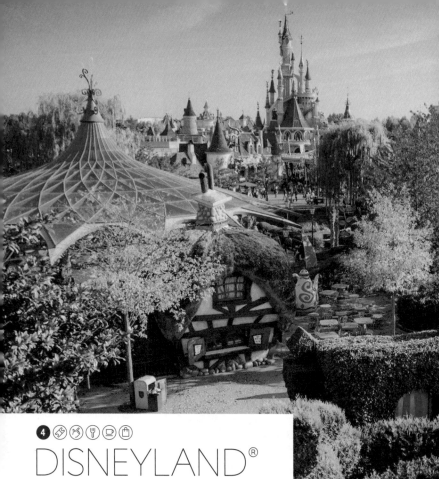

④ 🎟️ Ⓜ️ 🍴 🛒 🎁

DISNEYLAND® PARIS

🏠 Marne-la-Vallée 77777 🚌 Disneyland® Paris Express from Gare du Nord, Opéra and Châtelet 🚇 Marne-la-Vallée/Chessy ⏰ Disneyland® Park: 10am–11pm in high season (closes earlier in low season); Walt Disney Studios® Park: 10am–9pm in high season (closes earlier in low season) 🌐 disneylandparis.com

Unbeatable for complete escapism, combined with vibrant excitement and sheer energy, Disneyland® Paris offers extreme rides, gentle experiences and phenomenal visual effects.

The resort is built on a massive scale – the 2,230-ha (5,510-acre) site encompasses two theme parks; seven hotels; a shopping, dining and entertainment village; an ice-skating rink; a lake; two convention centres; and a golf course. The theme parks are split into Disneyland® Park and the Walt Disney Studios® Park. The former, with more than 60 rides and attractions, celebrates Hollywood folklore and fantasies, while the latter highlights the ingenuity involved in cinema, animation and television production with interactive exhibits and live shows.

DISNEY VILLAGE

The fun does not have to end when the two parks close. Disney Village offers a host of evening entertainment options – including a cinema, concerts and Buffalo Bill's Wild West Show – as well as numerous restaurants and shops. Seasonal events take place all year, including celebrations for Easter, Halloween and New Year.

Did You Know?

Sleeping Beauty's castle was designed to contrast with the grey Parisian skies.

↑ The view from Alice's Curious Labyrinth in Disneyland® Park

1 The entrance to Crush's Coaster® in Walt Disney Studios® Park.

2 The Mad Hatter's Tea Cups in Disneyland® Park's Fantasyland®.

3 The parade in Disneyland® Park features characters from films such as *Toy Story*.

DISNEYLAND® PARK

Disneyland® Park is comprised of five areas. Main Street represents a fantasy small-town America, its Victorian façades fronting interesting stores and food outlets. Frontierland®, a homage to America's Wild West, hosts some of the park's most popular attractions, while wild rides and Audio-Animatronics are the draw at Adventureland®. The buildings in Fantasyland® are modelled on those in animated movies, and contain many attractions for younger children. Science fiction and the future are the themes at Discoveryland®, home to the popular multi-loop ride Star Wars Hyperspace Mountain.

←

The park, home to rides such as Indiana Jones™ and the Temple of Peril (below)

TOP 3 RIDES IN DISNEYLAND® PARK

Star Wars Hyperspace Mountain
Formerly known as Space Mountain®, this iconic rollercoaster draws crowds from the outset but at the end of the day you can often walk straight on.

Big Thunder Mountain
This wild rollercoaster ride on a speeding runaway mine train is a crowd favourite.

Pirates of the Caribbean
This boat ride takes you on a thrilling journey through underground prisons and past fighting galleons.

The entrance to Walt
Disney Studios® Park,
with the Earful Tower ↑

↑ The four-wheeled
Cars Quatre Roues
Rallye attraction

↑ The underwater
animated world of
Crush's Coaster®

WALT DISNEY STUDIOS® PARK

The four production zones at Walt Disney Studios® Park reveal the secrets of movie-making. Inside the giant studio gates on the Front Lot, Disney Studio 1 houses a film set boulevard, complete with stylized street façades and venues such as the 1930s-style Club Swankedero. Toon Studio® contains rides and exhibits inspired by various iconic Disney and Pixar characters, and includes La Place de Rémy, home to the 4D experience Ratatouille: A Recipe for Adventure. The Production Courtyard® offers the chance to see behind the scenes on the Studio Tram Tour®, among other attractions; while the Backlot focuses on special effects, film music recording and dare-devil stunts.

→ Mickey Mouse casting
his magic over the
Toon Studio® zone

EXPERIENCE MORE

5

La Défense

🏠 1 Parvis de la Défense
Ⓜ/RER La Défense ☉ La
Grande Arche: 10am–7pm
daily 🌐 grandearche.com

This skyscraper business
district on the western edge
of Paris is one of Europe's
largest modern office
developments and covers
80 ha (198 acres). It was
launched in 1958 to create
a new home for leading
French and multinational
companies. Since then, a
major artistic scheme has
transformed several of the
squares into fascinating
open-air museums.

In 1989, one of Paris's most
striking landmarks, La Grande
Arche, was added to the
complex – an enormous
hollow cube large enough to
contain Notre-Dame cath-
edral. This was designed by
Danish architect Otto von
Spreckelsen as part of major
construction works, or *Grands*

Travaux, which were initiated
by (and are now a memorial
to) the late President François
Mitterrand. You can take a lift
to the top of the arch for some
great views. There's also a
restaurant and an exhibition
space for photojournalism.

6

Musée Marmottan-
Monet

🏠 2 Rue Louis Boilly 75016
Ⓜ Muette ☉ 10am–6pm
Tue–Sun (to 9pm Thu)
🚫 1 Jan, 1 May, 25 Dec
🌐 marmottan.fr

In 1932, art historian Paul
Marmottan bequeathed his
19th-century mansion and
his Renaissance, Consular
and First Empire collections
of paintings and furniture to
the Institut de France, and a
museum was established. The
focus of the museum changed
in 1934 after the bequest by

↑ Claude Monet's
glasses, Musée
Marmottan-Monet

Michel Monet of 65 paintings
by his father, Claude Monet.
Some of Monet's most famous
paintings are here, among
them *Impression – Sunrise*, a
beautiful canvas from the
Rouen Cathedral series, and
several *Water Lilies*.

In addition, part of Monet's
personal art collection passed
to the museum, including
paintings by Camille
Pissarro and works by the
Impressionists Pierre Auguste
Renoir and Alfred Sisley.
The museum also displays
some exquisite medieval
illuminated manuscripts.

↓ Shiny modern office
blocks at La Défense
business district

Tombs within the Basilique-Cathédrale de St-Denis

7

Basilique-Cathédrale de St-Denis

📍 1 Rue de la Légion a'Honneur, 93200 St-Denis Ⓜ St-Denis-Basilique 🚉 St-Denis ⏱ Apr–Sep: 10am–6:15pm Mon–Sat, noon–6:15pm Sun; Oct–Mar: 10am–5:15pm Mon–Sat, noon–5:15pm Sun 🚫 1 Jan, 1 May, 25 Dec 🌐 saint-denis-basilique.fr

Constructed between 1137 and 1281, the cathedral is on the site of the tomb of St Denis, the first bishop of Paris, who was beheaded in 250. The building was the original influence for Gothic art. From Merovingian times, it was a burial place for rulers of France. During the Revolution, many tombs were desecrated and scattered, but the best were stored, and now represent a collection of funerary art. Memorials include those of Dagobert, Henri II and Catherine de Medici, and Louis XVI and Marie-Antoinette.

8

Potager du Roi

📍 10 Rue du Maréchal-Joffre, 78000 Versailles ⏱ 10am–6pm Tue–Fri (plus Sat & Sun Apr–Oct) 🚉 Versailles-Château-Rive Gauche 🌐 potager-du-roi.fr

When Louis XIV built Versailles, he decided that it would be prudent for a king to have his own vegetable garden (poisoning was a constant threat in the château). Jean-Baptiste de La Quintinie developed the *potager* – vegetable patch – for Louis in 1678. At first, the swampy ground proved difficult to master, but eventually La Quintinie was producing all sorts of fruits and vegetables for the king, including summer produce in the winter. The garden continued to function in several capacities after the Revolution, becoming a centre for education and horticultural schools. In 1991, the Potager du Roi opened up to the public for visits. There is a shop selling seasonal produce pulled from the garden.

9

Marché aux Puces de St-Ouen

📍 Rue des Rosiers, 75018 St-Ouen Ⓜ Porte-de-Clignancourt, Garibaldi ⏱ 10am–5:30pm Sat–Sun, 11am–5pm Mon; reduced hours during summer 🌐 marcheauxpuces-saintouen.com

This is the oldest, most expensive and largest of the Paris flea markets, covering 6 ha (15 acres). In the 19th century, rag merchants and tramps would gather outside the city limits and offer their wares for sale. By the 1920s, there was a proper market here, where masterpieces could sometimes be purchased cheaply from the often uninformed sellers. Today, it is divided into specialist markets. Known especially for its profusion of furniture and ornaments from the Second Empire (1852–70), few bargains are to be found these days, yet some 150,000 people still flock here to browse among more than 2,000 stalls.

10

Marché aux Puces de la Porte de Vanves

📍 4 Ave Georges Lafenestre 75014 Ⓜ Porte de Vanves ⏱ 7am–7:30pm Sat & Sun 🌐 pucesdevanves.typepad.com

Every Saturday and Sunday, bargain-hunters descend on this lively outdoor flea market. Visitors can pick through a wide selection of glassware, furniture, artworks, and a seemingly endless variety of odds and ends. There are always surprises. In 1989, the very first portrait ever taken by Louis Daguerre sold here at this market for the equivalent of €500, a modest sum for such a monumental piece of photographic history. There are real finds to be had if you look hard enough – go early to beat the crowds and prepare to spend a few hours browsing.

Did You Know?

Less than a quarter of Paris's 10.5 million inhabitants live within the 20 arrondissements.

NEED TO KNOW

The Metro whizzing across the Pont de Bir Hakeim

BEFORE
YOU GO

Forward planning is essential to any successful trip. Be prepared for all eventualities by considering the following points before you travel.

AT A GLANCE

CURRENCY
Euro (EUR)

AVERAGE DAILY SPEND

SAVE
€60

SPEND
€165

SPLURGE
€300+

BOTTLED WATER
€1

COFFEE
€2.50

BEER
€5

DINNER FOR TWO
€60

ESSENTIAL PHRASES

Hello	Bonjour
Goodbye	Au revoir
Please	S'il vous plaît
Thank you	Merci
Do you speak English	Parlez-vous anglais?
I don't understand…	Je ne comprends pas

ELECTRICITY SUPPLY

Power sockets are type C and E, fitting two-pronged plugs. Standard voltage is 230 volts.

Passports and Visas

For a stay of up to three months for the purpose of tourism, EU nationals and citizens of the US, Canada, Australia and New Zealand do not need a visa. For visa information specific to your home country, consult your nearest French embassy or check online.
France-Visas
W france-visas.gouv.fr

Travel Safety Advice

Visitors can get up-to-date travel safety information from the **UK Foreign and Commonwealth Office**, the **US State Department**, and the **Australian Department of Foreign Affairs and Trade**.
AUS
W smartraveller.gov.au
UK
W gov.uk/foreign-travel-advice
US
W travel.state.gov

Customs Information

An individual is permitted to carry the following within the EU for personal use:
Tobacco products 800 cigarettes, 400 cigarillos, 200 cigars or 1 kg of smoking tobacco.
Alcohol 10 litres of alcoholic beverages above 22% strength, 20 litres of alcoholic beverages below 22% strength, 90 litres of wine (60 litres of which can be sparkling wine) and 110 litres of beer.
Cash If you plan to enter or leave the EU with €10,000 or more in cash (or the equivalent in other currencies), you must declare it to the customs authorities.
If travelling outside the EU limits vary, so always check restrictions before departing.

Insurance

It is wise to take out an insurance policy covering theft, loss of belongings, medical problems, cancellation and delays.

To receive discounted or free emergency medical care in France, EU citizens should ensure they have an **EHIC** (European Health Insurance Card).

Visitors from outside the EU must arrange their own private medical insurance.

EHIC

🆆 europa.eu/youreurope/citizens/health/unplanned-healthcare/temporary-stays

Vaccinations

No inoculations are needed for France.

Money

Most establishments accept major credit, debit and prepaid currency cards, but it's always a good idea to carry some cash too. Contactless payments are widely accepted in Paris.

Booking Accommodation

Paris offers a huge variety of accommodation, including luxury five-star hotels, family-run B&Bs, budget hostels and private apartments.

The city is busiest during Christmas, New Year and France's school breaks. Tourists pour in from May to September, but Parisians pour out en masse in August.

Travellers with Specific Needs

Paris's historic buildings and cobbled streets can make the city tricky to navigate. However, there are a number of organizations working to improve accesibility in France's capital.

The **Office du Tourisme et des Congrès** has a useful guide that lists easily accessible sights and routes for visitors with mobility issues, while **Jaccede** has details of accessible museums, hotels, bars, restaurants and cinemas in Paris and other French cities.

The **Vianavigo** website provides detailed information on accessible public transport, including a route planner that can be tailored to your specific needs, and SNCF's **Accès Plus** website is a useful source of information regarding accessible train travel.

Les Compagnons du Voyage will provide an escort for persons with limited mobility or visibility on public transport, for a small fee. For further information, contact the **GIHP**.

Accès Plus
🆆 accessibilite.sncf.com
GIHP
🆆 gihpnational.org
Jaccede
🆆 jaccede.com
Les Compagnons du Voyage
🆆 compagnons.com
Office du Tourisme et des Congrès
🆆 parisinfo.com
Vianavigo
🆆 vianavigo.com

Language

The French are fiercely proud of their language, but don't let this put you off. Mastering a few niceties goes a long way though you can get by without knowing the language at all.

Closures

Lunchtime Some shops and businesses close for an hour or two from around noon.
Mondays Some museums, small shops, restaurants and bars are closed for the day.
Tuesdays National museums are closed for the day, except Versailles and the Musée d'Orsay, which are closed on Monday.
Sundays Most shops are closed.
Public holidays Public services, shops, museums and attractions are usually closed.

PUBLIC HOLIDAYS 2020

1 Jan	New Year's Day
13 Apr	Easter Monday
1 May	Labour Day
8 May	Victory 1945
21 May	Ascension Day
1 Jun	Whit Monday
14 Jul	Bastille Day
15 Aug	Assumption Day
1 Nov	All Saints' Day
11 Nov	Armistice 1918
25 Dec	Christmas Day

GETTING AROUND

Paris has an efficient public transport system that will allow you to navigate the city's many sights with ease.

AT A GLANCE

PUBLIC TRANSPORT COSTS

Tickets are valid on all forms of public transport.

SINGLE
€1.90
(zones 1-3)

DAY TICKET
€13.20
(zones 1-3)

3-DAY TICKET
€29.40
(zones 1-3)

SPEED LIMIT

MOTORWAY
130 km/h (80 mph)

MAJOR ROADS
80 km/h (49 mph)

RING ROADS
70 km/h (43 mph)

URBAN AREAS
50 km/h (30 mph)

Arriving by Air

Paris has two major airports, Charles de Gaulle (also known as Roissy) and Orly, and one secondary airport, Beauvais, which serves mainly budget airlines. All three are well connected to the city centre by train, bus and taxi. Car rental facilities are also available, although driving in Paris is not recommended. For information on journey times and ticket prices between Paris's airports and the city centre, see the table opposite.

Airport Shuttle provides a door-to-door transfer service between all three airports and individual hotels. It costs €70 for one person, or €21–5 each for two or more people. Book at least 48 hours ahead, then call them after landing to confirm your journey.

The **RATP Roissybus** operates regular services from Charles de Gaulle, and RER trains (Line B) leave regularly every 5–15 minutes, calling at Gare du Nord, Châtelet-Les-Halles and several other major stations. **Le Bus Direct** runs a reliable service from both Charles de Gaulle and Orly.

A shuttle bus operates between Beauvais and Porte-Maillot. Trains run from Beauvais station to Gare du Nord, but the station is a 15-minute taxi ride from the airport, and the train journey into Paris takes at least 1 hour 15 minutes.

Airport Shuttle
W airportsshuttles.com
Le Bus Direct
W lebusdirect.com
RATP Roissybus
W ratp.fr/en/titres-et-tarifs/airport-tickets

Train Travel

International Train Travel

Regular high-speed trains connect Paris's six international railway stations to numerous major cities across Europe. Reservations for these services are essential, as seats get booked up quickly, particularly during peak times.

You can buy tickets and passes for multiple international journeys from **Eurail** or **Interrail**; however, you may need to pay an additional

GETTING TO AND FROM THE AIRPORT

Airport	Transport	Journey Time	Price
Charles de Gaulle	Le Bus Direct Line 2	45–70 mins	€18
	Le Bus Direct Line 4	1 hr 20 mins	€18
	RATP Roissybus	1 hr 10 mins	€12.50
	RER	25–30 mins	€10.30
	Taxi	25–45 mins	from €45
Orly	Le Bus Direct	20–60 mins	€12
	GOC	30 mins	€35
	RATP Orlybus	25–30 mins	€8.30
	Orlyval/RER	30–40 mins	€13.25
	Tram Line T7	30 mins	€1.90
	Taxi	25–45 mins	from €25
Beauvais	Shuttle bus	1 hr 15 mins	€17
	Taxi	1 hr – 1 hr 30 mins	from €100

reservation fee. Always check carefully before boarding that your pass is valid on the service you wish to use.

Eurostar runs a fast, regular service from London to central Paris via the Channel Tunnel.

Students and those under 26 can benefit from discounted rail travel both to and within France. For more information on discounted travel, visit the **Eurail** or **Interrail** website.

Thalys runs a high-speed service between Paris, Brussels and Amsterdam ten times a day, with a variety of special offers, package deals and half-price last-minute deals.

Eurail
w eurail.com
Eurostar
w eurostar.com
Interrail
w interrail.eu
Thalys
w thalys.com

Domestic Train Travel

Paris has a number of main train stations situated at various points across the city, all of which serve different regions.

The French state railway, **OUI SNCF**, has two services in Paris: the Banlieue suburban service and the Grandes Lignes, or long-distance service. The suburban services all operate within the five-zone network. The long-distance

services operate throughout France. The TGV offers a reliable high-speed service which should be booked in advance.

Before boarding a train, remember to time-punch (*composter*) tickets to validate your journey; this does not apply for e-tickets. Tickets for city transport cannot be used on Banlieue trains, with the exception of some RER tickets to stations with both SNCF and RER lines.
OUI SNCF
w oui.sncf.com

PARIS'S MAIN STATIONS

Station	Destinations Served
Gare de Lyon	Southern France, the Alps, Italy and Switzerland
Gare de l'Est	Eastern France, Austria, Switzerland and Germany.
Gare du Nord	Northeast France, Britain and Northern Europe
Gare St-Lazare	Channel ports and Normandy
Gare d'Austerlitz	Southwest France, Brittany ports and Spain
Gare Montparnasse	Brittany ports and Spain

Public Transport

The Metro, RER, buses and trams are all run by **RATP** (Régie Autonome des Transports Parisiens).
RATP
🔲 ratp.fr

Tickets

The Paris metropolitan area is divided into five ticket zones. Central Paris is zone 1, Charles de Gaulle airport is in zone 5, Orly airport and Versailles in zone 4. The Metro serves zones 1–3.

Ordinary Metro and RER tickets (called t+) can be bought either individually or as a group of ten. These tickets are also valid on trams and buses and can be used for transfers within 1 hour 30 minutes of first use.

Bus-only tickets can be purchased on board from the driver. All bus tickets must be validated using the machine on the bus. Anyone travelling without a valid ticket may be fined.

Visitors can enjoy unlimited travel on the Metro, RER and Paris buses with a Paris Visite pass or a one-day Mobilis card, both valid for travel on most forms of public transport, and both available from RATP. There is also the **Passe Navigo Découverte**, a prepaid contactless smart card that costs €5.
Passe Navigo Découverte
🔲 navigo.fr

Metro and RER

The Paris Metro has 14 main lines and two minor lines. The RER is a system of five lines of commuter trains that travel underground in central Paris and above ground in outlying areas. The two systems overlap in the city centre. RER trips outside the centre require special tickets; fares to suburbs and nearby towns vary.

Buses and Trams

Most buses must be flagged down at designated stops. A single bus ticket entitles the bearer to a single journey on one line only. If you want to make a change, you'll need another ticket. (Exceptions to this rule are the Balabus, Noctambus, Orlybus and Roissybus services, and lines 221, 297, 299, 350 and 351.)

There are 48 night bus lines, called Noctilien, serving Paris and its suburbs. The terminus for most lines is Châtelet.

There are seven RATP tramways operating in Paris – T1 (Gare de St-Denis–Noisy le Sec), T2 (La Défense–Porte de Versailles), T3 (Pont du Garigliano–Porte d'Ivry), T5 (Marché de Saint-Denis–Garges-Sarcelles), T6 (Châtillon-Montrouge–Vélizy-Villacoublay), T7 (Villejuif-Louis Aragon–Athis-Mons) and T8 (Saint-Denis-Porte de Paris–Épinay-Orgemont). The T4 (Aulnay-sous-Bois–Bondy) is run by SNCF and is a tram-train line.

Long-Distance Bus Travel

The main coach operator to Paris is **Eurolines**, based at the Gare Routière Internationale. Its coaches travel from Belgium, the Netherlands, Ireland, Germany, Scandinavia, the UK, Italy and Portugal. Low-cost alternatives are **Ouibus**, **Flixbus** and **Isilines**, all of which which connect Paris to other towns in France and to London, Brussels, Amsterdam, Milan and Barcelona.
Eurolines
🔲 eurolines.eu
Flixbus
🔲 flixbus.com
Isilines
🔲 isilines.fr
Ouibus
🔲 ouibus.com

Taxis

Taxis can be hailed in the street unless there is a taxi rank nearby. The meter will show an initial starting charge (around €2.50). If you order a taxi, the meter will show the charge from where the driver started their journey to collect you.

Vélo taxis are motorized tricycle rickshaws that offer a green alternative to traditional taxis. Taxi apps such as Uber and Taxify also operate in Paris. The following services can be booked by phone or online:
Citybird
🔲 city-bird.com
Taxis G7
🔲 taxisg7.com

Driving

Driving in Paris is not recommended. Traffic is often heavy, there are many one-way streets and parking is notoriously difficult, not to mention expensive.

Driving to Paris

Autoroutes (motorways) converge on Paris from all directions. For those travelling from Britain to Paris by road, the simplest way is to use the Eurotunnel trains that run between the terminals at Folkestone and Calais, which both have direct motorway access.

Paris is surrounded by an outer ring road called the Boulevard Périphérique. All motorways leading to the capital link in to the Périphérique, which separates the city from the suburbs. Each former city gate, called a *porte*, now corresponds to an exit onto or from the Périphérique. Arriving motorists should take time to check their destination address and consult a map of central Paris to find the closest corresponding *porte*.

To take your own car into France, you will need to carry proof of registration, valid insurance documents, a full and valid driving licence, and passport at all times.

Car Rental

To rent a car in France you must be 21 or over and have held a valid driver's licence for at least a year. You will also need to present a credit card to secure the rental deposit.

Driving licences issued by any European Union member state are valid throughout the EU. International driving licences are not needed for short-term visitors (up to 90 days) from North America, Australia and New Zealand. Visitors from other countries should check the regulations with their local automobile association before they travel.

Moov'in.Paris is a self-service electric car rental service that operates throughout Paris and the Paris region. You can pick up a car from one parking station, make your journey and park at any other station in the region. The service is open to everyone 18 years old or over who holds a valid driving licence.

Moov'in.Paris
w moovin.paris

Driving in Paris

Paris is a limited traffic zone and it is compulsory for all vehicles to display a Crit'Air sticker with a number ranging from 1 to 5, which denotes the level of pollution in ascending order. In the event of high pollution levels, vehicles with certain stickers may be banned from the road. The stickers can be purchased from the **Air Quality Certificate Service**.

Park in areas with a large "P" or *payant* sign on the pavement or road, and pay at the parking meter with *La Paris Carte* (available from any kiosk), a credit or debit card, or using the **PaybyPhone** app *(p315)*.

Paris has numerous underground car parks, signposted by a white "P" on a blue background.

Air Quality Certificate Service
w certificat-air.gouv.fr

Rules of the Road

Always drive on the right. Unless otherwise signposted, vehicles coming from the right have right of way. Cars on a roundabout usually have right of way, although the Arc de Triomphe is a hair-raising exception as cars give way to traffic on the right.

At all times, drivers must carry a valid driver's licence, registration and insurance documents. The wearing of seat belts is compulsory, and it is prohibited to sound your horn in the city. For motorbikes and scooters, the wearing of helmets and protective gloves is compulsory. In the city centre, it is against the law to use the bus lanes at any time of day. France strictly enforces its drink-drive limit *(p315)*.

Cycling

Paris is reasonably flat, manageably small and has many backstreets where traffic is restricted. For details of the city's cycle lanes, download the free **Paris à Vélo** map.

Paris à Vélo
w paris.fr/velo

Bicycle Hire

The **Vélib'** shared bicycle scheme is available 24 hours a day. For regular bikes, the first half-hour is €1, increasing by €1 for every additional half-hour; for electric bikes the first half-hour is €2, increasing by €2 for every additional half-hour. A one- or seven-day card is also available online.

Vélib'
w velib-metropole.fr

Bicycle Tours

Fat Tire Tours offer trips to Paris's most famous landmarks. **Paris à Vélo C'est Sympa!** runs multilingual tours to more offbeat locations.

Fat Tire Tours
w fattiretours.com
Paris à Vélo C'est Sympa!
w parisvelosympa.fr

Boats and Ferries

Arriving by Sea

The following companies run passenger and vehicle ferry services from the UK:

P&O Ferries runs services from Dover to Calais, **Condor Ferries** operates between Poole and St-Malo and **DFDS Seaways** runs routes from Newhaven to Dieppe and from Dover to Dunkirk. **Brittany Ferries** makes crossings from Plymouth to Roscoff, from Poole and Portsmouth to Cherbourg, and from Portsmouth to Le Havre and Caen. They also run an over-night service from Portsmouth to St-Malo.

Driving to Paris from Cherbourg takes about four hours; from Dieppe or Le Havre, about two and a half hours; and from Calais, two hours.

Brittany Ferries
w brittany-ferries.co.uk
Condor Ferries
w condorferries.co.uk
DFDS Seaways
w dfdsseaways.co.uk
P&O Ferries
w poferries.com/en/portal

Paris by Boat

Paris's river-boat shuttle, the **Batobus**, runs every 20–45 minutes, with more frequent services in spring and summer. Tickets can be bought at Batobus stops, RATP and tourist offices.

Batobus
w www.batobus.com

PRACTICAL
INFORMATION

A little local know-how goes a long way in Paris. Here you will find all the essential advice and information you will need during your stay.

AT A GLANCE

EMERGENCY NUMBERS

GENERAL EMERGENCY	FIRE SERVICE AND AMBULANCE
112	**18**

POLICE	MEDICAL EMERGENCY
17	**15**

TIME ZONE
CET/CEST
Central European Summer Time (CEST) runs 29 Mar–25 Oct 2020

TAP WATER
Unless stated otherwise, tap water in France is safe to drink.

TIPPING

Waiter	5–10%
Hotel Porter	€1 a bag
Housekeeping	€1 a day
Concierge	€1–2
Taxi Driver	Round up fare

Personal Security

Paris is generally a safe city and most visits are trouble-free. However, beware of pickpockets on the Metro and on buses during the rush hour and in major tourist areas.

If you have anything stolen, report the crime as soon as possible to the nearest police station, and bring ID with you. Get a copy of the crime report in order to claim on your insurance.

When travelling late at night, avoid long transfers in Metro stations such as Châtelet-Les-Halles and Montparnasse. The last RER trains to and from outlying areas should also be avoided.

Contact your embassy if you have your passport stolen, or in the event of a serious crime or accident.

Health

If you fall sick during your visit, pharmacists are an excellent source of advice – they can diagnose many minor ailments and suggest appropriate treatment.

For English-speaking visitors, there are two private hospitals with bilingual staff and doctors: the **American Hospital of Paris** and the **Franco-Britannique Hospital**. The **Centre Médical Europe** is an inexpensive private clinic, which also has a dental practice.

All EU nationals holding a European Health Insurance Card (EHIC) are entitled to use the French national health service (p309). Patients must pay for treatment and can then reclaim most of the cost from the health authorities. The process may be lengthy – travellers should consider purchasing private travel insurance.

For visitors from outside the EU, payment of hospital and other medical expenses is the patient's responsibility. It is therefore important to arrange comprehensive medical insurance before travelling.

American Hospital of Paris
W american-hospital.org
Centre Médical Europe
W centre-medical-europe.fr
Franco-Britannique Hospital
W ihfb.org

Smoking, Alcohol and Drugs

Smoking is prohibited in all public places, but is allowed on restaurant, café and pub terraces, as long as they are not enclosed.

The possession of narcotics is prohibited and could result in a prison sentence.

Unless stated otherwise, alcohol consumption on the streets is permitted. France has a strict limit of 0.05 per cent BAC (blood alcohol content) for drivers.

ID

There is no requirement for visitors to carry ID, but in the event of a routine check you may be asked to show your passport. If you don't have it with you, the police may escort you to wherever your passport is being kept.

Local Customs

Etiquette *(la politesse)* is important to Parisians. On entering a store or café, you are expected to say *"bonjour"* to staff, and when leaving to say *"au revoir"*. Be sure to add *"s'il vous plaît"* (please) when ordering something and *"pardon"* if you accidentally bump into someone.

The French usually shake hands on meeting someone for the first time. Friends and colleagues who know each other well greet each other with a kiss on each cheek. If you are unsure what's expected, wait to see if they proffer a hand or a cheek.

Visiting Churches and Cathedrals

Dress respectfully. Cover your torso and upper arms; ensure shorts and skirts cover your knees.

Mobile Phones and Wi-Fi

Free Wi-Fi hotspots are widely available in public spaces. Cafés and restaurants usually permit the use of their Wi-Fi on the condition that you make a purchase.

Visitors travelling to Paris with EU tariffs will be able to use their devices abroad without being affected by data roaming charges. Users will be charged the same rates for data, SMS and voice calls as they would pay at home.

Post

Stamps *(timbres)* can be bought at post offices and *tabacs*. Most post offices have self-service machines to weigh and frank your mail.

Taxes and Refunds

VAT is around 20% in France. Non-EU residents can claim back tax on certain goods. Look out for the Global Refund Tax-Free sign, where the retailer will supply a form and issue a *détaxe* receipt. Present the goods receipt, *détaxe* receipt and passport at customs when you depart to receive your refund.

Discount Cards

Entry to some national and municipal museums is free on the first Sunday of each month.

Visitors under 18 years of age and EU passport holders aged 18–26 years are usually admitted free of charge to national museums, and there are sometimes discounts for students and over-60s who have ID showing their date of birth.

The **Paris Pass** offers access to over 60 attractions for 2, 4 or 6 days. It also offers unlimited travel on the Metro, buses and RER within central Paris, and a ticket for a hop-on hop-off bus tour. It is worth carefully considering how many of the offers and discounts you are likely to take advantage of before purchasing.
Paris Pass
W parispass.com

WEBSITES AND APPS

en.parisinfo.com
    The official tourist board website.
Le Fooding
    No matter where you are in the city, find the nearest recommended restaurant in an instant.
PaybyPhone
    Pay for on-street parking quickly and easily with this app.
RATP
    The official app from RATP, the city's public transport operator.

INDEX

PHRASE BOOK

IN AN EMERGENCY

Help!	Au secours!	oh sekoor
Stop!	Arrêtez!	aret-ay
Call a doctor!	Appelez un médecin!	apuh-lay uñ medsañ
Call an ambulance!	Appelez une ambulance!	apuh-lay oon oñboo-loñs
Call the police!	Appelez la police!	apuh-lay lah poh-lees
Call the fire brigade!	Appelez les pompiers!	apuh-lay leh poñ-peeyay
Where is the nearest telephone?	Où est le téléphone le plus proche?	oo ay luh tehlehfon luh ploo prosh
Where is the nearest hospital?	Où est l'hôpital le plus proche?	oo ay l'opeetal luh ploo prosh

COMMUNICATION ESSENTIALS

Yes	Oui	wee
No	Non	noñ
Please	S'il vous plaît	seel voo play
Thank you	Merci	mer-see
Excuse me	Excusez-moi	exkoo-zay mwah
Hello	Bonjour	boñzhoor
Goodbye	Au revoir	oh ruh-vwar
Good night	Bonsoir	boñ-swar
Morning	Le matin	matañ
Afternoon	L'après-midi	l'apreh-meedee
Evening	Le soir	swar
Yesterday	Hier	eeyehr
Today	Aujourd'hui	oh-zhoor-dwee
Tomorrow	Demain	duhmañ
Here	Ici	ee-see
There	Là	lah
What?	Quoi, quel, quelle?	kwah, kel, kel
When?	Quand?	koñ
Why?	Pourquoi?	poor-kwah
Where?	Où?	oo

USEFUL PHRASES

How are you?	Comment allez-vous?	kom-moñ talay voo
Very well, thank you.	Très bien, merci.	treh byañ, mer-see
Pleased to meet you.	Enchanté de faire votre connaissance.	oñshoñ-tay duh fehr votr kon-ay-sans
See you soon.	A bientôt.	byañ-toh
That's fine	C'est bon	say bon
Where is/are...?	Où est/sont...?	ooay/soñ
How far is it to...?	Combien de kilometres d'ici à...?	kom-byañ duh keelo-metr d'ee-see ah
Which way to...?	Quelle est la direction pour...?	kel ay lah deer-ek-syoñ poor
Do you speak English?	Parlez-vous anglais?	par-lay voo oñg-lay
I don't understand.	Je ne comprends pas.	zhuh nuh kom-proñ pah
Could you speak slowly please?	Pouvez-vous parler moins vite s'il vous plaît?	poo-vay voo par-lay mwañ veet seel voo play
I'm sorry.	Excusez-moi.	exkoo-zay mwah

USEFUL WORDS

big	grand	groñ
small	petit	puh-tee
hot	chaud	show
cold	froid	frwah
good	bon/bien	boñ/byañ
bad	mauvais	moh-veh
enough	assez	assay
well	bien	byañ
open	ouvert	oo-ver
closed	fermé	fer-meh
left	gauche	gohsh
right	droite	drwaht
straight on	tout droite	too drwaht
near	près	preh
far	loin	lwañ
up	en haut	oñ oh
down	en bas	oñ bah
early	de bonne heure	duh bon urr
late	en retard	oñ ruh-tar
entrance	l'entrée	l'on-tray
exit	la sortie	sor-tee
toilet	les toilettes, le WC	twah-let, vay-see
free, unoccupied	libre	leebr
free, no charge	gratuit	grah-twee

MAKING A TELEPHONE CALL

I'd like to place a long-distance call.	Je voudrais faire un appel á l'étranger.	zhuh voo-dreh fehr uñ apel a laytroñ-zhay
I'd like to make a reverse charge call.	Je voudrais faire une communication en PCV.	zhuh voo-dreh fehr oon komoonikah-syoñ oñ peh-seh-veh
I'll try again later.	Je rappelerai plus tard.	zhuh rapeleray ploo tar
Can I leave a message?	Est-ce que je peux laisser un message?	es-keh zhuh puh leh-say uñ mehsazh
Hold on.	Ne quittez pas, s'il vous plaît.	nuh kee-tay pah seel voo play
Could you speak up a little please?	Pouvez-vous parler un peu plus fort?	poo-vay voo parlay uñ puh ploo for
local call	la communication locale	komoonikahsyoñ low-kal

SHOPPING

How much does this cost?	C'est combien s'il vous plaît?	say kom-byañ seel voo play
I would like ...	Je voudrais...	zhuh voo-dray
Do you have?	Est-ce que vous avez	es-kuh voo zavay
I'm just looking.	Je regarde seulement.	zhuh ruhgar suhlmoñ
Do you take credit cards?	Est-ce que vous acceptez les cartes de crédit?	es-kuh voo zaksept-ay leh kart duh kreh-dee
Do you take traveller's cheques?	Est-ce que vous acceptez les cheques de voyages?	es-kuh voo zaksept-ay leh shek duh vwayazh
What time do you open?	A quelle heure vous êtes ouvert?	ah kel urr voo zet oo-ver
What time do you close?	A quelle heure vous êtes fermé?	ah kel urr voo zet fer-may
This one.	Celui-ci	suhl-wee-see
That one.	Celui-là	suhl-wee-lah
expensive	cher	shehr
cheap	pas cher, bon marché	pah shehr, boñ mar-shay
size, clothes	la taille	tye
size, shoes	la pointure	pwañ-tur
white	blanc	bloñ
black	noir	nwahr
red	rouge	roozh
yellow	jaune	zhohwn
green	vert	vehr
blue	bleu	bluh

TYPES OF SHOP

antique shop	le magasin d'antiquités	maga-zañ d'oñteekee-tay
bakery	la boulangerie	booloñ-zhuree
bank	la banque	boñk
bookshop	la librairie	lee-brehree
butcher	la boucherie	boo-shehree
cake shop	la pâtisserie	patee-sree
cheese shop	la fromagerie	fromazh-ree
chemist	la pharmacie	farmah-see
dairy	la crémerie	krem-ree
department store	le grand magasin	groñ maga-zañ
delicatessen	la charcuterie	sharkoot-ree
fishmonger	la poissonnerie	pwasson-ree
gift shop	le magasin de cadeaux	maga-zañ duh kadoh
greengrocer	le marchand de légumes	mar-shoñ duh lay-goom
grocery	l'alimentation	alee-moñta-syoñ
hairdresser	le coiffeur	kwafuhr
market	le marché	marsh-ay
newsagent	le magasin de journaux	maga-zañ duh zhoor-no
post office	la poste, le bureau de poste, le PTT	pohst, boorah duh pohst, peh-teh-teh
shoe shop	le magasin de chaussures	maga-zañ duh show-soor
supermarket	le supermarché	soo pehr-marshay
tobacconist	le tabac	tabah
travel agent	l'agence de voyages	l'azhoñs duh vwayazh

SIGHTSEEING

abbey	l'abbaye	l'abay-ee
art gallery	la galerie d'art	galer-ree dart
bus station	la gare routière	gahr roo-tee-yehr
cathedral	la cathédrale	katay-dral
church	l'église	l'aygleez
garden	le jardin	zhar-dañ

ACKNOWLEDGMENTS

The publisher would like to thank the following for their kind permission to reproduce their photographs:

Key: a-above; b-below/bottom; c-centre; f-far; l-left; r-right; t-top

123RF.com:
Jon Bilous 18tc, 114-5cl; Francesco Bucchi 303br; Nattee Chalermtiragool 32br; Christian Mueller 267bl; Inna Nerlich 89cra.

4Corners:
Antonino Bartuccio 6-7c; Pietro Canali 11crb.

Alamy Stock Photo:
Todd Anderson 186cr; Andrzej Gorzkowski Photography 299bl; ART Collection 60bl; Peter Barritt 185cr; Martin Beddall 303bl; Piere Bonbon 24tl, 262-3; Eden Breitz 219cb; Helen Cathcart 119tr; Chronicle 70br, 131tr; Daisy Corlett 49b; Crowdspark / Newzulu / Dan Pier 134tc; De Rocker 156cra; Delmarty / Alpaca / Andia 26crb; Directphoto Collection 23tl, 234-5; Beth Dixson 189tr; Chad Ehlers 302cla; Everett Collection Inc 283cr; PE Forsberg 99tc; Giovanni Guarino Photo 46-7b; GL Archive 60br, 131ca; Granger Historical Picture Archive 62cr; hitandrun / Greg Meeson / © Succession Brancusi - All rights reserved. ADAGP, Paris and DACS, London 2018 *Brancusi's studio being exhibited at the Pompidou Centre in Paris* 91crb; Hemis / Arnaud Chicurel 232bl, 247tl; Bertrand Gardel 36b, 36-7t, 43tr, 213tl, 221cra, 221crb, Henri Bouchard *Apollo* © ADAGP, Paris and DACS, London 2018 222tr; Gilles Rigoulet 270bl; Pascal Ducept 28bl; René Mattes 28crb, 289tl; Sylvain Sonnet © Succession Picasso / DACS, London 2018 *Femmes à leur toilette (Women washing)* 88-9b; Bertrand Gardel 8-9cr, 106-7b, 143tr; Bertrand Rieger 137br, 245br; Sylvain Sonnet 96tl; Heritage Image Partnership Ltd / The Print Collector 61tl; IanDagnall Computing 131crb; Iconotec / Arthur Leroy 120b; JaiHoneybrook 294cr; Boris Karpinski 8cla; John Kellerman 92-3b, 121t, 165br, 242b, 242-3t; Keystone Pictures USA 131br; Elena Korchenko 297t; Lautaro 221bl; Lebrecht Music and Arts Photo Library 104br; Iugris 105; Centre Pompidou in Paris: Studio Piano & Rogers; courtesy of Fondazione Renzo Piano and Rogers Stirk Harbour + Partners / Luciano Mortula 90-1b; National Geographic Creative 83tl; Niday Picture Library 61bc; John Norman 28cr; Paris 94crb; Pawel Libera Images 300-1t; William Perry 26t; Photo 12 / Gilles Targat 136cr, 176bl; PhotoAlto / Laurence Mouton 58cla; Photononstop / Christophe Lehenaff 42-3b; Daniel Thierry 270-1; Pierre Pochan 136t; Henri Cochet Statue outside Roland Garros; Paris / Paul Quayle 293br; National Museum of Modern Art in the Pompidou Centre, Paris / Mervyn Rees Xavier Veilhan © Veilhan / ADAGP, Paris and DACS, London 2018 *Le Rhinocéros* 91cra; Robertharding / Godong 33ca; RossHelen editorial 223; Peter Schickert 96-7b; Science History Images 61cla; Shawshots 219crb; SJH Photography 301bl; Sergey Skleznev 267cr; Splash News/ Lionel Urman 41tl; William Stevens 40b; Street Art 18bl, 126-7; Claude Thibault 121br; / Tuul and Bruno Morandi © Succession Picasso / DACS, London 2018 *Head of a Woman* 88tr; Perry van Munster 48tc; Frédéric Vielcanet 51br; Don White 84-5cb; Tracey Whitefoot 287br; Gari Wyn Williams 274bc.

AWL Images:
Jon Arnold 1; Tour eiffel- Illuminations Pierre Bideau 21t, 196-7cl; Jan Christopher Becke 8clb, 173cla, 239tr; Walter Bibikow 39cr; Danita Delimont Stock 297cl; Bertrand Gardel 12-3bc; Carlos Sanchez Pereyra 17t, 84-5.

Candelaria:
Fabien Voileau 53b.

Cité Des Sciences et de L'industrie:
EPPD CSI / JP 145bl; E Luider 144-5t.

La Cuisine Cooking:
8cl.

Depositphotos Inc:
packshot 299clb, wjarek 209br.

Disneyland® Paris:
303t; © Disney / Pixar: 301clb, 301br.

Dorling Kindersley:
Neil Lukas 283clb, © Succession Brancusi - All rights reserved. ADAGP, Paris and DACS, London 2018 *The Kiss* 282br; Musee Marmottan / Susanna Price 304tr; Alphonse Terroir *Denis Diderot* (1925) / Neil Lukas / CNHMS, Paris 253tr; Jules Selmes 77t, 233crb; Valerio Vincenzo 208b.

Dreamstime.com:
Adisa 82bl, 258-9b; Georgios Alexandris 43cl; Andersastphoto 193b; Andrey Andronov 191tr; Antoine2k 51tr, 118-9b, 306-7b; Apn68140 55cla; Valentin Armianu 13cr, 22tc, 190-1, 214-5; Astormfr 16c, 66-7; Bargotiphotography 218; Christian Bertrand 11tc; Ilona Melanie Bicker 30t; Lembi Buchanan 133t, 209t; Michal Cervenansky 284b; Christianm 176tc; Ionut David 24cb, 278-9; Maurizio De Mattei 184-5t; Nicolas De Corte 159t; Digikhmer

210-1b; Matthew Dixon 206b; Yury Dmitrienko 41cr; Dennis Dolkens 75cr, 124-5b, 296-7b; Chris Dorney 230bl; Viorel Dudau 173tr; Evolove 220-1t; Fayethequeen93 146crb; Ruslan Gilmanshin 172-3b; Gornostaj 167cra; Ioana Grecu 225bl; Alberto Grosescu 13br; Guillohmz 119cla, 298crb; Bensliman Hassan 146b, 275bl; Dieter Hawlan 302b; Infomods 229t; Javarman 269tr; Valerijs Jegorovs 174-5b; Jeromecorreia 194bl; Joymsk 158bl; Juliengrondin 44-5b; Aliaksandr Kazlou 131tl; Kmiragaya 286-7t; Sergii Kolesnyk 30bl, 173tl; Maryna Kordiumova 185crb; Nikolai Korzhov 187 br; Denys Kuvaiev 135br; Liudmila Laurova 46-7tl; Bo Li 185bl; José Lledó 30crb; Madrabothair 76b, 132bl, 132-3b 177t; Tomas Marek 10ca, 282-3t; Meunierd 293crb; Minacarson 113br, 261tl; Daniel Buren © DB-ADAGP Paris and DACS, London 2018 *Les Deux Plateaux, Palais Royal* 188-9bl; Luciano Mortula 23cb, 248-9; MrFly 200clb; Neirfy 2-3; Nui7711 94-5t; William Perry 74bl, 75tr, 79tr; Kovalenkov Petr 109b, 224t; Mathias Pfauwadel 25tc, 290-1; Photofires 298-9t; Photogolfer 225br, 305tr; Ekaterina Pokrovsky 13tc; John Queenan 12clb; Redlunar 254bl; Eq Roy/ Architect Dominique Perrault © ADAGP, Paris and DACS, London 2018 *The Bibliotheque Nationale de France* 274-5t; Jozef Sedmak 192tr; Dmitry Shishkin 57cr; Siraanamwong 239cla; Smontgom65 28t; Alena Sobaleva 256b; Spytsekouras 255b; Darius Strazdas 17bl, 100-1, 104clb, 107tc, 130-1b; Petr Švec 32-3tl; Worakan Thaomor 204br; Tupungato 207tr; Ukrphoto 238cra; Valio84sl 12tc; Dennis Van De Water 266-7, 268bl; VanderWolfImages 20t, 168-9; Ivan Varyukhin 303clb; Vitalyedush 253tl, 257t, 304b; Vvoevale 78-9bc, 160t; Dirk Wenzel 285tl; Jason Yoder 73bl; Zatletic 75c.

Getty Images:
AFP / Eric Feferberg 58cl, 59tr; Kenzo Tribouillard 59bl; Lionel Bonaventure 58bl; Atlantide Phototravel / Stefano Amantini 33bc, / Massimo Borchi 204cl; Bettmann 283br; BSIP 285br; Centre Pompidou in Paris: Studio Piano & Rogers; courtesy of Fondazione Renzo Piano and Rogers Stirk Harbour + Partners / Busà Photography 91c; Guillaume Chanson 238-9b; Christophel Fine Art 45cl, 62tl; Corbis / VCG / Robert Holmes / 48-9tc; Corbis Documentary / P Deliss 73cra; Ian Cumming 48bl; Bruno De Hogues 10-11bc, 26bl, 276bl; De Agostini / Biblioteca Ambrosiana 219bl; C. Sappa 70bl; Stephane De Sakutin 267br; Simona Dumitru 292-3t; Neil Farrin 288cl; Owen Franken 56b, 195tl; Gallo Images / Ayhan Altun 73cr; Bertrand Guay 108tr, 213br; Francois Guillot 41br; Daniel Haug 59br; Heritage Images 219cra; Boris Horvat 219cl; Hulton Archive 200bl; Corbis Historical 61tr, 70fbl; John Sones Singing Bowl Media 98bl; Julian Elliott Photography 246bl;

Keystone 283cb; Lo Chun Kit 58br; Pascal Le Segretain 40tl; Philippe Le Tellier 63bl; Lonely Planet Images / Russell Mountford 104cla; MathieuRivrin 200-1; Michael Ochs Archives / Waring Abbott 73tr; Nicoolay 60t; NurPhoto 59cr; Maksim Ozerov 38-9t; Gregor Erhart *Mary Magdalene or 'La Belle Allemande'* (early 16th century) / Photo Josse / Leemage 186bl; Photolibrary / Julian Elliott Photography 19bl, 152-3; Marc Piasecki 45t; Joe Daniel Price 204-5cr; Jean Victor Schnetz 61br; Sizun Eye 35cra; Pierre Suu 63br; Topical Press Agency 222bl; ullstein bild Dtl. 283tr; Universal Images Group 62br; Ivan Vukelic 20cb, 180-1cl; Bruce Yuanyue Bi 47crb.

iStockphoto.com:
AlexKozlov 166bl; Orbon Alija 4; AlpamayoPhoto 162-3; anouchka 38bl; asab974 30cr; AzmanJaka 52-3t; B&M Noskowski 54-5b; Silvia Bianchini 11br; borchee 252cl; brenac 50crb; Calinat 110-1; conejota 63cra; Dirk94025 55crb; DKart 230-1t; efired 59cl; espiegle 80-1, 211tl; Mario Guti 240-1bl; Gwengoat 50tl; Michel Hincker 122-3; Ihor_Tailwind 179tl; instamatics 157; isatis 293bc; isogood 178cla; jacoblund 37cla; JASCKAL 277cr; johnkellerman 244-5t; JoseIgnacioSoto 50-1b, 70crb; LembiBuchanan 34-5t, 57tl; Valerie Loiseleux 164-5t; MarcelloLand 34cb, 112-13bl; mmac72 259tl; Pavliha 226-7; Razvan 58cra; sasasasa 124clb; Sean3810 70cra; Tomas Sereda 228-9b; serts 39cl, 64-5; Neil Sidhoum 58cr; Starcevic 54-5tr; Tolga Tezcan 71; Veronique de Viguerie 70fbr; VvoeVale 47cla; zheltikov 10clb.

La Fine Mousse:
Alexandre Martin 52br.

Le Musée du Quai Branly - Jaccques Chirac:
Lois Lammerhuber 202-3b; Exterior by Jean Nouvel / Vincent Mercier 202clb; Patrick Gries / Bruno Descoings 203cra.

Musée Antoine Bourdelle:
Dorine Potel 286bl.

Musée de Cluny:
M. Chassat 254tl.

Musée de Louvre:
©Pyramide du Louvre, arch. I. M. Pei 11tl, 20cb, 32br, 180, 184-5t, 185bl.

Musée de Montmartre:
Jean-Pierre Delagarde 161b.

Parc de la Villette:
William Beaucardet 142-3b, 143cla; Pierre-Emmanuel Rastoin 150-1t.

Philharmonie de Paris:
William Beaucardet / Architect Jean Nouvel © ADAGP, Paris and DACS, London 2018 147t.

Picfair.com:
Benis Arapovic 260bl.

Rex by Shutterstock:
Granger 62bc; Moviestore Collection 44tl.

RMN:
Tre ésor de l'abbaye de Saint-Denis / Grand Palais (Musée du Louvre) / Peter Willi 187tl.

Robert Harding Picture Library:
Stuart Dee 239cl; Julian Elliott 35bl; Jakob+MacFarlane - Cite de la mode et du design, Quai de Austerlitz; Paris / Javier Gil 272-3b.

SuperStock:
4X5 COLLECTION / © Succession Picasso / DACS, London 2018 *The Kiss* (1969) Musee Picasso 89br; Francisco de Zurbaran *Lying-in-State of St Bonaventura* (c.1629) 186tl; age fotostock 53cla; Heinz-Dieter Falkenstein 75br; T. Papageorgiou 42tl, Carlos S. Pereyra 26cr; Javier Larrea /Vassily Kandinsky *With the Black Arc* (1912), Centre George Pompidou, 91tl; eps / Marka 62-3tr; Hemis / Bertrand Gardel 57br, 59tl, 63tr, 294bl, 295; Architect Jean Nouvel © ADAGP, Paris and DACS, London 2018 *Le Parc de la Villette, Philharmonie de Paris*, 19tl, 138-9; Architect Jean Nouvel © ADAGP, Paris and DACS, London 2018 *Paris Philharmonic Concert Hall* 148-9; Hervé Hughes 150br; Hervé Tardy 267crb; Jean-Pierre Degas 56tl; Lionel Montico /Architect Adrien Fainsilber © ADAGP, Paris and DACS, London 2018 *La Geode*, Parc de la Villette 145br; / Maurizio Borgese 220br; Stéphane Lemaire 297cra; imageBROKER / Stephan Gabriel /Architect Jean Nouvel © ADAGP, Paris and DACS, London 2018 *Exterior of Musee Du Quai Branley* - Jacques Chirac 203tl; Photononstop / Architect Adrien Fainsilber © ADAGP, Paris and DACS, London 2018 *Cite des Sciences et de L'industrie* 145clb; Universal Images 299crb.

THATMuse: Daisy de Plume 37br

Cartographic Data ERA-Maptec Ltd (Dublin) adapted with permission from original survey and mapping by Shobunsha (Japan)

Front Flap:
Alamy Stock Photo: Piere Bonbon bl; John Kellerman cb; **Dreamstime.com:** Ionut David cra; Darius Strazdas cla;

iStockphoto.com: Esperanza33; **Picfair.com:** Benis Arapovic t.

Sheet Map Cover:
iStockphoto.com: Esperanza33.

Cover images:
Front and Spine: **iStockphoto.com:** Esperanza33.
Back: **4Corners:** Antonino Bartuccio t; **La Cuisine Cooking:** c; **Dreamstime.com:** Rosshelen cla; **iStockphoto.com:** Esperanza33.

All other images © Dorling Kindersley

For further information see: www.dkimages.com

Penguin
Random
House

Main contributers Bryan Pirolli, Alan Tillier

Senior Designer Owen Bennett

Senior Editor Ankita Awasthi Tröger

Project Editor Elspeth Beidas

Project Art Editors Dan Bailey,
Toby Truphet, Stuti Tiwari Bhatia,
Bharti Karakoti, Priyanka Thakur

Design Assistant William Robinson

Factchecker Lyn Parry

Editors Ruth Reisenberger,
Lucy Sienkowska, Penny Walker

Proofreader Christine Stroyan

Indexer Zoe Ross

Senior Picture Researcher Ellen Root

Picture Research Susie Peachey,
Harriet Whitaker

Illustrators Stephen Conlin,
Stephen Gyapay, Maltings Partnership,
John Fox Nick Gibbard, David Harris,
Kevin Jones Associates, John Woodcock

Senior Cartographic Editor Casper Morris

Cartography Andrew Heritage,
Zafar ul Islam Khan, James Mills-Hicks

Jacket Designers Maxine Pedliham, Bess Daly

Jacket Picture Research Susie Peachey

Senior DTP Designer Jason Little

DTP Coordinator George Nimmo

Senior Producer Stephanie McConnell

Managing Editor Hollie Teague

Art Director Maxine Pedliham

Publishing Director Georgina Dee

This edition updated by
Hansa Barbra, Elspeth Beidas, Lyn Parry,
Lucy Sara-Kelly, Christine Stroyan

First edition 1993

Published in Great Britain by Dorling Kindersley Limited,
80 Strand, London, WC2R 0RL

Published in the United States by DK Publishing,
1450 Broadway, Suite 801, New York, NY 10018

Copyright © 1993, 2019 Dorling Kindersley Limited
A Penguin Random House Company
19 20 21 22 10 9 8 7 6 5 4 3 2 1

A CIP catalog record for this book
is available from the British Library.

A catalog record for this book is available
from the Library of Congress.

ISSN: 1542 1554
ISBN: 978 0 2413 6876 3

Printed and bound in China.

www.dk.com

**The information in this
DK Eyewitness Travel Guide is checked regularly.**
Every effort has been made to ensure that this book
is as up-to-date as possible at the time of going to
press. Some details, however, such as telephone
numbers, opening hours, prices, gallery hanging
arrangements and travel information, are liable to
change. The publishers cannot accept responsibility
for any consequences arising from the use of this
book, nor for any material on third party websites,
and cannot guarantee that any website address in
this book will be a suitable source of travel
information. We value the views and suggestions of
our readers very highly. Please write to: Publisher, DK
Eyewitness Travel Guides, Dorling Kindersley,
80 Strand, London, WC2R 0RL, UK, or email.